The Covert Colour Line

'Raises a fascinating question: what if the biggest failures of intelligence are not the factual errors, but the inbuilt biases that shape what types of information is deemed useful, or even legible, to the state?'
—Lisa Stampnitzky, University of Sheffield and author of *Disciplining Terror: How Experts Invented 'Terrorism'*

'A ground-breaking contribution to the field. Elegantly written, the book decodes a plethora of declassified documents showing the racialised assumptions underlying the use and abuse of intelligence in contemporary Western politics. This is a must-read for anyone interested in democratic politics, recent armed conflicts in the Middle East or asymmetrical global power relations.'
—Elisabeth Schweiger, University of York

'Your jaw will drop and your heart will break. We urgently need this reckoning with the role of race-thinking in international politics. Lives depend on it.'
—Gargi Bhattacharyya, co-author of *Empire's Endgame: Racism and the British State*

The Covert Colour Line

The Racialised Politics of Western State Intelligence

Oliver Kearns

First published 2023 by Pluto Press
New Wing, Somerset House, Strand, London WC2R 1LA
and Pluto Press Inc.
1930 Village Center Circle, 3-834, Las Vegas, NV 89134

www.plutobooks.com

British Library Cataloguing in Publication Data
A catalogue record for this book is available from the British Library

ISBN 978 0 7453 4730 1   Paperback
ISBN 978 0 7453 4733 2   PDF
ISBN 978 0 7453 4732 5   EPUB

This book is printed on paper suitable for recycling and made from fully managed and sustained forest sources. Logging, pulping and manufacturing processes are expected to conform to the environmental standards of the country of origin.

Typeset by Stanford DTP Services, Northampton, England

Simultaneously printed in the United Kingdom and United States of America

Contents

List of Figures

Acronyms and Abbreviations

CBW	Chemical and biological weapons
CIA	Central Intelligence Agency
CIG	Central Intelligence Group
CPS	Crown Prosecution Service
DARPA	Defence Advanced Research Projects Agency
DIS	Defence Intelligence Service
FO	Foreign Office
JIC	Joint Intelligence Committee
JIS	Joint Intelligence Staff
MENA	Middle East and North Africa
MI6	Military Intelligence Section 6 [SIS]
MoD	Ministry of Defence
NFZ	No-fly zones
NIE	National Intelligence Estimates
NSC	National Security Council
ONE	Office of National Estimates
OPR	Office of Political Research
ORE	Office of Reports and Estimates
PAID	Production Assessment and Improvement Division
RGS	Royal Geographical Society
SIS	Secret Intelligence Service [MI6]
SNIE	Special National Intelligence Estimate
SRI	Stanford Research Institute
UNSCR	United Nations Security Council Resolution
WMD	Weapons of mass destruction

Acknowledgements

Parts of Chapters 3 and 4 were originally presented in a different form at a panel on contemporary intelligence at the European International Studies Association's (EISA) 13th Pan-European Conference on International Relations, on 14 September 2019 in Sofia. A portion of what would become Chapter 1 was presented at an EISA workshop on the same subject, on 3 July 2020 online. My thanks in both cases to Hager Ben Jaffel and Sebastian Larsson for organising the events and providing feedback on my ideas, and also to Marco Munier for acting as a discussant. I was lucky to then collaborate with Hager, Sebastian, and Alvina Hoffmann on furthering the discussion of re-thinking Intelligence Studies. I can only applaud all three for their original, ongoing research in this area and for our fruitful work together. An early draft of Chapter 4 also received feedback from three anonymous reviewers through the journal *International Studies Review*, for whose comments and criticism I am most grateful. Thank you also to Andrew Neal for his thoughts and constructive criticism on the ideas for the book, and for supporting me since my doctoral days.

The team at Pluto Press have been wonderful to work with. My thanks to all of them and in particular to my editor Jakob Horstmann, whom I first met years ago, who saw this book's potential from the beginning, and who consistently applied the precise sort of critical eye that was needed to improve it.

I wrote much of this book while an honorary research fellow at the University of Bristol with SPIN, the Secrecy Power and Ignorance Network. I am part of a fantastic group of colleagues in SPIN. Clare Stevens, Amaha Senu, and Tim Duroux have always offered insightful and inspiring conversation on Secrecy Studies, as have Henrietta Wilson, Owen Thomas, Lisa Stampnitzky, Brian Rappert, and Thomas Leahy on researching state violence and its archives. Thank you to Elisabeth Schweiger for always helping me see the political stakes of our work. Finally, thank you to Elspeth

Van Veeren and Jutta Weldes for their mentorship and advice as I planned the writing of the book, and for our great discussions on secrecy, power and ignorance. Obviously any errors in this final text remain mine alone.

Some words on sources: Because I started drafting this book in earnest in the middle of the COVID-19 pandemic, much of the archival research was done remotely, something which would have been impossible even a few years ago. Declassified US records were accessed through the CIA's Electronic Reading Room (www.cia.gov/readingroom) and the State Department Office of the Historian's Foreign Relations of the United States series (https://history.state.gov/historicaldocuments). UK National Archives documents were accessed from a number of sources: Taylor & Francis' Secret Files from World Wars to Cold War (www.secretintelligencefiles.com); UAE National Library and Archives' Arabian Gulf Digital Archives (www.agda.ae/en); Adam Matthew's Archives Direct (www.archivesdirect.amdigital.co.uk); the Margaret Thatcher Foundation Archive (https://www.margaretthatcher.org/archive); and Gale's Declassified Documents Online: Twentieth-Century British Intelligence (www.gale.com/intl/c/declassified-documents-online-twentieth-century-british-intelligence-intelligence-empire). As these sources all reproduced UK National Archives material, I have referenced the National Archives' own catalogue in citations. My great thanks to Catherine Downs and Liz Cooper at the University of Bristol's Library Services for helping me access the Gale database.

I originally accessed the Iraq Inquiry's declassified intelligence material and hearing transcripts through the Inquiry's website. The website itself is no longer active and has been archived by the National Archives (https://webarchive.nationalarchives.gov.uk/ukgwa/20171123122801/ www.iraqinquiry.org.uk/the-evidence). The material referenced in this book is now accessible through the National Archives' UK Government Web Archive (https://webarchive.nationalarchives.gov.uk/search), by searching for material from the website 'www.iraqinquiry.org.uk', though it is unclear how much of the material has been preserved. This convoluted set-up is an example of how 'transparent government' and new technology can obscure as much as they can reveal. I therefore heartily recommend the Warnings from the Archive initiative by colleagues at the University of Exeter (https://warningsfromthearchive.exeter.ac.uk), which has reclaimed the Chilcot Inquiry material and gathered it into an easily-searchable database.

Thank you to my family for their support and love. And finally, thank you to Marie Yan for encouraging me from the beginning and helping me see the book's full potential. I should probably find myself an office now, shouldn't I?

Introduction
Ukraine, Iraq, and the failure
of intelligence failure

When do we think intelligence has failed, and what does it take for it to succeed? More than any other term, 'intelligence failure' sums up the popular understanding of what secret service analysts do and how they should be judged once their writings and discussions with politicians become public. It is seen as reflecting an objective measure of what makes intelligence good or bad, untainted by politics or cultural bias. And no intelligence failure has more public salience today than the false claim that Saddam Hussein was hiding weapons of mass destruction (WMD) in Iraq. The point of this book is to demonstrate that the intellectual tools used by practitioners to measure good or bad intelligence are most certainly biased, have been shaped by US and British imperial history, and prevent us from understanding how intelligence makes global inequalities and state violence appear plausible and legitimate.

THE LIMITS OF ACCURACY

Twenty years after the coalition invasion of Iraq, this event continues to cast its shadow on how we discuss intelligence. As I write in the autumn of 2022, it is over 200 days since Vladimir Putin sent Russian forces across the border into Ukraine on the spurious grounds of uprooting Nazism in the country's politics, although the Russian Government's objective now seems to be to annex large parts of Ukraine's south and east.[1] One small part of this horrific war's story has been the charges of intelligence failure thrown back and forth by both Russia and those states who are supporting Ukraine's government. As an invasion appeared more and more likely in early 2022, the intelligence services of the United

States, including the Central Intelligence Agency, calculated that Russian troops would overthrow the Ukrainian Government within two weeks. The director of the Defence Intelligence Agency later admitted that their officers had misjudged the state of Russia's military and underestimated Ukraine's defence capacity.[2] On the other hand, the same intelligence officials have claimed that Putin himself was badly misinformed before the war by his subordinates about the relative capabilities of Russian and Ukrainian forces, as well as the strength of resistance from Ukrainian society. Russia saw 'a failure of honest upward reporting of intelligence'. Two months later, Putin fired or arrested members of his secret service held responsible for this faulty analysis.[3] On all sides, then, intelligence failure has been defined in the most obvious way: being inaccurate about the world out there.

That is not quite how Iraq enters this story though. Why, in public debate about Russia and Ukraine, has Iraq kept coming up? At one level, it was simply a matter of remembering another time 'when US intelligence assessments have proven to be faulty', to warn US and other states' intelligence agencies not to become 'overconfident' in their judgements and 'exaggerat[e] claims, as happened in the run-up to the Iraq war'.[4] But past failure in Iraq was also framed as having political consequences, which the war in Ukraine was now rectifying. Intelligence agencies had been following Russian troops massing on the border for months, along with Russian support for separatists in Donbas. Weeks before Putin gave the order, President Joe Biden's administration began briefing that an invasion could be launched at any moment and that Russia had prepared hit-lists of political opponents. In the words of a London *Telegraph* commentator, the subsequent invasion was 'a very public vindication of Western intelligence capabilities'. More than this, it was 'a rebuff to those still stuck on the failures of Iraq'. Truly, having been 'mocked after Iraq', 'Western intelligence [...] has redeemed itself'.[5] US military observers agreed: '[d]omestically, the reputation of US and UK intelligence has been restored after the Iraq fiasco'.[6]

And the prize for this redemption and reputation? These intelligence services can now contribute to the public information war against Russia. Having left behind 'the use – and abuse – of intelligence to justify the US invasion of Iraq', agencies like the CIA were now regaining public trust through a 'novel declassification strategy' that has successfully 'colour[ed] public discourse and debate' around Putin's war rationale. Having learned the lessons of Iraq, according to former CIA analyst Jeff Asher, the intelligence community could now 'provide effective messaging in support of US foreign policy objectives'.[7] Their assessments also 'offered lead time to assist, equip, and train the Ukrainians'.[8]

The changed fortunes of intelligence in the aftermath of Russia's invasion demonstrates something well-understood by intelligence officers and scholars – often a very thin distinction – but that rarely gets stated explicitly in public debate. Intelligence failure, as the term is used today, is not just about inaccuracy. Two prominent scholars, both once employed by US intelligence agencies, point out that good intelligence is both accurate *and* useful for policy-makers. Gauging utility is not easy, either, since statespersons and their advisers vary in what they feel they need to make decisions.[9] Another scholar, this time a current US intelligence officer, has pushed back strongly against the popular idea that anything less than clairvoyance is a failure. Intelligence fails 'simply when the intelligence input into the decision-making process is lacking or unsatisfactory', which again depends on the decision-maker and the situation. The line between intelligence and policy suddenly looks blurrier: If policy-makers have unrealistic expectations of their analysts or end up downplaying the significance of the reports they are given, where does the blame for failure lie? For that reason, 'intelligence professionals must understand the needs and preferences of those to whom they provide intelligence products'.[10] This suggests an even starker definition: Intelligence success or failure has no essential link to accuracy or inaccuracy.

A pushback here would be to say that policy-makers obviously need accurate intelligence to guide their states through international affairs without bumping into unexpected disastrous events. Intelligence needs to reveal what is actually going on in the world. But the way that intelligence has fitted into the story of international efforts against Russia makes even this more complicated than it first seems. As late as December 2021, US intelligence officials believed that Russia's large troop deployments were designed to 'obfuscate intentions and to create uncertainty'. Across Europe, France's intelligence agencies demurred that an invasion was unlikely since 'the conquest of Ukraine would have a monstrous cost and [...] the Russians had other options'. In fact, a recent review of the intelligence war in Ukraine concludes that 'France may yet be proved right in that the invasion *has already* come at a "monstrous cost" to the Russians'.[11] Whether France's secret services were accurate, though, is not the point. It turns out that what often gets called accuracy is actually about which agency has the most useful evidence threshold, the point at which you decide to warn your policy-makers, like US analysts did, that something *could* happen.

The one crucial variable that this threshold could not be based upon was the inaccessible thought process of President Putin. Commentators have repeatedly emphasised that 'it is impossible to know the true state of Putin's mind' while lauding the valiant efforts of intelligence officers to do exactly that, to '[get] inside Putin's head' (Figure 0.1).[12] Figuring out 'the intentions of autocratic leaders' is always the problem. So observers turn to speculation. Perhaps those French agents had simply misjudged 'what costs the adversary was willing to take'. Maybe the 'values and concerns of Western governments' are 'not as relevant' in Putin's decision-making.[13] Those analysts who were more willing to adopt *this* hypothesis were the ones who came up with an intelligence success. Their reports allowed policy-makers to prepare for a war despite no one knowing what Putin was thinking. Notice how quickly the lack of access to Putin's mind segues into speculation about his non-Westernness and irrationality. If he does not value the things Western governments value, perhaps 'the mental state of the man' is at issue.[14] Even those who dismiss the idea that Putin has gone insane, like US Director of National Intelligence Avril Haines, argue that Putin's unrealistic ambitions are leading to 'more ad hoc decision-making' on his part, making it 'increasingly difficult for the intelligence community to predict' his actions.[15] If he is 'isolated in a bubble of his own making', as intelligence officials believe, he will have been 'stewing' in 'a strange view of the world' based around his 'mindset and obsessions [...] with Ukraine and the West'. Press coverage of such intelligence beliefs are accompanied by shots of a shirtless Putin hunting in the countryside, rifle in hand.[16] Perhaps, too, Putin's ambitions stem from such illogical, emotional sources as a belief in 'Ukraine's legacy as part of this Russian Empire' – hardly a promising prospect for negotiations.[17]

This kind of intelligence judgement can then be used to help the war effort. 'It increasingly looks [like] Putin has massively misjudged the situation', the head of Britain's Government Communication Headquarters reported in a public press conference. Whether this represents 'the full picture or a more selective one', choice declassifications like this were commended for contributing to a 'psychological war', designed to 'maintain support for the tough Western stand' and 'sow discord' in the Kremlin.[18] Never mind if these public humiliations 'risk further isolating Putin or mak[ing] him double down on his aim of restoring Russian prestige', to 'overcome the perceived [previous] humiliation of Russia' following the Soviet Union's collapse; according to a Biden official, 'Putin is going to do what Putin is going to do'.[19]

This risky contribution to the international war of words against Russia extends the link with Iraq even further. Back in 2003, intelligence officers felt confident enough to assign the same misjudgement to Iraq's President Saddam Hussein, on the basis not of material intelligence but of bigger ideas about race and geopolitics. The consequences of these ideas for the coalition's war in Iraq, and the lessons for how we should judge intelligence efforts on Putin and others, have not yet been given a place in public debate. The objective of this book is to make the case for doing so.

THE 20-YEAR SEARCH FOR THE SMOKING GUN

It is hard to overestimate just how much the invasion of Iraq two decades ago has utterly reshaped the country and the Middle East's political landscape. Inside Iraq, documented direct deaths from violence since the bombs began to fall in March 2003 stand at 288,000, with annual deaths today from armed conflict and terrorism remaining in the hundreds.[20] Iraqi protests in July 2021 against power outrages only hint at the country's wider social violence. Twenty years after the coalition invasion, Iraq suffers from 'the lack of clean water and electricity, widespread poverty,

"Nervous Kremlin watchers acknowledge they can't be sure what [Putin] is thinking or even if he's rational and well-informed."
John Leicester, 'What's Putin thinking? Tough to know for nuclear analysts', Associated Press, 4 October 2022, with accompanying photo of Putin watching Russian military exercises in 2021 (Kremlin.ru, Creative Commons CC BY 4.0. Image cropped.)

Figure 0.1 The effort by intelligence officers and others to understand Vladimir Putin's strategy has been framed as an attempt by objective Westerners to decipher an alien, culturally-fixed mindset.

"[Former CIA operative Glenn Carle highlights] the difference in how the West views international relations versus how Putin sees them [...] The Russian leader subscribes to a Eurasianist philosophy [which] sees foreign policy as a zero-sum game [...] 'He is behaving rationally within the confines of a fundamentally irrational set of beliefs.'"

Sonan Sheth and John Haltiwanger, "Rational, consistent and ruthless': National security veterans warn against painting Putin as an unhinged madman', Business Insider, 3 March 2022

"Russia's leader Vladimir Putin is trapped in a closed world of his own making, Western spies believe. And that worries them [...] [He is] a man angry and obsessed with Ukraine and the West."

Gordon Correra, 'Western agents seek to get inside Putin's head', BBC News, 20 March 2022

"Putin has concocted all of these threats in his mind to justify a war of aggression because his autocracy is threatened by Western values, by Western liberal ideas of civil liberties and individual freedom and self-determination."

Rolf Mowatt-Larssen, former CIA Moscow station chief, CBS News, 12 October 2022 high levels of unemployment, government corruption, and dismal prospects for the largely young population'. Mass privatisation and predatory contracts with multinationals during the occupation 'drained the country's resources', leaving 'a totally bankrupt economy' when coalition forces largely withdrew in 2011. Iraq's unprecedented 'lack of development, services and resources [...] food scarcity, poverty and unemployment' are reinforced by 'the West's political support of Iraq's corrupt political elite'.[21] Across the region, the Iraq War's public framing within a 'War on Terror' allowed governments of all stripes, from conservative monarchies to revolutionary autocracies, to position their own long repressions and counter-insurgencies as counter-terrorism efforts, gaining US and British backing in the process. The removal of Saddam paved the way for increased Iranian influence against Saudi Arabia, while Iraq's insurgency and then the Syrian civil war have helped to legitimise a sectarian view of regional power struggles, militarising many societies in the process.[22]

Intelligence did not cause all of this. But to the extent that intelligence rationalised the view of Saddam as a threat and the aim to remove him from office, analysts' ideas about who Saddam was, what Iraqi society was like, and how Middle East geopolitics worked were crucial. These ideas would have been part of US and British policy debates, even part of the atmosphere in each administration of what it was acceptable to think about as a possible policy action or not. Critics of the invasion have a stake in knowing how intelligence is likely to have shaped that atmosphere.

Yet critical discussion of this intelligence analysis has almost exclusively centred on the question not of ideas but of accuracy. When then British Prime Minister Gordon Brown announced an independent inquiry into the Iraq War headed by John Chilcot, to cover all events from 2001 to 2009, British intelligence on Iraq had already been the subject of four legislative and commissioned independent investigations. These past inquiries had each been tainted by accusations of deception and powerlessness: The Foreign Affairs Committee was refused access to documents and witnesses; the Intelligence and Security Committee was too trusting of officials and used the mildest language to rebuke them; the inquiry led by James Hutton prevaricated on the term 'sexed-up' – the accusation made by a BBC journalist about the public case for war – and was prevented from comparing government statements with the intelligence basis; and the review led by Robin Butler, aimed specifically at studying intelligence which had now been proven false, was seen to have pulled its punches on policy-makers' use of officers' analysis.[23] The momentum of these inquiries from 2003 to 2004 and the dissatisfaction that grew with them, especially once the WMD claim was disproven by inspectors in Iraq, filed the intelligence issue down to one sharp, narrow question: Had intelligence reports been truthful?

Lack of truthfulness has always been seen to have two possibilities: Was the intelligence analysis fallible at its roots, or was it distorted through public presentation? For those wanting to, in Chilcot's words, 'establish, as accurately as possible, what happened',[24] this suggests two possible culprits: Either intelligence officers incorrectly analysed the Iraqi Government's behaviour and miscalculated Saddam's acquisition or possession of WMD; or government officials, having received what was correct intelligence, misread or misrepresented these conclusions to the public to make the case for war. This way of understanding what went wrong feels like a strong critique of state power because it insists that the security services can be useless lackeys and politicians are often deceptive – 'Blair lied, thousands died'. Putting the question like this, however, has always been valued by many among the British political elite because they believed the answer would provide 'practical lessons' for policy-making, so that 'the failings that have been brought to light [...] are never repeated'.[25] This attitude fits the standard aim of any commissioned inquiry in a liberal democratic state: to resolve crises in public confidence; to re-legitimise institutions that are seen to have failed in their presumed right to govern; to make clear that the failing was temporary and not grounds for re-structuring state power.[26] This even became explicit: When Robin Butler was challenged in a British parliamentary committee on his wariness about criticising policy, he argued that his team 'felt the proper place where government should survive or fall was in Parliament or with the electorate', as 'it would have been improper for us to say the government should resign on this matter'. His inquiry's job was 'to give a balanced, factual picture' that would contribute to the normal workings of state representation.[27] If Blair lied, the fault was his alone; if thousands died, intelligence procedures could always be improved in future.

The two-part question of truthfulness gives two corresponding explanations: that flaws in intelligence assessment allowed for unjustified conclusions about the scope of Iraq's WMD programmes; or that the assessment was manipulated through political pressure or the addition of false statements on those WMD.[28] Both explanations put capabilities front-and-centre; they hinged on whether Iraq really had the things that intelligence attributed to them. And so a flurry of scholarship has been produced over 20 years, with intelligence officers, political scientists, and historians examining one or the other of these explanations and culprits, sometimes even combining them to propose a more complex process of failure.[29] Those who reject the idea of politicisation insist that intelligence officers started from a reasonable assumption that just happened to turn out to be wrong: that given his history of trying to produce WMD, Saddam was probably continuing to do so and had had some success.[30] On the other side, a lot of ink has been spilt over the issue of the 2002 'September dossier', a public presentation of British intelligence judgements, which included the now-infamous claim that Saddam Hussein could deploy chemical and biological weapons within 45 minutes of an order to do so.[31] Scholars have followed the trail of private correspondence and declassified minutes which emerged through public inquiries. That trail leads to evidence that policy-makers shaped the drafting of the September dossier to more robustly and emphatically assert Saddam's possession of WMD.[32] As more evidence has been released, this now includes the fact that a late piece of intelligence suggesting chemical agent production was inserted at the behest of Blair officials without being properly assessed.[33]

The problem with this attempt to establish what happened, with this way of asking the question of truthfulness, has always been that it plays on the turf already fully occupied by the defenders of the invasion. The only way of proving whether intelligence officers screwed up or political officials sexed up reports is if the people involved admit to it or if they left behind a documentary trail. These same people have been using this to their advantage for two decades. 'That is four inquiries now that have cleared me of wrongdoing', said Alistair Campbell, Tony Blair's former communications director, in response to Chilcot's report. 'I hope', he continued, 'that the allegations we have faced for years – of lying and deceit to persuade a reluctant parliament and country to go to war [...] are laid to rest'.[34] Campbell is skipping over what he *was* accused of, but on lying, he was indeed absolved by every inquiry's chair. If Blair and his acolytes are judged to have made no 'personal and demonstrable decision to deceive', as Chilcot himself concluded,[35] then the worst that can be said is that these people suffered from self-deception, a zealous belief in their own convictions that blinded them to alternative readings of intelligence.[36] The only way to get beyond that conclusion is to find a written record of deceit, what Anna Stavrianakis calls an analytical 'smoking gun' of 'that moment of decision' which reveals 'someone [...] in control of events'.[37] With many records of Cabinet discussions and conversations between Blair and Bush remaining classified even after Chilcot, this search for the smoking gun sets a very high bar for establishing what went wrong with the Iraq intelligence. It also risks keeping debate within the exact arena that most suits political elites: how to fix that temporary failure and re-legitimise the state.

I am not saying that the issue of whether political figures lied to make the case for war should be dismissed. Those classified records may yet reveal in more detail how that happened. Those records which *are* now in public, however, can reveal crucial aspects of intelligence's role in that war that have so far been overlooked. As a result of Chilcot's Inquiry, hundreds of previously secret documents have entered the public record. These include dozens of British intelligence assessments, along with discussions among and between analysts, their superiors, and politicians. In a system of government which normally keeps such records classified for decades, this revelation of documents from as recently as 15 years ago offers an unprecedented opportunity. The Chilcot Inquiry also produced thousands of pages of witness hearings, including with intelligence analysts whose rare discussions of their own work are now available for public consumption, even if the hearings themselves were held in private. The cosiness of the inquiry's proceedings may also have encouraged intelligence witnesses to speak as if chatting with colleagues of a similar mindset. Witness hearings involved no 'Iraqis, Americans, or foreigners of any sort' and were often run 'like a private conversation in a Whitehall club', with John Chilcot himself 'treat[ing] witnesses like a therapist with a nervous patient'.[38] One member of the intelligence services felt at home enough during their session to share a Latin quip from Virgil's *Aeneid*, to which Chilcot responded in kind.[39] This was a comfortably elite environment, making the witness sessions even more insightful for what they inadvertently reveal about intelligence analysts' thoughts and assumptions.

To uncover new lines of inquiry from this voluminous evidence, we need to use this declassified material to start going beyond what has been called juridical individualism. This is a way of discussing responsibility for crimes that centres on *intent* rather than *motive*. With intent, one asks whether a person meant to commit a certain action. With motive, one asks how they justified themselves. Law in liberal democracies reinforces societal inequality by focusing on intent: You can no longer get away in a courtroom with stealing a loaf of bread by explaining that you are poor.[40] Again, sticking only with the question of intelligence's accuracy and its causes can end up contributing to that same process, by only searching for elite duplicity rather than asking what they thought they were doing and what assumptions they made about today's vastly unequal international state system. Thinking instead about motive means considering *how* ideas about the world are formed over time. As Owen Thomas puts it, in the case of Iraq, it would mean examining 'the ways of thinking that made the British case for war possible', and that helped to bind together 'a political community' on the basis of a shared understanding of the world.[41]

For those who want justice for victims of state violence and a democratisation of societal power, it also means going beyond a definition of the security services by their organisational power. Critiques of security and intelligence agencies tend to imagine these agencies first and foremost as competing bureaucratic structures, tightly regimented groups in closed-off corridors that push for more control over the state apparatus against other political actors, such as elected politicians. The question of 'democratising' intelligence becomes one of avoiding two extremes: an autonomous agency carrying out its own surveillance and policy, a 'rogue elephant' as the CIA was famously charged in the 1970s; and a personal security service for a leader trying to avoid legislative accountability, a private army.[42] Scholars of intelligence have pursued this kind of typology of intelligence's position and power within the state.[43] Ironically, they share that interest with Anglosphere dissidents and critical social scientists. The latter tend to define security organisations' impact on politics using terms like a 'surveillance state', a high-tech panopticon encroaching on civil liberties, or a 'garrison state', where decision-making is dominated by what President Dwight Eisenhower famously called the military-industrial complex.[44]

The limitation of this critique is that it all-too-quickly reduces the political effects of intelligence to bureaucratic power plays. It risks overlooking the political effects of intelligence *beyond* these agencies' own relative hold on instruments of state power.[45] For one thing, no matter how secretive they may be, intelligence officers are also part of society, which means their view of the world will shape and be shaped by their societal background.[46] For another, that social context will be reflected in how those officers think and talk about what the state actually is. Intelligence analysis helps to make the state – not as a neutral organisational structure but as a political identity that gets attached to people, to laws, and to policies. The ways of thinking that create a political community also create the state that this community represents.

So as well as looking for the smoking gun, we should ask: How is intelligence likely to have contributed to the state's identity and to these ways of thinking? Instead of asking who had power over whom, the intelligence officers or the politicians, why not examine what kind of social ideas were reflected in intelligence assessments, and how those assessments might then have made certain policies seem possible to policy-makers? Could this have happened *before* deception or self-deception about WMD became a factor?

RACE AND GEOPOLITICS

Defenders of intelligence's role in Iraq keep bringing up something rarely acknowledged by intelligence's critics. Tony Blair raised it himself while giving evidence to Chilcot's Inquiry. For Blair, when the British Cabinet discussed how to address Iraq's non-compliance with United Nations Resolutions, '[t]here was not a great dispute about what we thought about the facts. The facts were he is continuing to develop WMD. *He has the intention of doing that. It is crucial to his regime*'.[47] In Blair's long speech to the House of Commons in March 2003, he began by noting that Saddam 'had used the weapons against Iran, against his own people, causing thousands of deaths', before arguing that '[w]e are now seriously asked to accept that in the last few years, contrary to all history, contrary to all intelligence, [Saddam] decided unilaterally to destroy the weapons. Such a claim is palpably absurd'.[48] Blair is talking here not just about capabilities but about Saddam's intent. And not just Saddam's supposed intent to have those capabilities but his motivations for doing so: that he needs WMD somehow for his own rule; that he has a strategy of using such weapons against political enemies.

Now consider an influential study of the Iraq intelligence by the late Robert Jervis, 'the dean of Intelligence Studies' in academia.[49] To date, Jervis' is one of the most in-depth appraisals of how US and British agencies came to their conclusions on Iraq. Jervis argues that although 'analytical processes were badly flawed', fixing them would *not* have led intelligence officers to a different conclusion. Why not? Jervis argues that analysts doubled down on 'inferences' that Saddam was pursuing WMD because of 'their plausibility in light of previous Iraqi behaviour and the sense they made of Saddam's goals and general capabilities'. They were relying less on 'specific signs of WMD activity' than on 'their sense of [Saddam's] political objectives and outlook'. The intelligence received by analysts made sense as evidence of Saddam pursuing WMD because this is exactly what he had done in the past. He had used those weapons, he had 'major incentives to rebuild his programs', he had the means to do so, and there was no other obvious reason why he would be trying to disrupt UN inspections. We can hardly fault analysts, says Jervis, for relying on plausibility.[50]

Intelligence agencies turned out to be wrong, Jervis argues, because their inferences presumed an actor who was 'rational' and who had 'a coherent strategy' over time. That was the problem: Saddam was not rational and had no coherent strategy. He was trying to please international observers by appearing to disarm, hoping this would get sanctions on Iraq lifted. But at the same time, he did not want to reveal to Iran and the US that he had no significant WMD programmes, because he thought those states would then smell weakness and seek to overthrow or assassinate him. So he continued with ambiguity and thereby invited an invasion. According to Jervis, Saddam failed to realise that a belief in WMD would not deter the US, while their lack did not make an Iranian attack inevitable. His behaviour was 'foolish and self-defeating', 'figuratively and perhaps literally suicidal'. How, then, were analysts supposed to put themselves in his shoes and understand the situation from his point of view? Analytical processes that can 'produce an accurate picture of normal adversary behaviour' do not work 'when the other's beliefs and behaviour are strange and self-defeating', when 'the country or situation is odd'.[51] Jervis goes further in an interview in 2008: 'Saddam's view of the world was really crazy' in that he underplayed in his own mind the threat of a US attack; he did not believe it would come to that. He therefore 'committed suicide, not only figuratively but literally', which is 'nuts' from the perspective of International Relations theory. 'A regime should *not* commit suicide; if something like a National Interest exists, committing suicide is definitely not part of it'.[52]

Jervis raises the role not just of accuracy but of ideas in intelligence. In his view, analysts had an idea of how states are supposed to act in international affairs, namely that they try to avoid their own destruction by not provoking others. And they had an idea of what Saddam Hussein wanted in the world, based on the history of his government. So their error was in thinking that Saddam's desires would fit appropriately within the normal behaviour of states. An intelligence failure, yes, but one that rested on Saddam's own irrationality rather than analysts' miscounting of missiles.

What exactly are these ideas that intelligence agencies suppos-edly held and which underpin Jervis' explanation of their failure? Jervis does not dig into them himself, but it is crucial to ask how they are defined. What is a normal state as opposed to an odd one? What does it mean to act rationally as opposed to being crazy? What makes a policy self-defeating or suicidal? And how do you know it when you see it? This book argues that to come up with a stronger and more fundamental critique of intelligence analysis, we need to answer these questions, and doing so means reaching into the origins and twentieth-century history of modern state intelli-gence services. It means looking at how those services constructed for themselves an idea of their purpose, their reason for existing and making analyses of the world, which then shaped what sort of ideas they thought they needed in order to do their work. And this mission and ideas came from a crucial but overlooked source: the experience of decolonisation.

British and US intelligence agencies took on their modern form and got a handle on their current activities at a moment in history when the number of independent states and self-governing pop-ulations was multiplying rapidly (Figure 0.2). When the United Nations was founded in 1945, there were 750 million people living in territories governed by colonial states, nearly a third of the world's population.[53] Between 1945 and 1960, more than 30 new states across the African and Asian continents would free people from European colonial rule by declaring autonomy or complete inde-pendence.[54] This epoch-defining shift in international relations conditioned how intelligence analysts saw their new role in US and British policy-making. This book argues that their efforts consti-tute an emergency intellectual response to decolonisation, where they provided policy-makers with ideas and arguments about what was happening in the world and how they could respond to it. Out of this long process of thinking and writing, from the end of the Second World War to the new millennium, came the ideas that Jervis then brings up in his study: of normal and abnormal states; of proper behaviour on the world stage that avoids self-destruc-tion; of when a statesperson is being rational and when they are being nuts. If Jervis' argument about the intelligence failure of Iraq is right in any substantive way, then that failure is a legacy of this intellectual history of responding to decolonisation.

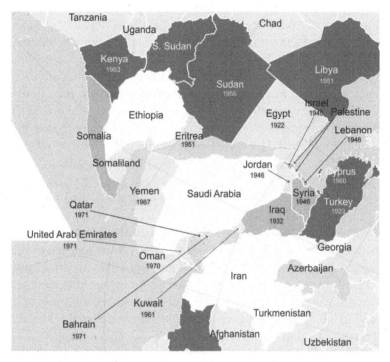

Figure 0.2 This map highlights the years when Middle East and North African (MENA) countries *de facto* escaped colonial sovereignty. Those shaded darkest (e.g. Sudan) were British colonies or under occupation; in medium shade (e.g. Iraq), British and French Mandate territories; the lightest (e.g. Yemen), British protectorates. The map uses the Dymaxion projection to preserve accurate scale. (Dymaxion map source: https://bit.ly/3z8ztJ1. Annotated by author)

Concepts of normal and abnormal states, of good statesmanship and ignorant, irrational actions, have a sharp rhetorical power whose logic is difficult to immediately pin down. Thinking about them in the frame of colonialism and decolonisation gives us a way of understanding this power: Their use reflects the continuing role of race in how political actors imagine and carry out international relations. The standard story of international relations describes a system of functionally identical units – nation-states – that are legally equal and politically stuck in the same boat, all trying to live together and protect their citizens without sufficient information to fully trust one another and without an overarching authority. Yes, colonialism once existed, but it was overcome through a natural liberal process of expanding the family of equal states beyond the competent 'givers', Europe and the US, to those 'learning' and 'catching up', the Global South. Since racism was therefore dismantled through the spread of state sovereignty, then today we have a neutral global order, albeit one which is tragically tough on the catching-up nations whose states simply don't function quite as well. This story erases the possibility that the long colonial history of tying populations to political territories defined the nation-states that later emerged in hierarchical, discriminatory ways, or that the multiplication of sovereignty left non-white-majority countries stuck, structurally denied access to equal power and wealth.[55]

When race is acknowledged in mainstream debate on world politics by white writers like myself, it tends to be reduced to the human body, as prejudice towards physical characteristics, as if racism can only exist in international politics when statespersons discriminate against people or populations who look different.[56] And to be sure, politicians in the Anglosphere *do* do this – Donald Trump's and Boris Johnson's infamous racist slurs against African peoples, for which neither have paid a political price, are only the most recent examples.

But the fundamental substance of race and racism in international relations mirrors the role of intelligence that I wish to explore in this book: the social construction of group boundaries and belonging.[57] This book focuses on a particular form of racialisation, of socially constructing racial groups, one with a colonial heritage. It is about imagining people's psyches and their innate ways of being in the world. Practices of racism make claims about people's sensibilities – that is, how others react to things with their mind and their senses, how they tend to think and feel about the world around them. Practices of racism decide that such sensibilities reflect people's *capacity* or competency for thinking and feeling, a capacity with a certain direction of travel and a certain limit. This is what defines people as having a common racial belonging: The idea is that they share inherent ways of experiencing and understanding things around them which predispose them to certain attachments and preferences, to different vices and virtues, even to levels of emotional control; these limits, moreover, are difficult to transcend. From formal colonialism to today, racist practices have tried to identify physical traits as surface markers of those capacities for thinking and feeling, linked in turn to projections of place, of where these capacities supposedly took root. Appearance and behaviour is supposed to reveal what people are really like 'underneath', an underneath which ties them to certain parts of the world where those psychological limits were engrained, and which makes them inferior to those who have no such limits, those doing the defining.[58] In the countries of Euro-America and their global relations, displaying an unconstrained psyche through your physique and emotional life is what lets you into the group 'white'. Does your body and behaviour show that you have the right kind of thoughts and feelings? This claim to a pristine mind and soul, not to mention the material privilege and protection society gives you for it, make these countries' racial majorities invested emotionally in their racial difference.[59]

During nineteenth-century European colonialism, when our modern ideas of race were codified and institutionalised, the physical surface markers that colonisers looked for were those associated with physiology and genetics. Racialisation was about categorising the human species into bogus biological subsets; anything from skin tone to facial features to ancestral lineage revealed your racial belonging and therefore your competence for taking part in 'civilised society'.[60] But identifying these surface markers was no guarantee that they would make any sense whatsoever when the people being marked actually lived their lives in the world. People can demonstrate capacities for thought and feeling that completely trounce or flummox those doing the categorising, making the latter anxious that their interpretations are not up to scratch. Equally, people who are supposed to belong to the superior group, the group without innate limits, can struggle to measure up, or even mingle and mix with their supposed inferiors.[61] So these categories had to be constantly re-made, their defining features scraped over again and again.

At the end of the Second World War, with Nazi Germany having brought colonial racism home to Europe,[62] racialisation based on bogus biology began to (somewhat) fall out of favour. Social change, not least decolonisation and the attendant growth of multicultural societies, was making this racism less tenable as a way of governing the emerging liberal international order. As this book will demonstrate, political elites in the English-speaking colonial and allied states – a self-conscious Anglosphere[63] – gradually accepted a different idea, of humanity being divided by civilisational culture. No longer were physique or genes an index of people's capacity for thought and feeling. Instead, outward appearance and behaviour marked people's *cultivated* capacities, cultivated by the social group they grew up in or their supposed links to other societies around the world. Defective biology becomes deficient cultural traditions. This shift has allowed elites to bat away the accusation that they or their policies are racist with the retort that they are merely singling out people's voluntary social values, not their uncontrollable biology. If others' values are inferior or unwanted in liberal societies or international order, discrimination is justified. But make no mistake: Because this singling out means identifying the bodily signs of people's overriding group cultures, markers of how people have been predisposed to think and behave, and because these cultures are supposed to be distinct, their differences insurmountable, this is a process of racialisation.[64] The Islamophobia which has accompanied the past 20 years of counter-terrorism is racist in the way it targets only certain bodies regardless of religious belief, those marked as looking or behaving 'Muslim-like', based on claims of those bodies' culturally-determined feelings and alien social bonds. Political practices which single out these markers are today policing ever-more-restrictive boundaries of belonging.

As this book travels from the 1940s through subsequent decades, this cultural racism will make up the bulk of my evidence for the role of race in intelligence agencies' deliberations on a post-colonial world. In the international politics of the past hundred years, racialisation has revolved around whether certain populations are able to govern themselves, to make their own geopolitical decisions, or whether instead they need international tutelage, guidance, even overrule. Those populations, with their supposedly inherent cultural pivot or limits, have frequently been defined as of 'the East', contrasting with 'the West'. This sweeping claim of enormous categories of belonging, of separate civilisations, grounds a grand narrative form of racialisation called Orientalism.[65] The birth of this narrative speaks to its future use by intelligence agencies. Europe of the fifteenth to eighteenth centuries comprised both Christian monarchies *and* a diverse, Islam-majority Ottoman Empire, which encompassed Anatolia and south-east Europe. Ottoman ideas, trade, and military actions existed *within* Europe's geopolitics, overlapping the rest of the continent. But as the Ottoman Empire weakened and other European states renewed their colonial expansion, the latter's politicians and historians re-wrote history. The Ottoman sultan was falsely characterised as despotic, his reign explained as foreign 'Turks' imposing autocracy on the Balkan people and others. This despotism, moreover, was used to explain the Ottoman Empire's disintegration. Going against the available evidence, political figures claimed that this political weakness was totally unlike European governance.[66] In this way, the Ottomans were defined as outside 'the West' on the grounds of their innate, racialised political practices. The stage was set for European empires to imagine themselves as torch-bearers for a lineage of civilisation stretching back to ancient Greece, while the forms of government they encountered across the eastern continent, from Turkey to China, were presumed to share in the Ottomans' decrepit tyranny.[67]

Despite having different guises since then, Orientalism always treats people beyond the West's imagined borders as being unable to think and act well in world affairs due to their inferior cultures. It has allowed politicians and analysts to make sense of unfamiliar forms of governance in what is now called the Middle East, by assuming that this difference reflects others' *lack* of properly-functioning state structures, ones which the West is presumed to have.[68] Scholar Dina Rezk has recently explored how historical Anglosphere intelligence successes and failures in the Middle East were influenced by changing ideas of Arab political culture. Rezk sees positive moves from the 1950s to the 1980s towards analysing cultural specificity.[69] This book extends such scholarship by looking at the flip side of specificity. As the above origin story indicates, this kind of racialisation also *contains* the geopolitical relations of the rest of the world, by defining the many alliances and conflicts of the Middle East as unrelated to, even disconnected from, the Anglosphere. The book argues that intelligence agents took on this lesson: that separate civilisations means separate explanations for political events. The material reality of the world has helped to validate the Orientalist story, as today's political-economic systems treat people differently and help make that difference acceptable. Disparities in preventable death and resolvable conflict make clear that international politics excludes some people from protection, from dignity, from the means to live, while giving others these material benefits. This lived inequality is used as evidence that some groups are deficient at thinking and feeling, that their faulty logic and unkempt emotions are to blame for people's woes.[70] As we shall see, the enduring inequalities between older and newer nations in the post-colonial period were translated by intelligence analysts into evidence for world populations' cultural and political inferiority.

In today's world politics, then, the key role of race is to reflect and reinforce how certain political actors believe the global social order should look. Racism simply *is* global inequalities and how they are explained away. It was the related political struggle over self-governing that led the sociologist W. E. B. Du Bois to insist that the twentieth century would be defined by the global colour line, a demarcation of the unequal political-economic 'relations of the darker to the lighter races [...] in Asia and Africa, in America and the islands of the sea'.[71] Throughout Du Bois' long life, from the late nineteenth to mid-twentieth centuries, he saw racist practices emerge from the 'close contact' between different national populations, not least because that contact resulted from the discriminatory 'territorial, political, and economic expansion' of Britain, the US and other states across the globe. Du Bois pointed out, however, that while these states had hoped to 'displace the native races and inherit their lands', the political consciousness and actions of world populations had 'rudely shaken' their belief.[72] The global colour line, in Du Bois' eyes, was violently unsustainable. As non-white populations around the world rose up to assert their dignity and then their independence from colonialism, Du Bois described their victories as the global colour line being 'crossed' in revolutionary ways, as challenging the mutual support between the concept of whiteness and the exclusive claim to civilisation: 'The magic of the word "white" is already broken'.[73] It is true that, like the colonial categories of old, the intellectual defence of a white world order kept being re-worked. Nevertheless, Du Bois' commitment to Pan-Africanist thought and organising reflected his assessment that just as race made international relations, so anti-colonialism could remake it in turn.[74]

This inter-relation is what makes race and racism a key constituent of world order today: The global hierarchy, where a few states' wealth and power vastly outweigh those of the rest, rests on and reproduces lived ideas of racial belonging, of who has the inner competency to lead and make decisions for the world and who does not. But in an era of decolonisation, the close contact between Anglosphere powers and world populations was constantly undermining the magic of the former's strategic thinking and the claim that the latter's politics were vacuous. 'I do not want to overstate my pessimism', reported former US Ambassador to India Chester Bowles in 1955. But after a trip to Africa and South Asia, he was 'seriously disturbed by the low state into which our position has fallen', as these continents' peoples expressed 'widespread admiration' on the one hand for those who 'participated in the common struggle against Western domination', and disdain on the other for the US's 'patronising and tactless' policies, including its government's 'compromise on the issue of colonialism'.[75] The most significant part of Bowles' dispatch for our purposes is to whom it was addressed: Central Intelligence Agency Director Allen Dulles. The global colour line was to be a key concern of intelligence agencies such as the CIA for decades to come.

INTELLIGENCE: A BANDAGE FOR DECOLONISATION

This book argues that British and US intelligence analysts saw their post-war mission as one of trying to secure the international position that their two states now found themselves in, a position which happened to be at the top of racial hierarchies of wealth and geopolitical influence. The book draws on historical documents

from US and British state archives, including intelligence assessments and meeting minutes, as well as material related to these
states' diplomatic offices since, as the Chester Bowles reference
above shows, diplomats produced open-source intelligence that
fed into the analyses presented by policy-makers. The book also
refers to the work of intelligence scholars, who have often been
an intrinsic part of this community and its debates. If intelligence analysts were going to be of use to policy-makers, they had
to explain how and why the geopolitical dynamics around them
threatened their position. Of course, there was a problem with this
mission: It was being engrained just at the moment when millions
of people worldwide were contesting these two states' position in
international hierarchies.

Anti-colonial movements called out Britain and the US, among
others, for their hypocrisy in lauding self-determination as a
principle of anti-Nazism while wishing to retain colonies and
stymieing independence struggles.[76] As the twentieth century
continued, the breadth of political philosophies and movements
that grew out of anti-colonialism posed an existential challenge to
British and US statespersons' image of their own power and legitimacy. Self-determination demands could include the freedom
to decide one's own foreign policy priorities and economic sovereignty, both frightening prospects for the material reach and
political influence of the Anglosphere, while new states made
world order increasingly difficult to manage. Policy-makers
and scholars were worried: What if populations proposed to use
their own natural resources without compensating foreign oil
companies that had reaped the benefits for decades? What if more
and more armed movements declared their own forms of independence?[77] In the 1960s, a writer in the elite US magazine *Foreign
Affairs* alluded to these problems as 'The Cacophony of Nations',
lamenting that while 'discontented nations and colonies clam-
our[ed] for independence', no longer did Great Britannia and its
Atlantic ally have 'the power to subdue turbulence and maintain
order in the world'.[78] As is discussed in the following chapters, this
danger of independent governance was especially significant in the
Middle East, understood to be a major source of British and US
privilege, owing to its geographical position and material wealth.

Any form of intelligence analysis worth institutionalising would have to address these questions, to provide an image of what was happening in this region and how these two states could navigate the decolonial challenge.

With this mission and challenge underlying their work, intelligence analysts began to make sense of decolonisation, for themselves and for policy-makers, by seeing it as evidence of two major new ideas about the world and the Middle East in particular. These ideas are addressed respectively in Chapters 1 and 2. Analysts gradually codified these ideas in their assessment reports and used them in turn to interpret new events, as the consequences of decolonisation stretched through the rest of the century. The first idea was that geopolitics in the Middle East region reflected a self-contained logic that tended towards stasis or continuity. The important political dynamics that shaped the region were located within the region itself, in the form of assertive monarchist leaders, compliant populations, and traditional cultures. The forces of anti-colonial nationalism destabilised this logic, by highlighting people's desire for change and the oppressiveness of their living conditions. Instead of adjusting their model, analysts judged that this movement's call for revolutionary change upset the dynamics of stasis and was therefore *the* cause of any regional 'instability' – not those dynamics themselves.[79] Intelligence analysis therefore justified the Anglosphere intervening in the region's geopolitics, by means both diplomatic and military, to try to restore that static equilibrium. Chapter 1 details how this played out in the 1940s and 1950s, from post-war discussions about the purpose of intelligence to the rise of anti-colonial organisations, the Suez Crisis, military interventions, and the 1958 revolution in Iraq.

The second idea was that the thoughts and actions of all these new political actors in a decolonising Middle East reflected something more than what it might appear on the surface, namely, a principled opposition to different forms of colonialism. Rather, these beliefs and behaviour were evidence that societies in the region were shaped by mindsets and emotions completely alien to the Anglosphere. The cultural background of these attitudes became the most important thing about anti-colonialism: They over there just do not think and feel the way we do. Over time, intelligence analysts disparaged any suggestion that people in the Middle East thought like so-called Westerners as an act of mirror-imaging. It was a fallacy, even arrogant and insensitive, to project your own mindset on to others. But mindsets were defined in racial terms, as innate competencies of thinking and feeling, bred by distinct cultures. So if the thought processes reflecting intelligence analysts' cultures were considered clear-sighted, objective, rational – well, the actions of Middle Eastern political actors must be something other than all these things. And they could not be *more* objective and clear-sighted. Chapter 2 traces the history of this idea of avoiding mirror-imaging. While its roots can be found in early intelligence assessments of the Soviet Union and of General Nasser's Egypt, the concept was formally inaugurated among a group whose influence here is rarely acknowledged: the US neoconservative movement in the 1970s. Despite intelligence scholars' claim today that to avoid mirror-imaging is to be culturally progressive, those who gave the concept to intelligence agencies put forward a racial view of world politics, one that argued in favour of Anglosphere supremacy.

Having detailed how these two ideas developed as key parts of analysts' post-war work, Chapters 3 and 4 detail their long post-colonial legacy in later intelligence assumptions about Iraq and Saddam Hussein. More than a history, the book explains how exactly intelligence analysts' ideas about Saddam made pro-war ways of thinking about him and Iraq acceptable and plausible before the 2003 invasion. Decades worth of intelligence analysis on Saddam's personality and his Ba'athist Government were structured by arguments about the political emptiness of Iraq's historical anti-colonialism, the culturally-based emotional xenophobia of Saddam, and the enduring irrationality of his government's actions on the world stage, that Iraq simply did not understand how geopolitics worked. These arguments were structured and backed up by the two major ideas which developed in intelligence circles during decolonisation – Iraq was considered a prime example of the need to preserve the Middle East's equilibrium and of the engrained ignorance of the Arab mind. This is what underlies the proposals raised by Robert Jervis in his explanation of the Iraq intelligence failure. And, as the Conclusion discusses, these arguments echo further through post-Iraq intelligence, into the 2011 intervention in Libya, the Arab Spring, and even recent intelligence on Putin and Ukraine.

The crucial consequence of these intelligence ideas is that they make it hard for analysts and policy-makers to imagine how their own actions might impact on the outlooks and behaviours of Middle Eastern states. Intelligence officers have promoted these stories of regional stasis and insular cultures during a decades-long period when populations around the world have had unprecedented opportunities to entangle themselves in and transform one another. Political life in the late twentieth and early twenty-first century is born out of global solidarities and interactions. This arguably gained perpetual motion during decolonisation, spurred on by forms of anti-colonial Third Worldist activism that crossed state borders.[80] Communication and exchange are better supported materially than ever before and accessible to a greater swathe of societies, boosting that global political life. You cannot understand political dynamics around the world without taking these global entanglements into account. Experts and non-experts alike find it hard to think so, however, because we tend to view the world in terms of discrete political objects, like nation-states, that emerge from within themselves like a seed and grow towards an ideal end like a flower. Only then do they interact.[81] This way of thinking has a colonial heritage: Nineteenth-century European citizens imagined empire in terms of 'here' and 'there', of a 'home' that was comfortably familiar and untainted by the disparaged cultures and political problems of 'away'.[82] But this was a political fantasy, as the societies that we call 'Britain' and 'the United States' with their 'developed' qualities have *always* come out of movements between and relations with other parts of the world.[83] Moreover, political ideas and their effects, like self-determination, burst over state borders, shaping the minds of disparate people who then act on them. These ideas and effects have origins around the globe and have helped to create the supposedly self-referential Western world.[84] State leaders and citizens alike have their world-views shaped by these constant global flows.

Intelligence has long disagreed. Its emergency response to decolonisation disavowed global conditions for politics, either 'at home' or in the rest of the world. If normal Middle East geopolitics is self-contained and political actors there are determined by their deficient cultures, then home-grown, sensible Anglosphere policy has no perceivable role in shaping how those actors think about the world and how geopolitical dynamics in the region become unstable. This is a necessary consequence of intelligence fulfilling its mission, of explaining how British and US superiority in international hierarchies can be preserved. Because if analysts try to account for the role of Anglosphere policy in attitudes and actions towards it in the region, the risk is that this role would turn out to be fundamentally crippling of that superiority. Perhaps, in other words, Anglosphere influence over politics and its material foothold in the region would turn out to be politically unsustainable. Perhaps it was a major cause of societal damage, institutional degradation, and political violence. As this book demonstrates, in those moments when intelligence analysis came close to highlighting just such a dynamic, this possibility was overruled by the strength of those ideas on which post-colonial intelligence has based itself – that the Middle East tends towards stasis, and that the outlooks of others come from their insular cultures. At key points in the run-up to the Iraq War, this overruling is exactly what happened. Similar to the way colonial administrators reacted to instability under their rule by re-structuring societies to suit their racial pre-conceptions, intelligence agents interpreted Saddam Hussein's reactions to escalating British and US threats as evidence of his engrained ignorant mindset, leading to assessments that justified continuing those threats.[85] Saddam Hussein was treated as being just as cut-off and self-deluded as Vladimir Putin.

This last comparison is not an idle one. Days before Russia invaded Ukraine, William Hague, Britain's former foreign secretary, wrote a remarkable piece of ventriloquism in *The Times* of London, writing at length on 'what [Putin] may be thinking'. 'I am about to make history', to bring forth 'the post-Western order', says Hague's imagined Putin. While 'Western Europeans' believe 'power comes from being interdependent', 'I think it comes from [...] following my own rules'. 'They think like traders; I think like an intelligence officer'. Hague implores the reader: Let us not make Ukrainians the latest 'people the West has abandoned and betrayed'.[86] This prose is all the more remarkable because of its author. Hague not only moved to dismiss an International Criminal Court bid to prosecute British politicians for war crimes in Iraq;[87] he also spearheaded Britain's role in the 2011 intervention in Libya that eventually ousted Muammar Gaddafi (which we will discuss again in the Conclusion). Those same press reports on intelligence efforts to understand Putin's mind note that the Russian president is convinced the Anglosphere wishes to overthrow him, leading to his 'obsession with watching videos of Libya's Col Gaddafi being killed after he was driven from power in 2011'.[88] Putin's obsession formed just as Anglosphere commentators were warning of Russia's gradual 'Turn to Its Asian Past', its 'nostalgia [...] for the eastern conquest of Genghis Khan'.[89] While one state leader interprets the world as bearing down on them and justifying violence, across the globe intelligence analysts and their political superiors look at this leader and see a backward alien culture disconnected from that world – justifying the use of force against him.

Over the last several decades, intelligence ideas of racial infe-riority and geopolitical good behaviour have bolstered the case for state violence abroad, by making paths towards de-escala-tion impossible to imagine as real opportunities and legitimate policies. As with Putin, intelligence judged that Arab leaders such as Saddam and populations such as Iraq's were simply going to do what they were going to do.

1

Whispering geopolitics
in a decolonising world

On 21 March 1946, an unusual memo was copied to members of Britain's Joint Intelligence Committee (JIC). The president of the Royal Geographical Society (RGS) had written to Prime Minister Clement Atlee asking for some clarification: What did the term 'Middle East' mean?[1] Having caught wind that Atlee was open to reconsidering the government's official use of the term, the RGS wanted to point out that for geographers, some countries were clearly within a 'Middle' and others within a 'Near' East. Might the prime minister then provide a supportive 'authoritative ruling' in public, before the less precise use of the term 'crystallises into accepted practice'?

On the face of it, this does not sound like an issue that should concern British intelligence officers, especially as their centre for intelligence analysis, only a decade old, was dealing with the fallout of a world war. But perhaps out of uncertainty or disinterest, the RGS president's letter had been forwarded to the JIC for them to provide a decent answer on the Middle East's scope and meaning. This gives a sense of how intelligence analysis would be treated in the mid-twentieth century: as a resource for establishing how exactly this changing world should be defined.

So, at their meeting the next day, the JIC discussed the letter.[2] It was felt that the term had already crystallised, meaning any new pronouncement was of little use. But the director of plans also insisted that the generally-accepted concept of 'Middle East', covering states from North Africa all the way to the Arabian Peninsula, comprised 'one strategic theatre' in which British forces operated, making it 'hardly [...] practicable' to divide it up. Indeed, doing so would even be 'danger[ous]', given that British strategic planning relied on it so heavily. When consulted, the Colonial Office agreed. Yes, the RGS were 'no doubt right' that 'historically speaking' some states were 'properly described' as 'Near' as opposed to 'Middle' East. But the term's current usage was 'confirmed and greatly reinforced' by all the regional organisations Her Majesty's Government had itself set up using that moniker, both at home and abroad. Plus, the Colonial Office insisted, considering Iraq and Jordan's recent independence, Britain's only colonial territories in the region were Palestine and Aden, and the RGS wanted them taken *out of* the Middle East definition. The Colonial Office left the ridiculousness of such an outcome unspoken but implicit.[3] No, only the present common usage would do. With this advice, the JIC wrote a reply to the prime minister's private secretary recommending exactly that.

What makes this discussion significant is that Britain's highest intelligence body – granted, still a heavily military one at this point[4] – was thinking about the make up of the world, of international politics, through the lens of how its government and preceding ones had already shaped it. Intelligence analysts shared this outlook with academic experts: A writer in the *Geographical Review*, citing the prime minister's reply to the RGS, agreed that wartime military bases implanted in the region had quite simply made it necessary to 'reorganise the political and economic life of the countries concerned', under the auspices of one term.[5] The Middle East made sense as a concept because its use reflected how British imperial power had treated those states and peoples. To change the concept meant risking a dent in the definition of the country's influence – to think, a Middle East with no British Empire territories in it! This was presented by analysts, however, not as self-important arrogance but as a level-headed assessment of how power was currently balanced – namely, in Britain's favour – and what was most desirable for the region in the future. Note the Colonial Office's argument: Geographers might be technically correct in their view of these countries, but accuracy was not really the point. Britain needed to strategically manage Middle Eastern geopolitics, and that meant keeping the term Middle East.

How quickly all this would change in a few years. Not the definition of Middle East itself: That of course would survive many decades. The politics of this definition, however, would come to attract uncomfortable scrutiny. By the 1950s, India's President Nehru was calling out the term as a Eurocentric legacy of impe- rialism, much to the ridicule of self-professed serious scholars.[6] By 1960, the term's increasing prevalence in the US prompted an assessment in *Foreign Affairs*, which bemoaned the Eisen- hower administration's inconsistent definition. Alas, 'the spread of Western civilisation and political influence' made some precision imperative when putting 'labels on distant lands'.[7] Even if such crit- icisms were conveniently dismissed, 'Western' specialists quickly needed to re-assess their immediate post-war claims of a shared 'community of sentiment' among 'Middle Easterners', character- ised by laziness, lack of public duty, and low political horizons (this from a review of reports by the Middle East Supply Centre, one of the organisations approvingly cited by the JIC to back up their view of the region).[8] People's horizons were, it turned out, multiple and dizzyingly high, and both British and US intelligence analysts would struggle to reconcile their model of how the world was *supposed* to work with these emancipatory ambitions, as colonies in the Middle East and across the European empires rapidly gained sovereignty and pursued their own political visions in the 1940s, 1950s, and 1960s.

This is the context for the present chapter: the blossoming of a post-colonial 'Middle East', just as US and British intelligence analysts were trying to get a handle on an international structure in which their two victorious governments were supposedly hegemonic.

SQUARING THE CIRCLE OF 'STABILITY'

The origin of Western intelligence analysis is typically told as a story of a pragmatic reaction to threat, of facing up to a Cold War power struggle. Britain and the US each get a variation on this theme. On one side, having evolved to coordinate the study of Axis strategy using intercepted decoded material, Britain's Joint Intelligence Committee was forced to learn how to do the same for the Soviets and Chinese communists but without access to anything like the same level of decrypted documents.[9] A lot is made of the coordi- nation role: After all, it is this organisation, much admired and emulated by other countries, that is said to have brought analysts' combined expertise from across different intelligence groups to bear on policy-making.[10] On the US side, President Truman was famously convinced of the Soviet Union's existential threat right after the Second World War; the first task of his newly-ordained peacetime Central Intelligence Group was to assess methods of spying on this wartime ally.[11]

There is a lot riding on this story. It explains twentieth-century intelligence analysis as a necessity, a valiant effort to combat existential threats – an explanation that conveniently fits its contemporary justification. It started as it meant to go on.[12] The idea that this intelligence scrutiny was necessary also nourishes an old neoconservative image of the Soviet Union – as fundamentally deceptive and suspicious, with spies needed to uncover its hidden expansionist machinations.[13]

But put these ideas alongside the above discussion of 'Middle East' confusion and another story emerges. British analysts in the mid-1940s had a stake in this discussion of labelling, not because the Soviets' presence or actions in the region gave 'Middle East' meaning, but because the British Empire had a chain of material interests – in the form of colonies and bases – and forms of political influence over the governments concerned. As Foreign Secretary Anthony Eden put it in 1945, the region was 'a matter of life and death to the British Empire' because 'it is there that the Empire can be cut in half'.[14] Analysts argued that the present concept of the Middle East gave policy-makers the best means for *preserving* those interests and influence. Regardless of Soviet relations, Britain had gained this position in the region and it was now simply a requirement to keep it. US officials, meanwhile, also guarded their newfound ability to bring 'our political and economic strength' to bear on the Middle East rather than be 'forced back to the Atlantic'.[15] The region's location and 'great mineral wealth' were reason enough for the US to now 'directly and indirectly' intervene in its 'political and economic development', to raise its 'economic and cultural levels' so that its strategic position and wealth stayed within the orbit of 'democratic civilisation'.[16] This would gradually come to mean vast US oil company concessions and bases of its own. The danger of the Soviet Union, as Anglo-American analysts saw it, was that it threatened this footprint and influence that their states had gained in the region (Figure 1.1). Without that presence and political power, the assessment of threat and how to deal with it would be upended.

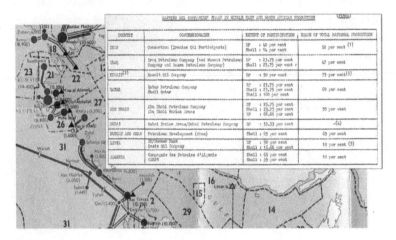

Figure 1.1 The question of oil was never far away in intelligence assessments of a decolonising Middle East. This table, from a mid-1960s Joint Intelligence Committee report, details British oil companies' financial stakes in different countries' oil reserves. The table accompanies a map of those concessions. (JIC (68) 24 (Final), 2 July 1968: pp. 15, 17)

This takes us to the other vital issue lying behind that 1946 debate over labelling – decolonisation. That same year, Jordan gained independence from British political oversight. Egypt and Iraq, two states whose influence would be felt throughout the region, had done so years earlier. The British Mandate in Israel ended in 1948. In 1951, Libya would leave the British Empire, followed by Kuwait in 1961 and Aden in 1967. Anti-colonialism fed uprisings in Oman, Aden, and Cyprus. With Syria and Lebanon gaining independence from France, by the 1960s the political landscape in the region would be transformed. This transformation was, however, more complicated than a switch from colony to post-colony: States such as Jordan and Libya remained dependent economically and militarily connected to their former colonial master, while others accepted, tolerated, or fell into informal US policy control.[17] And then there were those that chose different paths, with anti-colonial nationalists forming governments in Egypt and Iraq.

When historians talk of British and US intelligence's role in this transformation, they tend to focus on either the covert shenanigans of agents 'in the field' or the cultivation of local intelligence agencies to counter Soviet 'subversion'.[18] Both are vital lines of inquiry. But again, while historians are mindful of their story's moral resonance today – that Western intelligence may have given imperialism another gasp of breath – their focus ends up supporting the orthodox story of the Cold War. Intelligence agencies are described as countering, through good or bad means, Soviet encroachment on these newly independent states. Wittingly or otherwise, the 'Cold War' frame makes intelligence action against Russia appear an inevitability, again obscuring that there was nothing unavoidable about Britain and the US trying to stay in and dictate Middle Eastern affairs even with their perception of Soviet threat. That strategy was no will of God or nature.[19]

Whatever we think of the intelligence services' political outlook, the story of counter-espionage against an unavoidable foe does not give intelligence analysts of the time the intellectual credit that they deserve. As this chapter demonstrates, these analysts progressively understood their role as one of putting together different pieces of information to find patterns within them, patterns that pointed to possible future events and their consequences for the material footprint and political influence of these analysts' governments. This longer-term political assessment meant constructing a model, an intelligence picture, of how Middle Eastern geopolitics tended to work, in order to figure out how to preserve US and British power to shape those geopolitics. Intelligence analysts were trying to do this, however, right at the moment when a new political force, anti-colonial nationalism, was rewriting the apparent rules of how those geopolitics worked. The political vision of anti-colonialism allowed regional elites and populations to act in ways that did not fit British and US analysts' model.

Consider this chapter then a sketch of an intellectual biography of Anglosphere intelligence during decolonisation. This biography's central thread is the stability paradox. Analysts were invested in the presumption that an Anglo-American presence in the Middle East benefited 'political stability' in the region. Manifestations of anti-colonial politics, however, kept insisting on the opposite: that this presence destabilised regional geopolitics by provoking resentment and concerted resistance. The intelligence reports written by analysts squared this circle of what counted as stability by translating the relationship between Anglo-American power and nationalist sentiment into a simpler, more insular dynamic. Instead of considering how these two phenomena influenced one another, analysis overwrote their relationship with an image of the Middle East as a *self-contained* theatre of politics. Analysis described this theatre as having an internal logic, an equilibrium that kept to a regular pattern. Nationalism was seen as a force that disturbed this equilibrium, making a US and/or British presence necessary to contain this force and bring things back into balance. In this way, analysts equated stability with *continuity*, even as they acknowledged that nationalism was here to stay. This way of imagining the Middle East laid a foundation for understanding post-colonial governments and their interactions with the Anglosphere, echoing in the thoughts and words of those who decades later would study Saddam Hussein's Iraq.

POST-WAR CRISIS: WHAT USE IS A FACT?

In today's debates about international affairs and state security services, the reason for having a state intelligence agency is treated as obvious, as something that does not need spelling out. But an important aspect of the British and US agencies in the 1930s and 1940s is their soul-searching over their purpose. When talked about in intelligence history, this is described as a slow waking up to reality, as agencies getting to grips with the truth of external threats. Looking at analysts' internal discussions, however, reveals a debate over reality and empire, over whether analysis should try to make the best use of the facts to give an accurate picture of the world, or figure out how to preserve their states' new positions of pre-eminence – the implication being that these aims could be at odds.

Consider first Britain. In the 1930s and 1940s, Britain's political elite were largely dedicated to preserving their country's imperial presence, even in the face of a world war's ruinous impact on its finances and the possible need to defer to an ascending United States.[20] Intelligence's role in all this was unclear even before the Second World War. Germany was still disarmed and not yet 'Nazified' in the mid-1930s, and a lack of human intelligence sources on Hitler's strategic planning encouraged analysts to adopt 'rosy-tinted misconceptions' about its future threat.[21] When Nazi Germany did become an intelligence focus of the newly-minted JIC, the military-heavy committee was not yet allowed to set its own political assessment objectives. What early strategic estimates it did write were ignored when higher-ups deemed them too pessimistic.[22] Michael Goodman, the JIC's official historian, has described the late 1930s as the committee's 'Irrelevant Period': Not only was it rarely called upon by departments for reports, it did not itself offer political analyses that would broaden statespersons' horizons.[23]

So, how did the JIC find its purpose? By 1938, the JIC chair was making the point that military intelligence and political intelligence were two different things, each worthy of attention.[24] There was also a difference between intelligence 'facts' which 'speak for themselves' and those that are only 'intelligible' after being 'collated' with others and 'interpret[ed]' through critical thought. Surely the JIC was concerned with the latter.[25] Once war broke out, the JIC got the chance to present this kind of interpretive political intelligence at a high-policy level, giving assessments of enemy perceptions and of the broader consequences of ever-shifting battlelines. Intelligence officials saw a need to study 'the intentions of other enemy or potentially hostile countries' and so set up a section of the JIC for this purpose.[26] Some in the new committee, however, identified a problem here: How do you best write '[a]ppreciations from the enemy point of view'? Analysts' initial solution was to deny this new section access to any intelligence that they thought was not also possessed by Axis governments, literally forcing a narrowed enemy 'perspective'. This went so far as to discourage section members from attending other meetings where they might learn of new secret information.[27] But that raised another question: Who should be in the JIC anyway? Was economic expertise important in terms of enemy intentions? Did they need someone dedicated to 'general political questions'?[28] Analysts were wrestling with a challenge of imagination, with how to put themselves in the enemy's shoes, if this was to be the JIC's analytical edge.

These struggles led directly to the creation of the Joint Intelligence Staff, the JIC's main report-drafting body.[29] But the wrestling continued after the Second World War. The committee's chair argued that while they were 'well equipped' to write on 'enemy intentions generally', 'it would be foolish to pretend that even now [...] intelligence has not many critics'. One problem was sifting through all available information and making the best use of it. If a peacetime agency was going to give warning of other countries' 'development of warlike actions or policies', it would need to use the right intelligence sources.[30] But sources were now thin on the ground. Without intercepted decoded material on the Soviet Union and other countries, such as they had on Nazi deliberations during the Second World War, analysts would have to make their assessments despite their 'general lack of high level, reliable, and verifiable intelligence'.[31]

So, to deal with this lack, the JIC broadened its methods. In 1944, the committee was basing its Soviet estimates on large-scale measurements of Russia's economy and population: Such a large empire, with plentiful raw materials but a rapidly growing population, would choose to improve its internal standard of living rather than compete with other great powers militarily.[32] But by 1946, the Joint Intelligence Staff was openly 'speculat[ing]' not just on the Soviet Union's 'strategic interests' but on 'the intentions [...] of the Russian leaders'. Now the prime factors were not the material statistics of Russia – geography, 'development' status – but its elite's perception of their state's destiny: 'They are convinced' that they will reach 'greatness', 'an ultimate position of predominance in the world'.[33] As discussed more fully in the following chapter, this presaged a new mode of analysing 'adversary' governments. But for now, it is important to note that this change in method had an important consequence for imagining geopolitics. Tucked away in the 1946 discussion is a reflection on how Stalin's 'inner circle' might be interpreting the actions of Britain and the United States. It was likely, analysts thought, that Soviet leaders perceived the US and Britain to have 'harden[ed]' their attitude towards the USSR, as if both were trying to 'restrict Russia's aspirations'. This hints that the Soviet outlook is dynamically *connected* to the outside world, and that Britain and the US can *alter* that outlook. But this unspoken possibility gets overridden by explicit statements about race, of the Soviets' 'immense Asiatic element': Its leaders have 'an oriental regard for the maintenance of their dignity' which 'makes [them] uncompromising in all their actions which may affect Russia's position in the world'.[34] Intelligence 'expertise' felt more secure from this viewpoint, but the international looked much less dynamic.

And what of US analysts' view of their purpose during this time? By all accounts, the early work of the CIA on 'strategic assessment' was neither praised nor well-understood. Wartime precursors were initially forbidden from 'interpreting' facts, only 'reporting' them.[35] At the end of the Second World War, as the new US administration debated what, if any, peacetime agency should be preserved, President Truman suggested that such an agency only needed to collate information; facts would speak for themselves, if only they were in one place.[36] In 1946, the same year the British JIC were adjusting their methods, members of this new US Central Intelligence Group (CIG) were unsure how to balance the demand for 'daily summaries', made up of 'factual statements', with that for 'strategic [...] policy intelligence'. Nor did they know how to produce the latter. Who should write this strategic analysis, what it should contain, how it should be written – it was all up for debate. Even after the CIG was succeeded by the Central Intelligence Agency, other parts of the US Government did not put much stock in attempts by the new Office of Reports and Estimates to disseminate such analysis; they were seen as trivial reads with little bearing on policy.[37] As one officer saw it, the problem was that the agency's remit had expanded unchecked to include any and all political and economic research, a kind of 'omnicompeten[ce]' that produced 'nondescript intelligence' without 'clear concept of mission'.[38]

So how did the CIA overcome their analysts' seeming irrelevance? Like the JIC before them, they proposed a change in approach. In 1949, the CIA argued that it was being hampered by having both *'explicit'* and *'implicit'* (their emphasis) responsibilities that pulled in different directions: the first, to produce National Intelligence Estimates; the second, to simply be an 'intelligence facility', passing on information to the president and National Security Council. The latter responsibility, which had grown up over time, seemed far more policy-relevant to intelligence's consumers. To redress this imbalance, the CIA suggested that national intelligence, those assessments made by coordinating and interpreting multiple sources, be defined as something designed to 'reduce [...] surprise in foreign situations and developments which affect United States *national security*', and whatever else the National Security Council, set up two years earlier, decides is needed.[39]

National security had emerged among US military and policy officials as a key concept for post-war planning. Diplomats and policy-makers viewed the devastation in Europe and the immiseration of colonial populations in the Second World War's aftermath as potent sources of future social unrest and political breakdown. Economic development, fuelled by Persian Gulf petroleum, was therefore vital, not only to help the world recover but to link all these regions economically to the Anglosphere through their new purchasing power and oil company deals, placing them under the US's influence.[40] Military advisers, reaching similar conclusions about world recovery, argued that securing these much-needed resources in Asia and Africa, and responding to any revolutions by the immiserated, meant maintaining an extensive worldwide basing network, as had already emerged from the Second World War.[41] Having been officially inaugurated as CIG's successor through the 1947 National Security Act, the CIA was tied organisationally to the 'national security ideology'.[42] It was now drawing explicitly on this discussion, promoting a concept that emphasised active US involvement in world affairs in an effort to meet the 'security challenges' and 'responsibilities' of the country's new global position *and thereby maintain that position.*[43]

The CIA made a smart case for its importance: Unlike other US Government intelligence bureaus and departments, it argued, only this agency had the 'perspective' and the 'freedom from bias' to make up-to-date political assessments that spoke to this national security requirement, a 'delicate and significant function'. But this defence hinted at analysts' intellectual struggle over how they should relate to the US state. Was a 'national security' remit compatible with accurate intelligence? There was, the agency admitted, an outstanding question of 'what sort of estimates should emerge from the national intelligence structure'. Surely estimates needed to '*earn* [their emphasis] their distinction as the most authoritative intelligence available to the policy makers'. But at the same time, analysts needed those policy-makers to 'give the Central Intelligence Agency such guidance in matters pertaining to national policy that Central Intelligence Agency support will be more directly responsive to their needs'.[44] Being authoritative suggests estimates that have the potential to both open up *and* close off policy possibilities, to declare one strategy viable and another not. Being responsive suggests asking questions that do not risk frustrating policy-makers' aims.

While this debate over 'national intelligence' was taking place, another part of the CIA was providing an answer to its conundrum. The CIA's report series 'Review of the World Situation' took the US's position in international hierarchies seriously from the beginning. At the first meeting of the National Security Council, members discussed a memo on their own function, the creation of an advisory committee for the CIA, and the very first Review of the World Situation.[45] An internal review of the series years later commended the fact that the reviews' authors had 'reasonable latitude' to express conclusions without any 'modifications desired by the [other intelligence] Agencies'. Even more notably, these reviews 'boldly stated the theoretical basis' for their conclusions, as in their background thinking on 'US Security in general' and what it would mean to maintain it – that is, what constituted 'national security'.[46] On that front, the series' first author, CIA officer Ludwell Montague, defined the review as 'a responsible synthesis and interpretation of the developing global situation', while the retrospective described each issue as 'concentrating in essay form on one aspect of the total situation'.[47]

The global, the total: These reviews consciously approached the US's place within international hierarchies. In the agency's very first Review of September 1947, 'the Security of the United States' is affected not by the potential and will of the Soviet Union to directly attack the US, both of which are judged to be weak, but by the possible erosion of US global influence. Russia's attempts to worm its way into the Middle East would be 'unacceptable in the twentieth century for much the same reasons applicable to the nineteenth'.[48] Montague extends this imperial-heritage outlook on the region: Since the capabilities of the British Empire, 'formerly a major stabilising influence', are now sadly 'reduced', the objective of the US should be to try 'redressing the balance of power' in the Middle East, in order to protect 'the strategic position of the Western powers' in these areas – specifically, basing rights and oil production.[49]

At least one agency officer got it: Intelligence analysis worked when it considered 'security' as geopolitical stature. By 1949, the Executive Secretary of the National Security Council would publicly describe the CIA as 'the eyes and ears of the Council and the President for intelligence relating to national security'.[50] But while the USSR was the explicit rival to this stature in these reports, it was the supposed focus of the Soviets' scheming and manipulation, according to Montague's first review, which would become key to US and British analysis: the 'social unrest' and 'political instability' in 'colonial (or former colonial) areas'.[51]

EXPLAINING (AWAY) ANTI-COLONIAL NATIONALISM

In the early 1980s, in a reflective piece written for their colleagues, a US intelligence analyst looked back at the recent 1979 Iranian revolution for lessons on dealing with such surprising events. Thinking it through, the analyst remarked that their profession had taken a long time to give the concept of political instability the attention it deserves. The analyst tells their story through a lens rarely acknowledged in popular intelligence history: The post-war situation saw the US needing new ways to interpret 'the sudden collapse of colonial empires throughout what we now call the Third World'. This 'essentially benevolent nation' was now 'dealing with the millions of the world less fortunate than ourselves and only recently launched into independence'. And of course there would be those who 'would undermine the fruit of our benevolence'. But what about, as in Iran, 'riots, strikes, demonstrations, political assassinations, chaotic factional conflicts, insurrections' – how could they fit in? The problem was trying to discern and predict 'the erosion of political authority'.[52]

That erosion of authority was, this chapter argues, a major challenge to the self-made intellectual purpose of the post-war intelligence services. If British and US analysts were to study the world in a way that helped their states to keep their position in international hierarchies and, by implication, global inequalities, what to make of these growing political movements from Africa to Asia, which questioned both the material and moral bases of that position? Intelligence officials gradually reasoned that a narrow focus on the Soviets was inadequate. Uprisings in British colonies were blamed on a lack of intelligence, while the Joint Intelligence Staff pushed for the prioritisation of 'trouble spots' outside Soviet machinations.[53] A CIA agent working in their new Office of National Estimates later described his colleagues as 'acquir[ing] a knowledge and understanding of other problems the world faces which have little or no connection with communism'.[54]

From the perspective of these two governments' political interests in that ill-defined 'Middle East', there was a logical series of questions for intelligence analysts. First, how, if at all possible, could these movements for self-determination be satisfied or controlled *while* maintaining US/British political command, without the cost outweighing these movements' potential damage? Crucially, this question accepts that those two goals influence and counter-balance one another, the weight of pursuing one perhaps displacing the other. Second, would this response require some intelligence appreciation of these movements' political goals? And finally, in policy terms, would it ultimately require some repressive use of force?

Structuring these questions as if they are obvious, however, is misleading. British and US intelligence did not exactly ask them. Rather, they asked: How could nationalism be managed *in order to* maintain their states' position in the Middle East? This subtly different question makes the two goals sequential – one leads to the other. From the late 1940s through the 1950s, there was little to no sense in intelligence assessments that the dynamics of self-determination movements might necessitate a *reduction* in the presence and political power of a receding empire and an ascendant superpower, to avoid nationalism's perpetuation and even greater losses in future. The reason for this goes back to that newfound purpose. Because intelligence assessments held that their states should retain their presence and power, anti-colonialism's appearance in different forms across the region had to be interpreted as something that did not pose an intellectual challenge to that requirement, that did not explicitly undermine the case for retaining that position. If it did – if intelligence officers ever countenanced that anti-colonial nationalists represented an argument about the repression of democracy and self-government by the US and British regional foothold – then policy-makers would have to accept that unless they provided an answer to that argument, their material presence and influence in the Middle East would only intensify these movements and erode that foothold, erode their own political authority.

So, instead of facing that intellectual challenge, intelligence officers were predisposed to see nationalism within an image of geopolitics that had, at its core, the legitimacy of their states' regional presence. Nationalism *had* to be wrong in its thinking for that legitimacy to make sense. This led Anglosphere observers to interpret nationalism as irrational and unrepresentative. The position is summed up well by the Official Committee on the Middle East, a British Cabinet policy group that regularly consulted the Joint Intelligence Committee. Looking at events up to the late 1950s, the committee conceded that Arab nationalism did have a 'constructive side', focused on realising the theoretical 'good [post-war] doctrine' of 'the rights of nations'. The problem was that Arab nationalism tended 'to express itself practically' as paranoid 'resentment' and 'bitterness' towards 'external domination', along with 'a conscious sense of inferiority' towards 'Western [...] technical skill and economic power', especially Britain's 'large share of oil production'. Nationalism drew incorrect conclusions about Britain's effects on the region because of Arabs' irrational emotional humiliation. It would be fine if their nationalism was 'a straight issue', focused validly on achieving equality. But it is not: Arab nationalists see conspiracies by 'the old "imperialists"' everywhere, for instance, in relations with Israel. Because of this, any accusation that British policy has 'underestimated and mishandled Arab nationalism' is unfair, since under these conditions 'any policy in the Middle East runs the risk of enmity'. Britain and the US 'can [never] wholly gratify Arab nationalists'.[55] As detailed below, this dismissal of anti-colonial independence struggles developed in intelligence assessments over the 1940s and 1950s in response to displays of nationalist strength whose implications were too disruptive if thought about otherwise.

So how did this dismissal come about? In the late 1940s, as British intelligence was called upon to assess spiralling international crises and state-communist military manoeuvres,[56] the Joint Intelligence Committee put it to the director of plans that, if you want to assess how Soviet forces might take advantage of the balance of power around the world, you need to have a sense of what that world would look like geopolitically in the future – not just individual countries but as a whole, perhaps even looking ten years ahead.[57] It was a circular process of analysis: The Joint Intelligence Staff (JIS) were instructed to take into account current estimates of Russian intentions, while at the same time their new report was to underpin a *new* assessment of USSR intentions in the future.[58] Nevertheless, the JIS got on with its task and finally presented its report in June 1948, after several months' work, as a 'Forecast of the World Situation in 1957'.

The report is a comprehensive piece of work, but a general trend emerges in the analysis of the future for 'strategically important regions'. Acknowledging that forecasting so far ahead is a 'virtual impossibility', the report authors nonetheless gamely give 'best case', 'worse case', and 'intermediate' scenarios for each country, with respect to Britain and allied powers' global position, before picking the most 'probable' of the three. So, how would the Middle East look in ten years' time? The 'Arab world' would be 'in a state of political turmoil, largely owing to Communist and Nationalist agitation'. Despite this, however, these states and/or peoples (it is unclear who is being referred to) 'would be generally well disposed towards the Anglo-Saxon powers, as the lesser of two evils'. These 'territories and resources' – and there was no doubt that, economically, '[o]nly oil is important' in this region – would be 'at the disposal of the Anglo-Americans', as would the 'overseas possessions' of other European empires.[59] In other words, Europe would still have its colonies and those 'possessions' would largely appreciate the struggle with the Soviet Union. The overwhelming bet made by analysts was for an 'intermediate' outcome across the 'underdeveloped' world, with allegiances to the US and Britain enduring despite social unrest.

Read between the lines, however, and you can detect analysts' burgeoning unease at the possible meaning of 'instability'. The assumed 'best case' for the 'Arab world' is one where governments are 'politically anti-Communist *but* promoting necessary social and economic development'. That 'but' is important: It shows analysts are keenly aware that Soviet public policy *could* raise living standards and improve economic outputs, things that analysts did think were important for this part of the world. Analytically, this produced a problem. Beneficial social policies for Middle East states had to be rejected if they potentially reduced Anglosphere influence. Libya falling under an 'international trusteeship', for example, is a 'worst-case' because it would give the USSR political influence in the country. Better to stymie independence and try to promote 'development' through exclusively British trusteeship. Persia is judged to benefit from a '[p]opular and progressive Government', but this should not encourage any worst-case 'aggressive revolutionary minority' addressing the 'discontent of industrial workers and peasants'. The report does not explain how this delicate balance could be achieved.[60] The easiest way intellectually to deal with these struggles was to think of anti-colonial sentiment as politically unproductive, even undemocratic, and therefore not worthy of consideration. Analysts could not imagine that Arabs, Africans, and Asians were able to envision better political settlements than them. Discussing military capabilities, they note that 'the Arab is notably indolent, inefficient and technically incompetent', necessitating 'Western supervision'; the 'Arab mind' was 'totally unable to appreciate' certain military–economic matters. No surprise, then, that nationalism could only lead to 'turmoil', to 'chaos'.[61]

Finally, JIC higher-ups insisted that their Joint Intelligence Staff include a paragraph on what they called their 'cold war' in 'political and economic' affairs: If the US and Britain persisted in their 'firm line' on such affairs, then perhaps 'wavering or neutral' powers might come to our side. The paragraph's wording is vague but the JIC's discussions during the report's drafting make clear that they wanted to avoid an overly pessimistic or 'gloomy' outlook.[62] Surely, they were thinking, the Global South could be convinced of the benefits of an Anglosphere presence and influence.

US intelligence analysts, meanwhile, were also struggling with instability's meaning in their own assessments of the colonial world. Post-war US policy-makers, including President Roosevelt, had come around to the view that formal empires bred Soviet sympathies. But while they therefore had a disagreement with their British colleagues, they too preferred a form of trusteeship that could be managed – say, as part of the US-promoted Bretton Woods institutional arrangement – as opposed to formal independence. It was less a question of immediately ending empire than of adapting it.[63] Nevertheless, the title of a 1948 report by the CIA's new Office for Research and Estimates (ORE) would not have encouraged any British analyst who saw it: 'The Break-Up of the Colonial Empires' laments that European short-sightedness has made their global disintegration 'inevitable'. Looking from the perspective of the US's newfound world pre-eminence, the ORE argues that disintegration both weakens European allies and 'deprives the US itself of assured access to vital bases and raw materials in these areas', since independent states would be *free to choose their future alignments*. Considering the US's 'global [...] strategic needs and growing dependence on foreign military resources', this is 'an increasingly serious loss'.[64] Analysts were trying to figure out how the US could *secure* these assurances as the post-colonial wave continued. This underlying objective pushes US analysts, unlike their British colleagues, to recognise an immovable political object: European powers' '[b]elated concessions' to anti-colonial movements 'do not meet *the basic nationalist demand* for independence and are unlikely to be more than temporarily effective'. The US aim should therefore be to gain the 'good will' of 'emergent independent nations' by being 'sympathetic' to their 'national aspirations'.[65]

But while these aspirations were an inevitability that forced strategists to adjust, the ORE's analysts were working from a more fundamental assumption: that the US political power in the Middle East, having grown through the last world war, was legitimate in-and-of-itself. This too was an immovable object. Within this image of the world, the idea that independence movements would be correct in pushing for a reduction of the US presence in order to achieve real independence could not be computed. So it had to be translated differently.

CIA analysts had a key intellectual support to fall back on, albeit a wobbly and sometimes precarious one: race. The 1948 report tells a story of twentieth-century empire having inadvertently 'expos[ed]' colonised populations to the kind of socio-economic development that was customary in industrialised Europe. Those peoples now wanted the same quality of 'democratic' life. But the report then muddies this motivation by describing peoples' resentment of colonial inequality as having evolved into 'a deep-seated racial hostility', 'a reaction against "white superiority"' that was fostering solidarity between nations of the 'Orient [...] against the colonial powers and the US'.[66] By tracing anti-colonialism to 'an underlying racial antagonism', the analysis can side-step considering the intellectual merit of nationalist aspirations. In fact, the 'anti-whiteness' of nationalists blinds them to what analysts can plainly see, that '[t]heir relatively backward stage of political, economic, and social evolution' will keep them 'dependent upon outside help', i.e. the 'white overlords', for some time. That backwardness, that lack of political capacity, means that anti-colonialism's success against empire can only produce 'a political vacuum' in the region which the Soviet Union might enter into, by presenting itself as 'largely Asiatic' and by 'embarrass[ing] the US' on the latter's domestic treatment of African-Americans.[67] Indeed, the CIA reported elsewhere that Soviet propaganda made much of US segregation to demonstrate the latter's shallow anti-racist credentials.[68]

Now the issue of US interference in Middle Eastern politics is happily resolved. The US must '[fill] the gap'. These new states may be monocultures that still depend on their former occupiers as markets for raw material and agricultural exports. Their nationalist leaders may strongly desire 'economic independence' and 'tend to resent US economic dominance' through trade agreements. But if their states cannot survive without external economic assistance, and the US is 'the only nation able to supply it', then surely this need for private investment will 'temper [...] [their] antagonism'. Like the JIC, the ORE made a bet on the Global South coming around to their way of thinking.[69] Assumptions of anti-colonialism's race-based motivation allowed the ORE study to propose high-minded solutions to this social unrest that did not upset the idea of US hegemony.

SELF-DETERMINATION IN A WESTERN WORLD

How useful to US and British aims, though, was this (un)apprecia-tion of nationalism? Interpreting the massive political tide towards self-determination as something that these two states' material presence could smooth out, both politically through trusteeship and economically through investment, cuts analysts off from con-sidering what these movements had to say about the geopolitics of the Middle East, or even what their mere existence said about that presence. You cannot analyse the sociology and political discourse of anti-colonialism if one part of its dynamics, the political dominance of the Anglosphere, is off the table in terms of analysis. Nationalism therefore proves to be the problem concept that keeps coming up in analyses before being batted back down, described in a way that means it is never explained and policy-makers are not provided ways to reckon with it.

So, in a 1952 'Review of the Middle East and North Africa', a background report for Britain's Joint Planning Staff, the JIC argues that the region's populations have one uniting quality: a shared view of the region's political transformation as reflecting 'a gradual but inevitable process' of decolonisation, whereby the old colonial powers are seen, incredibly, as 'no more than [their] equals'. If these peoples agitate for this prophecy's fulfilment, the report warns, Britain and its allies will suffer as they have so much to lose. But this peculiar Middle Eastern desire for colonialism's retreat has no underlying principles, no intellectual history. It emerged with the wartime weakening of the Empires and is now simply 'infectious'. It 'thrives on success', as if nothing else could motivate it, yet its appearance *before* any success is unexplained. The review calls this 'the natural growth of nationalism'. Geopolitically, it has produced only territory disputes and violent campaigns against Anglosphere influence, as covers for the 'incompetence' of 'extreme politicians'.[70]

With nationalism reduced to a historical mystery, the JIC is able to suggest that their government intervene to promote improved living standards, so populations will be less resentful of Britain's healthily profitable oil companies, and ensure that regional military bases are 'strictly commensurate with their *needs* and are understood by the inhabitants as compatible with *reasonable* national aspirations'. It is a tragic irony, as analysts see it, that by blaming 'the "foreigners"' for people's ills, nationalist governments have turned populations against 'foreign assistance', the very thing which might improve standards of living.[71] The JIC cannot comprehend that anti-colonialism could, with any validity, reject their state's regional presence and influence.

More than a decade after this report, future JIC Chairman Bernard Burrows would propose a variation on this tragic historical narrative. Burrows, Britain's political resident in the Gulf before taking up this intelligence chair, placed Arab nationalism within a general category of natural societal progress, likening Arab anti-colonialism to 'the classic combination of Nationalism and Liberalism in 19th Century Europe': Arab populations, like Europeans before them, have come to believe that constitutional progress in their countries necessitates 'political freedom'. The problem with this natural process in the Arabian Peninsula as opposed to Europe is that these populations associate freedom with independence from 'the British Colonial Government', the very political body that could 'lead colonies into the forms of democracy'. This is 'particularly unfortunate', in Burrow's view, because any Arab democracy will have 'a strong tendency' to fall under the political influence of the anti-British United Arab Republic. Britain was lucky, says Burrows, that its 'support for the Shaikhs' in the Persian Gulf had maintained 'an established framework of society', not to mention a 'native and local force' dependent on British connections, that mediated against such political demands.[72]

The Joint Intelligence Committee wrestled with the idea that nationalism could be shaped by and in turn direct its ire at Britain's military foothold in the region. The JIC tries to think this through in a 1954 study on Britain's capacity to quell any future riots against their presence in Iraq. Britain at this point had much-valued basing rights and troops at two airfields in the country. Having approved military plans for potential unrest, the Chiefs of Staff thought to ask their intelligence analysts: How and why would this happen in the first place?[73] The committee's Assessments Staff identify 'two obvious issues' that might prompt 'anti-British feeling': the economic privileges given to the Iraqi Petroleum Company, owned by an Anglosphere consortium, and the Anglo-Iraqi treaty that guaranteed those bases. But to consider how British policy was therefore, by definition, causing political instability in Iraq was unthinkable. Analysts push this idea away by attributing it to Arab 'extremists': Any 'reasonable politician' in Iraq would only 'blame' Her Majesty's Government out of political 'convenien[ce]', or if other statespersons made an 'emotional [...] appeal'. In fact, this is the report's definition of 'nationalism'. The Joint Intelligence Staff insist that the Hashemite monarchy deal with low standards of living, popular political frustrations and the misuse of oil revenue, to reduce the likelihood of protest and 'extremist' inroads. Left unexplained is what to do if 'social development schemes' are hampered by the 'safeguard[ing]' of 'British interests', the oil production and military facilities that are producing inequality and political anger.[74] Britain's influence twists in and out of view, pinned down but then covered up as analysts try to fulfil their purpose.

This dance continued across the Atlantic, where throughout the early to mid-1950s the CIA interpreted the Middle East's political turbulence as necessitating foreign manipulation and control. While they might have given up on the story that all nationalism in the region was Soviet-inspired manipulation, the agency struggled to explain the staying power of self-determination movements. CIA Director Allen Dulles, for instance, was perplexed by the 1955 Bandung Conference, which brought together the elites of 29 nations and colonies to formulate shared decolonial policy. 'The nearest thing to a common denominator we can find', Dulles reported, is their 'experience [...] of Western imperialism'. With this exasperated political analysis, Dulles is reduced to decrying the 'emotionalism of Nationalist Asian leaders' and the supposed irony of the conference being conducted in English.[75] The CIA's later 'Estimate of the World Situation' of 1957 begins by acknowledging 'an acceleration of the processes of change' and cautions that it is unclear whether 'the phase of rapid movement' has abated. But among the 'main forces at work' here, '[t]he force of nationalism' in the Middle East represents 'an almost fanatic desire to eliminate the special foreign privileges and influences associated with colonialism', reflecting 'xenophobic' anti-white-Westernness. Given the difficulty of fulfilling its political and economic expectations, this force will only create more 'political tension'. From this stunned and disapproving assessment, the estimate's author reasons that post-colonies will nonetheless need foreign assistance to pursue their ambitious development goals. The challenge is therefore to insist on giving that assistance, which will require Arab leaders 'courageous enough to oppose extremist political elements' and policies to moderate nationalist aspirations. But there is no sense that US objectives might inflame anti-colonialism and undermine any such leaders and policies.[76]

In a rare moment, one of these many analysts noticed the knot they all might be tying themselves in here. During a September 1951 meeting of the JIC, Committee Chair D. P. Reilly put it to his colleagues that perhaps one problem with trying to study future developments in the Middle East was that the future depended on 'what *we* were doing or trying to do in the area'. And since Britain could not 'take all the action' required, it would also depend on the actions of 'other Powers having our interests'. This went outside 'current intelligence'. How then to prepare studies that were 'clear[ly] [...] required' for planning?

While JIC meeting minutes do not record silences or awkward pauses, the secretary's notes hint at how analysts saw their purpose and Britain's place in the world. A fellow committee member, Major General Shortt, replies that yes, this is a difficult problem. But there might still be 'considerable benefit' in producing an Intelligence Estimate of 'pending' changes in 'the Arab world' and their effects on 'the rest of the Arab countries' – that is, changes from within that world. This kind of estimate would help 'in any [future] study of Middle East problems'. Reilly is satisfied with this answer: Perhaps, he says, the report should therefore focus on '*sources* of trouble *for the Western Powers* in the area, with the object of foreseeing such trouble'. This formulation neatly passes over the initial troubling question. Negative developments in the Middle East are now caused internally and impact *on* Britain and its allies. The secretary records 'general agreement' with this solution and the initial proposed outline of the study is '[d]eferred'.[77] The discussion's conclusion points the way for the intellectual project US and British intelligence would embark on as decolonisation continued: enforcing a model of how the Middle East normally works.

EVERMORE VIOLENT STABILITY

If intelligence officials thought that their judgements about the world would help secure the current international hierarchy of states, the 1950s would prove disheartening. Anti-colonialism was not letting up. A 1955 review of colonial intelligence bemoaned that London's analysts had failed to foresee various indigenous rebellions. Britain's Colonial Office was brought fully on board the JIC, in the hope that analysts would now have the on-the-ground intelligence they needed to plan 'counter-subversion' operations – that is, black propaganda, infiltration of anti-colonial groups, and covert intervention.[78] Much of this 'plausibly-deniable' action failed to produce enduring 'pro-Western' governments in the Middle East and only increased popular discontent towards Anglo-America.[79] Moreover, the pro-development approach weaved through intelligence analysis unavoidably clashed with policy-makers' opposition to the free choice of independent nations. Britain's Official Committee on the Middle East, an interdepartmental group to which the JIC contributed, warned in 1957 against trying to divert the region's oil revenues towards development programmes 'for the benefit of the poor countries', since those countries were currently 'unfriendly' – political unrest be damned.[80] If development meant political and economic disentanglement from US and British influence, then it was less appealing than either autocracies or military intervention. The latter were pursued extensively: In the next few years, Britain and the US sent troops, officially or otherwise, to fight in Syria, Jordan, Libya, Lebanon, Kuwait, and Yemen, all in defence of autocratic rulers. Those policy preferences only further inflamed regional anger (Figure 1.2).[81] The US and Britain (along with the Soviet Union) found it increasingly difficult to convince Middle Eastern political actors to follow their line of thinking on international affairs, as states and populations prioritised an international struggle between revolution and conservatism.[82] People, said Britain's Saudi Ambassador, remained

untouched and unmoved by 'Western civilisation', while nationalist leaders like Nasser 'did not understand the importance' of 'the
defence interests of the Middle East'.[83]

Figure 1.2   Beirut citizens regard the US Marines who had arrived that day,
18 July 1958, to defend the embattled Lebanese Government. The soldier in
the centre is reading a newspaper whose headline reports Egyptian President
Nasser's support for the new Iraqi Government, which had just overthrown the
pro-Anglosphere Hashemite monarchy. (Bettmann/Bettmann via Getty Images)

Intelligence analysts adopted an updated remit: How could their
states ingratiate themselves within these Middle East currents, so
as to dictate policy and maintain political and military influence
as far as possible? In other words, given the purpose that they had
adopted after the Second World War, analysts were exploring how
to retain their countries' international superiority through these
increasingly-unstoppable changes in the region.

Analysts attempted to provide this 'useful' intelligence against a background of wider policy shifts in reaction to those changes. British policy-makers had long been debating whether clinging on to every last colony was worth it: Perhaps forcefully defending its administrations, military bases, and privileged role in oil production against uprisings was so corrosive to foreign relations that it made more sense, as Anthony Eden suggested in 1953, to 'harness these [nationalist] movements' and let them 'at least appear to have a determining voice' in the region, in order to 'maintain our position in the Middle East'.[84] Ministers and officials were far from endorsing decolonisation though, and right into the 1960s most were keen to maintain Britain's footprint in the region despite financial costs.[85] A debate had also developed in the US State Department and executive over ally Britain's attempts to maintain its imperial status in the Persian Gulf. Seeing Britain's declining influence as inevitable and its response increasingly desperate, US officials weighed up whether it was better to try to develop links with decolonial Arab nationalists or to bet that the British Empire would endure. Few were keen to replace Britain's protective role outright towards the Gulf sheikdoms.[86] From the Eisenhower administration to the post-Kennedy years, however, the aim of anti-colonial movements and 'Third-Worldism' to *shape* regional affairs themselves largely proved difficult for the US to accept.[87] Geopolitical independence was always the sticking point.

Against one's trenchant decline and the other's reluctance to fill imperial shoes, the analysis branches of the intelligence services tried to stabilise statespersons' knowledge. What seemed to be needed was an image of how politics in the Middle East operated, what were its most important variables, and what would it take to push and prod those variables in the right direction. Out of this challenge, there gradually emerged a model of the region as a self-contained equilibrium.

Among British analysts, this came about as a way of picturing the country in a position of dictating Middle Eastern affairs even with a reduced footprint. By 1956, ambassadors in the region saw Britain's military presence as useless at defending commercial interests, while those in Britain's colonial architecture retorted that any unhappy populations should be made to 'accept our position here as one of the facts of life'.[88] For the JIC's part, that same year its Chair Patrick Dean co-wrote a study on 'The Future of the United Kingdom in World Affairs', saying that Britain should 'take advantage' of the present low likelihood of world war to reduce military 'burdens' while maintaining 'our vital interests overseas'. Because Dean and his co-authors saw the Middle East as 'now the most critical theatre politically', there was 'no question of reducing the (very limited) amount of force we maintain in the Persian Gulf'. Nonetheless, shaping the oil flows through the region now depended less on 'physical strength' than on keeping states 'friendly' by helping in 'the rapid development of their economies' – so long as states accepted the political objectives of this assistance. Therefore, Dean and co recommended retaining basing facilities, 'to exercise military power if our interests are threatened', while reducing long-term troop numbers stationed there. Judged economically, they saw this footprint to be small anyway. Local discontent with what it politically represented was not considered. Instead, the authors obliquely noted the need to promote 'education on the right lines', to improve 'local security forces', and to boost 'counter-subversion'.[89]

So how did the analysts under Dean's command think this approach would fare within the political dynamics of the Middle East? Through the end of the 1950s, analysts kept trying to assess ways for Britain to retain its political, economic, and military privileges through these methods even while considering, albeit in a particular way, what Dean's co-authors had overlooked: that a material British presence stoked resentment and protest. A 1958 study of the political outlook for the Persian Gulf warns that 'the rising tide of pan-Arabism' was '[i]nevitably' targeting 'the absolute, or near-absolute, rule of the present regimes and the extent of foreign, particularly British, influence'. In Kuwait and Qatar, 'sabotage' of oil fields and 'riotous demonstrations' are all possible. But analysts take Britain's defence of these absolutist monarchies as a given – their existence supports 'British interests'. In the analysts' terms, that mutual support becomes the same as stability in the region, which means any trend in society that strains these monarchies cannot be part of stability. '[S]ocial reform' in these countries is therefore bundled alongside Pan-Arabism and 'Nasserism', since the 'chief targets' of all three are autocracy and British influence. Social reform – which might otherwise be seen as a move towards political societies more aligned with their vaunted Anglo-European cousins – is now a perverse Arab ideology that threatens the stable monarchist Gulf. The more 'extreme' elements of this movement even threaten to 'undermine the absolute rule of the Shaikhs [sic] and to liberalise the government'![90]

What might be needed, then, to re-establish stability? As the 1958 report saw it, in Kuwait, if 'local security forces' are inadequate, then 'British intervention might be required', *even though* this would, analysts state, 'discredit the British connection in the eyes of all classes'. Socially, it seems, stability can co-exist with popular anger and illegitimacy, if the latter are repressed. In a state like Bahrain, the report judges the government to be almost universally unpopular, but since dissidents are not thought able to 'achieve any effective resistance', the report concludes that there is no need to consider this unpopularity further. In Oman, which by 1958 had seen months of rebellion, the sultans are thought to have 'no real popular support'; a 'political settlement' giving rebel groups some sovereignty is probably needed. But 'such a settlement' might actually necessitate further 'intervention by British forces' and will nevertheless increase the risk of the sultans' overthrow. These challenges too are not commented on further in the report.[91] This kind of strategising was not a one-off. Stability's definitional shiftiness would persist right through to Britain's formal withdrawal from the Arabian Peninsula a decade later. Indeed, by that point, the JIC emphasised the common interest of allied Gulf states as being to 'preserve stability' as far as 'British interests' were concerned, but simultaneously spoke of the danger posed to this common interest by 'the endemic instability of the area'. The latter notion of instability was not elaborated.[92]

The CIA was also trying to produce an image of the Middle East's various parts, which it acknowledged moved quicker and quicker. By the end of the 1950s, the agency was producing more National Intelligence Estimates on the Middle East than they were on the Soviet Bloc.[93] A lack of self-awareness, however, made analysis more difficult. In the 1957 'Estimate of the World Situation', the National Intelligence Estimate authors emphasise from the start the 'desire of the peoples in underdeveloped countries for social and political opportunity and for the fruits of rapid economic development', which leads to their conclusion about the need for US assistance. Within the Soviet Union, they acknowledge the dichotomy that this desire is creating between centralised policy and 'national sentiments and interests'. Political liberalisation had allowed for 'the unleashing of open opposition in Poland and Hungary', reflecting a 'basic conflict between Soviet requirements and popular demands' in its European satellite states. But in the Middle East and elsewhere in the Global South, '[t]he withdrawal of Western authority' – that is, decolonisation – which has accompanied 'expectations for political and economic development' can only be seen as something that threatens the *goal* of 'retaining [US] overseas bases' on terms that assure their effectiveness 'in case of need'. That authority and accompanying military footprint is not considered as a *variable* affecting current political dynamics; as analysts see it, there is no 'basic conflict' here. US support does not figure in the 'developing struggle' between 'revolutionary elements' and 'traditional elites'.[94] Fifteen years later, the JIC would view Soviet encroachments in the Middle East in a similar manner. Russia, the committee argued, faces 'recurrent trouble with Arab nationalism', 'merely as a result of their involvement' in an area 'basically unsympathetic or hostile ideologically'. That basic fact might force Russia into an 'essentially conservative role of upholders of particular [...] régimes'.[95] The committee made this observation a year after Britain had formally withdrawn from the Arabian Peninsula for precisely this reason!

Such oversights would already have sore repercussions by the time of the CIA's next World Situation Estimate in 1958. By January, the National Security Council had come around to the idea that the reason US and allied prestige was declining was that '[i]n the eyes of the majority of Arabs the United States appears to be opposed to the realisation of the goals of Arab nationalism' by 'seeking to protect' its oil privileges and by 'supporting the status quo and opposing political and economic progress'.[96] The CIA agreed in their March estimate for the Council, warning in a section dedicated to 'The psychological impact of US and Soviet policies' that while the USSR's 'well-advertised economic and scientific progress' is seen by many populations as 'a demonstration of the effectiveness of Communist methods', the US is 'increasingly accused of indifference' regarding 'peace and social progress'. There is unease bubbling underneath this short statement: Analysts felt the danger that non-capitalist development could be proven successful. They note that 'our shortcomings – because of our democratic society – are more obvious to the world', pointing out that 'we cannot with the same ease as our competitors hide our race problem'.[97] Domestic anti-black racism had become an international issue: The CIA had long recognised that there was strong worldwide identification of the US with European colonialism on the basis of the country's continuing anti-black state violence and repression.[98]

According to the 1958 estimate's professed author, CIA officer Willard Matthias, his assessment of the US's standing was so dissonant that CIA Director Allen Dulles objected to the paragraphs describing US decline and a 'rising respect being accorded to the Soviet Union'. It took meetings with Office of National Estimates members to convince Dulles, who later explained that he 'simply had not believed that world support was turning away from what the United States was trying to do'.[99] Luckily, CIA analysts had a remedy. Quickly undercutting their damning appraisal of the US's international prestige, the estimate argues that '[u]nfortunately, some of our most cherished traditions – our respect for the rule of law, our desire not to offend our old friends' – that is, the European empires – 'and even our high regard for human life – are often regarded as unrealistic in these countries where the struggle for existence and the social tradition do not encourage such attitudes'. In other words, Middle Eastern populations' antagonism to the US comes out of a regrettable incompatibility between underdeveloped living and liberal democracy, a racialised Hobbesian dilemma. Calls for social reform are actually cries against humanist values! Therefore, with the Soviets continuing to have 'major problems' themselves, the US and its allies simply needed to calculate how to best place their 'political, economic, and military resources'.[100]

BOTH IN AND NOT IN THE MIDDLE EAST

With these strained assessments of the possibility of furthering Britain's and the US's privilege, analysts were pushing up against the possible inevitability of social change and its political consequences. Acting JIC Chairman C. R. Price, speaking on his committee's behalf, argued in August 1958 that the presence of British forces in the Arabian Peninsula was necessary for two reasons: first, 'to permit prompt intervention', a somewhat circular logic; and second, 'to deter trouble-makers and to help stabilise the political position in all areas, in particular those of economic importance to the UK'. Stability was again being equated with the continuity of Britain's political influence and power in the region.[101] This reaches its most absurd conclusion in the JIC's assessment of future events in the Arabian Peninsula. The assessment begins by listing Britain's 'chief interests' in the Middle East: The first listed is 'to maintain political stability in the area'; the second, 'to maintain British influence and prestige' along with 'the confidence of the present rulers'. Listing objectives in this way makes it unclear whether influence and prestige are a means to an end – say, securing oil production and 'essential bases', also listed – or an end in themselves. It Are also passes over how stability, influence and prestige are related: they caused by different phenomena? Can they conflict with one another? Which might overrule which?[102]

The Joint Intelligence Staff are even less inclined here to consider the long-term viability of Britain's footprint. As a result, they begin to picture the Middle East as a set of political dynamics that Britain might *insert* itself into at any time, rather than being *already* integrally involved in its evolving dynamics. So a revolt in one Arab country, they assess, could spark a 'chain reaction' of anti-monarchist uprisings. But 'a swift and effective intervention by British forces' might cut off that enthusiasm. In fact, 'the very presence' of British troops in the region might 'prevent situations arising which would require their use', as if deterring trouble-makers keeps the region's geopolitics running at their more 'usual', desirable pace. The possibility that British troop presences might slowly erode the viability of basing facilities and influence on oil production is effaced, since that footprint is characterised here as something neutral or passive until called upon in response to 'unstable' elements.[103]

Moreover, if actions detrimental to British power in the region are a subversion of normal relations, then analysts are right to judge whether other political actors understand this and act appropriately. In the 1957 memo by the Official Committee on the Middle East, governments which had 'maintain[ed] a friendly relationship with the United Kingdom' despite the Suez Crisis are described as having possessed the sense to 'hold firm', even, the report admits, 'tak[ing] certain risks with public opinion in the maintenance of this attitude'.[104] A JIC assessment the following December perpetuates this attitude. Outlining possible futures for Iraq's newly installed government, the assessment asserts that any communist takeover of the country, while deadly serious, might nonetheless 'mak[e] the Persian Gulf Rulers more aware of the value of the British connection'. Analysts feel no need to explain or examine that value.[105]

Across the Atlantic, US intelligence analysts were also adopting an image of the Middle East as a self-contained equilibrium, in part as a way to think through the push for social change. A National Intelligence Estimate in August 1959 outlines what analysts called 'the principal forces at work in the Arab world', its 'fundamental political and social factors' (Figure 1.3). While this again produces awareness of the dominant international struggle in the region, 'between defenders of the status quo and advocates of change', the dynamics of that struggle, its range and depth, extend only to a rivalry between the new Iraqi Government and Nasser's Egypt over who has the most 'radical' answer for 'social change'. Iraq's possibly communist policy-making make the Soviet Union relevant too, forming in analysts' eyes regional 'battle lines [...] between Arab nationalism and Soviet aspirations'. The CIA's analysts feel qualified to comment on how the players should best adjust to those lines: Nasser now 'appears' to Arabs a 'moderate reformer' and his 'future in the Arab World will largely depend on the success' of the United Arab Republic, the union between Egypt and Syria made the previous year.[106]

But in this analysis of reformist battle lines and best geopolitical practice, the US and Britain are nowhere to be seen. For sure, the

NATIONAL INTELLIGENCE ESTIMATE

MAIN CURRENTS IN THE ARAB WORLD

NOTE: This is an advance copy of the conclusions of this estimate
as approved by the United States Intelligence Board. The
complete text will be circulated within five days of this
issuance.

- Fundamental political and social factors
- Main domestic political patterns
- Roles of Iraq and the UAR
- The Soviet and Western positions

Figure 1.3 This 1959 National Intelligence Estimate clearly delimits 'the
Arab world' with its front cover map. Its 'fundamental political and social
factors' come this far, no further.

estimate concludes that the chances for 'Western influence' have
'improved', with any Soviet inroads in Iraq giving 'opportunities for
[...] influence elsewhere in the area'. There is, however, no assessment of the role of US–British support and defence commitments
to the monarchies of Kuwait, Saudi Arabia, Iran, or Libya, nor of
the cascade of recent military interventions, including 14,000 US
Marines sent to Lebanon the previous year. Instead, the estimate
simply bemoans that 'Arab nationalists, *whether radical or reformist*',
would continue trying to 'eliminat[e] special Western privileges in

the area and regimes identified with the West'.[107] Given the recommendation on improved opportunities, the estimate does not read
as a caution toward interventionist policy-makers. This assessment of the Middle East's inter-state dynamics and the positions
of its leaders presents those policy-makers with a self-contained
system of geopolitics, a set of states and populations whose ideas
and actions push against one another, the consequences of which
analysts can observe from afar, as if unentangled.

When those military interventions did come up, though, their
implications proved too troubling for analysts to completely
fit within a model of how the Middle East 'should' behave. The
1958 JIC assessment of Iraq's future considers which states might
militarily intervene were the new government to be struck by a
Nasserist or communist coup – and among those considered by
the aloof British analysts are regional states, Russia, and finally
'UK/United States'![108] Not unreasonably: The two governments
had discussed invading following Iraq's coup d'état earlier that
year, and another coup attempt in December had increased their
concerns that Iraq would turn Nasserist or communist.[109] While
the other potential interveners are ascribed motivations and calculations that implicate them in the political dynamics of the Middle
East, analysts' own states would simply invade to protect nationals
abroad or for some unelaborated 'other purpose'. But at this point
the report anxiously lists potential blowback effects on 'Western
interests', including Soviet and Arab attempts to force an 'igno-
minious withdrawal and loss of prestige'. That 'value' of the British
connection spoken of earlier sits uneasily with analysts' admission
that an intervention could hurt what they refer to as 'our position
in Kuwait and the Gulf'.[110]

As for interventions which actually went ahead, the Joint Intelligence Staff made a combined assessment of Britain and the US's
planned withdrawals from Jordan and Lebanon following their
respective military actions. Responding to the Iraq coup, the
British Cabinet had seen intervention in Jordan as a last stand
against 'the expansion of nationalist sentiment [...] before it was
too late', in order 'to retrieve our position in the Arab world'.[111]
Throughout the assessment, the JIS project any deterioration of
social order caused by these interventions on to the actions and

ideologies of others. Lebanon's status following withdrawal hinges, says the JIS, on whether 'law and order' efforts by the Lebanese security forces had 'stabilise[d] the internal situation' or whether social conditions were still 'unsettled' before withdrawal. The implicit admission here is that British troops have an impact on social unrest. But all the JIS can suggest is to keep a lid on that unrest. And while 'politically conscious Arabs' and 'nationalist opinion' in the Arabian Peninsula might 'interpret [withdrawal] as a defeat for "imperialism"', the inverted commas make clear that such a view would come from political ideology, a *misreading* of Britain's actions. But how to analyse Britain's effects if it is definitely not a part of a repressive regional hierarchy? The JIS warn that the Soviets will brand Jordan's monarchy 'a Western satellite' for propaganda purposes. Again, the implication is that such a view is analytically unsustainable.[112]

Consequently, the assessment makes no effort to analyse the British military presence and political manipulation of the region – say, its bases in Iraq, its unwavering support for Jordan's King Hussein – in terms of whether it has a political effect commensurate to a hegemonic imperial power. That kind of effect is now a *character trait* of this self-contained Arab world, a lamentable predisposition toward 'anti-Western opinion in the area'. Analysts' assessments avoid this trait. As JIC Chair Patrick Dean writes, what the committee believe is needed now is for 'relations between the West and Arab countries' to 'settl[e] down', implying this region can return to a natural equilibrium after these isolated interventions.[113] Such a reading creaked loudly, however, against other acknowledged facts. Britain's intervention, although aimed squarely at dissuading the revolutionary example of Iraq, needed the shaky pretext of a looming United Arab Emirates Republic invasion. It caused friction with regional states whose airspace was used illegally. And its end came about through a UN resolution initiated by the Egyptians.[114] Moreover, as the assessment states from the outset, British and US aid to King Hussein would have to continue indefinitely, since without it 'Jordan could scarcely survive for long'. Hussein's rule would remain, they stated, 'a weak and unstable regime [...] relying on Western support'.[115] Ministers also recognised that British forces might end up 'turning some of the local population against the King' and could not see 'how this intervention could be turned to our advantage in the long run'. But not intervening would 'expose our interests in the Gulf to great risks' and 'gravely weaken' Britain's 'political position'.[116] The problem, of course, was that this position in the Gulf was sacrosanct.

As for the CIA, their analysis of these interventions faced its own problems. The implicit model of the region as having a self-dependent logic goes hand-in-hand with outsiders' ability to judge the good sense of those within. As a Special National Intelligence Estimate (SNIE) on the invasions states, '[t]he Arab world is in a period of revolutionary ferment and is likely to continue to undergo periods of violence and irrationality'. Calling events irrational puts a helpful spin on various '[a]nti-Western demonstrations and attacks' taking place against allied monarchies. Even the syntax does some spinning: The landing of US forces in Lebanon 'has been interpreted as further identifying the US as the opponent of pan-Arab nationalism'. The wording carefully avoids pinning this interpretation on anyone in particular, while its convoluted structure only makes things more confusing – what is the difference between being *identified* with anti-nationalism by local populations and just being *interpreted* as being identified that way? The estimate acknowledges that '[t]he conflict between the West and the pan-Arab nationalists will intensify nationalist suspicion of Western motives'. It is not clear why this obvious consequence should be attributed to people's suspiciousness. '[E]vents' have also boosted the confidence of those opposed to conservative monarchies – perhaps interventionist events, perhaps not.

The SNIE then reviews the region's states, going over each government's likely feelings towards US and British moves, along with what some might become 'compelled' to do because of geopolitical dynamics, such as acquiesce to 'the onrush of Arab nationalist success'. But in this assessment, the US has no potential future influence on these feelings, since it is not part of 'the Arab world'. Nor is the US compelled by the logic of regional dynamics to make any diplomatic adjustments. Revolutionary fervour is simply an 'infection' that the US can try to prevent from 'spread[ing]'.[117] By the end of the 1950s, then, analysts were long past considering anti-colonialism's causes.

The intelligence services' reaction to the 1958 coup in Iraq brings us close to the point when Saddam Hussein would appear on analysts' radars. As they assessed this post-coup government and then the Ba'athist ones that would follow it, members of the CIA and JIC would draw on their implicit schematic of the Middle East – that awkward term that Clement Atlee had asked for advice on – as a place that had its own separate way of working, a social and political balance which favoured the US and Britain but which the latter only intervene in from without, to preserve continuity, rather than exist as part of from within, as a cause of instability.

Before we get to Iraq, though, there is one other crucial part of this story of intelligence and decolonisation. Because if Middle Eastern politics were self-dependent, then how should analysts study the post-colonial governments that were multiplying across it? If intelligence was supposed to scrutinise the actions of others, then how did these new actors' internal politics fit into the image that 'explained' this part of the world?

2

Dragons and tigers and bears, oh my: The invention of the mirror-image problem

In the spring of 1958, William A. Tidwell had what he gave the title of a 'Horrible Thought'. Tidwell, a CIA senior staff officer, would in a few years help to identify Soviet missiles in Cuba, now widely considered 'a major intelligence success'.[1] Before that, though, he drafted an article for the agency's in-house journal on the horribleness of thinking. In an age of '[g]ames, alcohol, tran-quillisers, TV, and business routine', Tidwell told his colleagues, it is easier than ever to avoid the effort of 'ever having a creative thought'. But when confronted with this complex world, agents of espionage need creative thinking now more than ever. So Tidwell obliges. Consider, he says, that while analysts in the past studied 'surface phenomena', reading the world by looking straight at it, nowadays they use 'standard techniques of [social] sciences' that give them new ways of interpreting that world, like how to measure the strength of another state's military or economy. The confounding thing, though, is that this ability to 'report the facts' rarely convinces politicians to plan for future likelihoods. Analysts are producing 'accurate' and 'timely' intelligence but are still failing! What is needed, Tidwell suggests, is intelligence *beyond* the immediate facts – '[t]he bold analysis, the sharp intuition, the long step ahead, and the provocative ideas' that speculate on future possibilities and their international effects. Analysts need to push the big vision under politicians' noses and tell them, 'these are the decisions that must be decided'.[2]

When Tidwell was writing, 'intelligence failure' was not the much-valorised concept that it would become. In this respect, his argument was prescient: Decades later, the 9/11 Commission would blame the intelligence surprise of al-Qaeda's terrorist attacks on a lack of CIA imagination – an inability to see commercial planes as potential weapons, a failure to connect the dots.[3] But what makes his horrible thought truly interesting is that Tidwell himself would follow his own advice later that summer, demonstrating the importance of imagination but in a way that is rarely acknowledged in today's literature on failure. In a further address to his colleagues, Tidwell discusses how to think your way into the mind of people outside the West. The intelligence community, he says, 'is not only responsible for knowing what the people of other cultures think, but for knowing *how* they think and *why*'. It therefore needs those agents on assignment abroad to integrate with 'people whose culture is radically different from the American culture'. The barriers to this cultural mixing are formidable, not least the CIA's insistence that its recruits conform to 'American moral standards, social mores, and conventionalities of behaviour'. Nonetheless, officers need to 'endure the discomfort' of the unfamiliar and amoral so as to better understand 'backward and unwesternised people throughout the world'.[4]

Not everyone agreed with this suggestion. A 'Ralph Riposte' lives up to their chosen name in an accompanying article, warning that Tidwell's suggestions for integration would risk agents sticking out even more. In Riposte's view, getting inside an alien culture is an act of subterfuge. The problem today is that '[i]t is no longer possible, with the aid of [a] makeup kit and a soiled burnoose, to slip shadow-like among the Arabs and ferret out their plots'. No, says Riposte, '[t]he only way in which we can learn about Arab plots today is to ask Arabs'.[5] Another officer later wrote to *Studies in Intelligence* complaining that Riposte had missed the point entirely: 'Mr. Tidwell', they say, was suggesting how to make it '*easier* and more profitable to ask Arabs about Arab plots', by first 'think[ing] our way into another culture'. Understanding others is a matter of great policy importance, and 'if American intelligence personnel do not understand them' in this way, 'nobody else will'.[6]

In this back-and-forth on overseas intelligence, the qualities of the sharp intuition and the long step ahead, much-coveted by Tidwell, depend on agents delving into foreign cultures. Imagination is necessary for that deep dive and in turn rewards the diver, letting them explore how others think. But notice how quickly this desire to know others becomes specific: Tidwell wants to understand the underdeveloped of the world, which Riposte narrows down further to 'the Arab'. There is an assumption of difference: Mixing with these people is so hard because the undeveloped do not share the agent's civilised social mores, their humanist morality. And there is secrecy involved: the sneakiness of the Arabs with their plots; and the supposedly more noble secrecy needed to gain their trust. As in the previous chapter, this reflects how knowledge-building bleeds into a strategic requirement, how a goal of objectivity becomes knotted together with a desire to secure the Anglophone's superiority, 'to accommodate' the United States 'adequately to world developments', in Tidwell's words.[7] This knot was no bastardisation of social science: Current and former intelligence officials like the CIA's William Langer were rubbing shoulders with civilian experts across academia in the 1950s and 1960s, founding new Middle East Studies programmes that prioritised knowledge of customs and traditions as a way to shape a new generation of national security-minded officials and intellectuals.[8] And all this was happening just as that concept that Tidwell anticipated, the intelligence failure, began to be confronted in the world of analysis.

This chapter continues the story of intelligence's intellectual response to decolonisation by exploring how analysts imagined the internal logic of newly independent Middle East countries and the mindsets of their state leaders. This ultimately becomes a story of attempts to re-script the history of decolonisation. Having imagined a self-contained equilibrium in the Middle East, one that the Anglosphere merely intervenes in to promote 'stability', intelligence analysts had to deal with all those political dynamics that seemed to negate this model. How to explain the fact that Middle East statespersons did not follow the script, that they seemed to disprove the equilibrium? If intelligence reports and assessments were to be of any use for policy-making, they had to give some insight into the political strategies of other governments, so that Anglosphere elites could pre-empt those governments' actions and maintain an (im)balance of power. Britain and the US may have been proven innocent, in analysts' minds, of causing Middle East instability, but were they smart enough to see into the minds of the guilty?

Gradually, the JIC and the CIA replaced a universal problem of epistemology – namely, that it is generally difficult to perceive from a distance the thought processes of people you don't know – with an ascription of Oriental uniqueness – that certain state leaders were *by their very nature* inscrutable. Through the efforts of intelligence experts and reviewers, this general challenge of doing international analysis turned into a confident description of other populations' internal qualities: *their* obtuseness, *their* secrecy, and their *irrationality*. By accepting this conclusion, analysts of the time ended up worrying that Westerners are so civilised and reasonable in global affairs that they often cannot imagine a different strategic outlook, one that is irrational and unreasonable. Officers feared that they and their political colleagues tended instead to assume that other people have good sense, just like they obviously do. They called this tendency the mirror-image fallacy.

The identification of mirror-imaging is now universally praised as an important corrective to bad intelligence habits. The prerogative to avoid mirroring, to instead try to see things from the perspective of mindsets other than your own, is considered a progressive and just acknowledgement of cultural pluralism: As the world consumes more and more of 'Western culture', the concept is used to warn against naively applying the 'cultural background' of the 'US or Western Europe' on to 'incomplete data' about other societies.[9] An influential list of 'axioms for intelligence analysts' calls mirror-imaging 'one of the greatest threats to objective intelligence analysis', since '[n]ot everyone is alike, and cultural, ethnic, religious, and political differences *do* matter'.[10] Almost none of these appraisals, however, acknowledge the origins of this idea of avoiding mirroring: first, in post-war judgements of the irrationality of Russia and newly independent states; and then, in internal reviews motivated by neoconservative policy preferences and a belief in the reasonableness of Anglosphere geopolitics. This right-wing claim to see others as they really are plays perfectly into the racial logic discussed in the Introduction. To identify and correct mirror-imaging, you would have to be able to get out of your own cultural preferences, to analyse the world without your perception being warped or constrained. And those you then see clearly would be revealed to have cognitive limits, ways of interpreting the world that were uniquely theirs – ways that stopped *them* from avoiding mirroring themselves. Time and again, the act of pre-empting or detecting the mirror-imaging error proved, in officers' eyes, that in the end they had superior analytical skills. And so post-colonial history is re-written: The US and British approach to Middle Eastern geopolitics has always been the correct approach, being shaped by people who can see the world clearly, while the unique cultural blinkers of decolonial elites has tragically led their fledgling independent states astray.

Analysts tried to narrate history in this way just as international relations were becoming ever more entangled, the beliefs and strategies of distant actors inextricably connected. The 1955 Bandung Conference of post-colonial actors produced all sorts of new solidarities: from decolonial groupings in the United Nations General Assembly, to the revolutionary Afro-Asian Peoples' Solidarity Movement, and to a series of state summits that would become the Non-Aligned Movement. These dialogues and alliances, though not without their own frictions, emphasised support for national liberation movements and a refusal to assist or legitimise the military footprints of 'Great Power' contests. Its participants insisted that they were trying to rethink international affairs outside of a Cold War framework.[11] Anti-colonial insurgencies were fuelled by, and reverberated back on, their international connections: the 1960s uprising in the Aden Protectorate, in what would become South Yemen, where rebels were inspired by Nasserist Pan-Arabism and supported by international advocacy;[12] through the 1960s and 1970s, the insurgency in Oman, where revolutionaries were shaped by the wider Movement of Arab Nationalists, by anti-colonial victory in Yemen, and by support from Maoist China;[13] and war in Algeria and Vietnam, which played out across international media and transnational solidarity movements.[14] Post-colonial states also offered new geopolitical precedents by intervening in international violence: India's halting of massacres in East Pakistan; Tanzania's toppling of the genocidal Idi Amin Government in Uganda; and Vietnam's overthrow of the Khmer Rouge in Cambodia.[15] As international relations scholar Siba Grovogui reflects, these dynamics together evoked a 'spirit of Third World engagements' that 'continue[d] to invite re-examinations of the intellectual, political, and moral foundations of the international system'.[16]

But Anglosphere policy-makers were dismissive of these initiatives, calling non-aligned states anti-Western hypocrites and denouncing their security actions.[17] Intelligence bodies were also largely uninterested in the lived significance of these interconnections and what they said about how political ideas and ways of living were nurtured and shared internationally rather than within strict national borders. Instead, agencies used their imagination to describe the internal mechanics and machinations of post-colonial states, mapping how they ticked in-and-of-themselves, in order to then ask, 'how fit are these governments to be part of the international community'. Obviously, you need an idea of what it means to play such a role in order to ask that question, and analysts were only too happy to supply one: their own view of how the world worked. These officers only cared about international links insofar as they might prove a self-contained Middle East and its waves of political ignorance. We might call this geopolitical whiteness: an image of how states should behave that will always support the superior position of the Anglosphere in international hierarchies. Before long, Saddam Hussein, Muammar Gaddafi, and other targets of regime change would be judged along these criteria.

THE TIMELESSNESS OF TOTALITARIANISM

In 2018, an author in the *American Intelligence Journal* wrote of the 'Return of the Bear', arguing that analysts should look back to historical successes and failures in assessing the USSR in order to better understand Vladimir Putin's Russia. There are 'many differences' between the two governments, he says, but also 'extensive parallels'.[18] The image of the Russian Bear, a hulking aggressor roaming the north, rarely turns up in intelligence work but does frame its scholarship: An in-house history of the CIA's approach to the USSR is titled *Watching the Bear* and opens with a drawing of Uncle Sam, staring through binoculars at a bear with massive fangs and claws; a wider review, by the future historian of the JIC, is called *Spying on the Nuclear Bear*.[19] Even without the explicit image, though, Anglosphere analysts built up an imaginative picture of the Soviets that carried the image's key implication: This was an utterly distinct political beast, shaped by and indigenous to that part of the world. The foundations of the avoiding-mirroring concept, later applied to Middle East governments, lie here.

In Chapter 1, we saw how intelligence analysts' approach to the Soviet Union shifted from an emphasis on statistical material factors – the country's economy, the composition of its armed forces – to speculation on the USSR's political elite, with those material qualities underpinning larger ideas about the attitudes of the leadership. In the March 1946 report discussed in the previous chapter, the Joint Intelligence Committee (JIC) highlighted their use of the term 'the Russian leaders'. For the committee, this referred to 'the inner circle controlling the communist party of the Soviet Union who are alone responsible for the framing of policy'. '[A]bove all', it meant 'Generalissimo Stalin'.[20] Two factors in this definition already stand out as having future consequences for the idea of avoiding mirroring. First, the JIC defined the leaders in symbiosis with the system they were leading. The two things shape and support one another: The leadership has an organisational 'position' which gives them political power, but which also ensures continuity, so that if Stalin were to die, there might be 'some slight difference in emphasis of Russian policy' but no change to 'the policy itself'. Second, this relationship between leader and system was seen as unique, as distinguishing Russia from the democratic West. Within the 'firmly established' Russian 'régime' where the government has 'steadily maintain[ed] its authority', '[d]ecisions are taken by a small group of men' and 'far less than in the case in the Western Democracies are the opinions of the masses taken into account'. This apparently makes it more difficult to '[obtain] intelligence on Russian intentions'.[21]

If this is meant to imply that Britain's or the US's foreign policy could be read from popular opinion at this time, then it is highly misleading: As these governments' internal discussions on intervening in the Middle East show, the masses were more an inconvenience to work around than a guide to follow. Moreover, considered by itself, the fact that the Russian Government has kept its authority is not particularly distinctive or insightful. What this description does, however, is establish that the USSR is most definitely *not* like Western Democracies in how it thinks. Expressing frustration with reading others' mindsets is here becoming a way to define their fundamental difference from us.

Two themes began to develop in so-called Sovietology, or the study of the Russian policy process: the determining weight of their history and the ill-tempered psychological predisposition of their leaders. As noted before, racial belonging played an explicit role in early assessments of the Soviet outlook. This was an analysis of time immemorial, of how people over there are predisposed to think. So, the Soviet leaders, 'many of them, like Stalin, not of Russian race', have both 'an oriental fondness for bargaining' and 'an oriental regard for the maintenance of dignity in all their dealings'. While the JIC made much of the communists' ideological faith in their long-term destiny, analysts' assessments carried their own faith in the innate preferences and behaviour of 'Asiatic' peoples.[22]

Intelligence analysts' belief in the weight of history, however, had a bumpy relationship with their idea of the Soviets' ideological distinctiveness. A follow-up JIC report in 1947 insists that Soviet policy 'can only be understood' if one accepts that the USSR is 'not merely, like Nazi Germany, a totalitarian dictatorship' but 'a unique and *abnormal member of international society* inspired by a dynamic ideology'. This Marxist ideology misreads 'the capitalist system' as 'contain[ing] the seeds of its own decay', which it is the Soviet duty to 'direct and hasten'. The Joint Intelligence Staff (JIS) see this 'long-term principle' as 'underlying' Russia's 'immediate search for security' around its borders. But when they actually describe this more immediate 'preoccupation', the JIS argue that 'Soviet leaders [are] influenced by old motive forces in Russian history altogether independent of Marxist history', namely Russia's historical vulnerability to invasion due to the lack of natural defensive borders around the country. It is this vulnerability, not a Soviet mindset, which encourages Russia's leaders throughout time to 'push out her frontiers as far as possible'.[23] The effort to establish an inherent source of Soviet aggression leads to severely muddied causation in this analysis.

It is also not obvious from the report that giving special attention to ideology or history rewards you with great insight into their effects. For what is the 'Resultant Policy' of the Soviets' swirling Marxist-meets-Russian-meets-geographical mindset? They will 'co-operate in international affairs' if it is in 'the direct furtherance of [Russia's] own national and ideological interests'. This includes supporting the United Nations and other international bodies insofar as 'they serve these ends'. This conclusion is virtually identical to British policy-makers' self-avowed international objectives over this period. What *is* different, as analysts try to '[look] outwards, as if from a window in the Kremlin', is the description of Russian leaders' *attitude*, of their emotions and willingness to take risks. Their unique ideology supposedly leads the Kremlin to cherish 'constant friction and struggle' in their relations, adopting 'a completely callous attitude in the promotion of chaos' outside their borders, quite unlike British clear-headedness.[24]

By the 1950s, this approach to the Soviet Union had permeated both British and US intelligence circles to a degree that undermined any hint of international influences on Soviet actions. Connections to global geopolitics were always translated into the essential way-of-being of a non-Western government. At a 1952 meeting of the US's Intelligence Advisory Committee, attended by the different intelligence branches and many of the CIA's analysts, those present discussed a report on 'Probable Soviet Courses of Action', noting that the authors had disagreed over how the Kremlin perceived US responses to their actions. The director of central intelligence interjected by sharing a recent suggestion to him that the community should study 'Russian history', in order to identify any 'patterns' from 'the Czarist' to the 'post-revolutionary periods'. The meeting's secretary notes a 'sense' from those present that such a study would help overcome 'the difficult[y] [...] of estimating Soviet appraisals of Western actions'.[25] Like the JIC around the same time (see Chapter 1), US intelligence was translating the problem of understanding their own impact on others' perceptions into a different challenge, of understanding the more fundamental character of an adversary. The first problem thereby recedes in importance: Why struggle with international sociology when you can speculate on timeless character traits?

This approach to analysis would face its own challenge the following year with the death of Josef Stalin. The relationship between personality and system needed to be clear if analysts were going to predict the future of Soviet policy-making. A provisional CIA estimate judged the ex-leader a 'ruthless and determined' autocrat, but one who had never 'allow[ed] his ambitions to lead him into reckless courses of action in his foreign policy'. Stalin's replacement, however, may be too weak to overcome 'established Soviet positions'. The estimate here implies a deterministic Soviet system, restraining all but the strongest wills. This was important, analysts thought, because it meant that the new elite might end up being 'compelled to react more strongly to what it regarded as new aggressive moves of the West'. What kind of moves might be read this way? '[P]articularly those involving long-range air forces or military forces close to the Bloc frontiers'.[26] Ideas of psychology and state system, then, allowed analysts to assess the actions of others without having to weigh up the validity of international influences, including from their own state, on those actions.

But a rough estimate was not enough: Agency higher-ups wanted a deeper assessment of how events might progress. So the following month, they turned to their so-called Princeton Consultants. These were a group of think tanks and academic staff outside state intelligence bureaucracy, who met throughout the year to discuss and comment on draft papers by the Office of National Estimates. Members could even gain promotion to the ONE's Board.[27] At their April 1953 meeting, the Princeton Consultants disagreed with the CIA's prediction of an orderly transfer of power after Stalin. They demurred, according to the meeting's minutes, 'largely on the basis of historical analogy'. Those present pointed variously to how 'divided leaderships' had 'historically' behaved, to the disorderly 'history of revolutions', to Lenin's own views on 'Russian history', and to the inevitable 'degenera[cy]' of 'modern totalitarianism' – 'Stalin had become more and more like Hitler'.[28] Despite the minutes' summary, however, those in attendance actually relied less on historical parallels than on discursive detective work. What did one Soviet elite's speech at Stalin's funeral, and its differing tone from another's, suggest about policy differences? Why was one political figure suddenly more in the public eye? Perhaps different party 'factions' were discernible in all these word games and spotlight changes. The Princeton Consultants' detective work told a story of Soviet foreign policy as resulting from the 'personalities' at the top and the '[d]ifferences among the top leaders'. Even though the Princeton Consultants define these personalities' differences as differences over *how to respond* to Anglosphere 're-armament', their story represents Soviet opinion as fixed objects to be pinned down, not viewpoints that would potentially change in response to geopolitical actions. US and British diplomacy only has the potential to 'split [these divisions] wide open', rather than temper re-armament suspicions.[29]

The Princeton Consultants' discussion ties psychology and system together to the point of their being self-referential. Each causes the effects of the other, with a hierarchy of power prompting suspicious jostling for more hierarchical power. This back-and-forth idea would become prominent in later analyses of Middle Eastern so-called 'regimes' (Chapter 3). The concept of the intelligence failure, meanwhile, would take these methods of connecting the dots from the halls of the Kremlin to the palaces and offices of the Gulf and the Arabian Peninsula.

AVOIDING MIRRORS IN THE EAST

'Away With Capabilities!', British analyst Alan Crick tells his US colleagues in 1956. Crick, the JIC's representative to the CIA, is worried that intelligence officers never agree on whether capabilities refers to untapped potential ('does this person have the power to do that') or, like an Agatha Christie crime story, to conscious desired actions ('who would be capable of such a thing!'). Forget this confusion, says Crick; as analysts, we should be focused not on capabilities but on 'the *course most likely to be adopted*', in other words, 'probable intention'. In making his case, Crick imagines the rebuttal that it is the commander on the field of battle – or, by analogy, the policy-maker in the Cabinet – who knows their own resources and battle plans, making them the one best placed to judge how the enemy will respond. '[I]ntelligence is useless', the commander feels, for 'he knows his enemy' already through 'his operational "hunch"'. Crick hints here at the archetype of two military equals facing one another across combat lines, each aware of how the other thinks because they are of the same breed, both generals, warriors. Analysts, however, do not just rely on the commander's 'measurable physical facts'; they know that 'evidence can take [you] only a small part of the way'. You need to use your imagination.[30] By rejecting the commander's superiority, Crick predicts the intelligence theory to come over the next 20 years. In this theory, analysts reject mirror-imaging, that is, the assumption that they are facing strategists like them. Underneath this premise lies another: You are not facing a warrior on the same plain of understanding; you are not facing an equal.[31] The other therefore cannot be expected to understand the rules of the game, of right and proper geopolitical behaviour.

While the concept of intelligence failure came first in this theory's development, the idea of success and failure smuggled the concept of a mirror-image dilemma in its shadow. It also linked Sovietology to the lesser-developed analysis of the Arabic and Asian worlds. In 1951, the JIC decided to undertake 'its first serious retrospective analysis', reviewing all estimate papers over the last few years on the intentions of the Soviet Union.[32] These really were estimates of Crick's 'most likely course': 36 papers in all, covering everything from probable Soviet policy in Berlin to events in satellite states to the likelihood of another world war. They were also papers on communist intentions more widely. Panicky analysts and policy-makers of this period viewed Marxist political movements through a wide-angle racial lens: The Russians were supposedly infiltrating the Eastern world through an appeal to their own Asiatic heritage, while East Asian populations were easily incited by revolutionaries through racial submissiveness and cross-country loyalties.[33] As a later JIC paper put it, 'underdeveloped' Asia was ripe for manipulation as it had 'no established democratic tradition' and was prone to 'a fervid and emotional nationalism'.[34] These dismissive judgements reflect the cross-over of biological and cultural racism, with Asia's popular politics traced sometimes to inbred political weakness and sometimes to a native, backward culture that stymied democratic thought and emotional control.

In their December 1951 review, the Joint Intelligence Staff were fairly complimentary of past efforts: All but three assessments had turned out correct, or at least had not yet proved incorrect. But of the three that did not make the grade, '[i]t is significant', the JIS said, that they 'were all concerned with the Far East': a study that underestimated communism's momentum in China; an incorrect assessment that the Chinese Communist Government would not intervene in Korea; and a further paper which misread subsequent military build-ups. Why had these failures occurred? Apart from intelligence gaps, the JIS emphasised that 'we do not yet understand the mind of the Chinese communist leaders'.[35] Given that each failure was around China's military policy or internal politics, this curt statement implicates irrationality – these opaque people fell for communism, and then took unreasonable military risks. The report's structure leaves no doubt that British analysts were reasonable in thinking the Chinese communists would not carry out such actions. There must, then, be something about *their* minds that led them to their unpredicted actions and which makes them hard to read. The irrationality comes out of their region and people. This represents a quick but powerful racialisation of world politics.

When Britain and the US sent troops to Jordan and Lebanon later that decade, Britain's ambassador in Peking reported on mass demonstrations outside his embassy. The ambassador blamed these on secret coordination by unnamed authorities, one part of wider Chinese Government efforts not just to display 'the vast size and angry spirit of the Chinese dragon', but to whip up 'a perpetual atmosphere of crisis' and 'international tension'.[36] Pro-Egypt protests during the Suez Crisis two years earlier were dismissed in a similar fashion, with only partial accuracy (Figure 2.1).[37] In 1959, the US analyst Cyrus Peake, who had worked in the National Estimates team, made sense of China's unpredicted invasion of Korea through its leaders having 'ignored [their own] inadequate capabilities'. The case proved that intelligence colleagues needed to appreciate 'personality attributes and characteristics', for instance, 'the psychological [boost to] the Chinese people of fighting in defence of "the motherland" against "imperialist" America'.[38] Diplomats and analysts therefore certainly did develop a view of the singular Chinese mind, in a way that conveniently batted away the possibility of cross-country criticism and political solidarity by focusing on an idea of the Chinese population's inherent emotional irrationality.

Figure 2.2 A protest in China, most likely Beijing, against British and French military action during the Suez Crisis, November 1956. (Keystone-France/ Gamma-Keystone via Getty Images)

The other case that Peake presented as proof of personality's importance was the nationalisation of the Suez Canal by Egyptian President Gamal Nasser in July 1956. As Dina Rezk has detailed, US and British intelligence on the Middle East through the late 1950s and 1960s was often steered by ideas of Nasser's regional ambitions and leadership of Pan-Arab nationalism.[39] These ideas further entangled the concept of the intelligence failure and the fear of mirror-imaging, in a process which foreshadows how Saddam Hussein would later be analysed. The 1952 coup that brought Colonel Nasser and General Naguib to power in Egypt, Nasser's later promotion to president, an arms deal between Egypt and Czechoslovakia, and finally Suez were all surprises that analysts felt they should have predicted. Given early CIA and State Department links to Nasser, the first two events were possibly British surprises alone.[40] In any case, in assessments and regular meetings, analysts turned to their model of the Middle East's equilibrium and the Sovietology lens of historical, delusional leadership cults. So when it came to 'learn[ing] valuable lessons' from intelligence's failure to foresee the Egyptian coup, the JIC extended the coup's secrecy to the personality of Egypt's new leadership. These coup officers would carry their deceptiveness with them into their 'future actions'.[41] They must be 'deliberately' misleading Britain, given their 'past records' of violent intentions. They would likely follow 'the evolution of past generations of Egyptian politicians' in becoming tangled up in 'internal problems'.[42] They were under the control of hidden 'extremist elements with an anti-British record'. And they were inept, 'a people who cannot govern themselves', prone to 'ill-considered' aggressive foreign policy which 'reduce[s] still further their own field of manoeuvre' simply 'to maintain themselves in power'.[43] The failure to predict Egypt's events proved something, agents thought, about a lineage of Egyptians' bad governing skills. And of course, what makes their foreign policy actions ill-considered is that Britain and the US respond to them punitively.

Colonel Nasser, publicly '[n]icknamed "Tiger" for his toughness', was approached through this frame of irrational power struggles.[44] The JIC traced Nasser's rise to Egypt's deceptively layered power structure – as they put it in one meeting, 'it had always been known that Colonel Nasser was the power behind [Naguib]'.[45] This layers-of-power lens obscured Nasser's international relations. When Egypt signed a Czech arms deal in 1955 and Committee Chairman Patrick Dean ordered another intelligence review, the question of *why* Nasser had considered the deal beneficial was twisted around.[46] Committee members concentrated on Nasser's lack of domestic governance savvy – he was 'well and truly in the toils' and 'required successes' to stay in power.[47] The committee dismissed the idea that Nasser's dealings had been a signal to Britain and the US for concessions. No, the latter had surely been 'lulled into a sense of false security'.[48] When one member suggested 'fear of Israel' as a motivating factor, Chairman Dean responded that Nasser's 'real reason' for taking such 'considerable risks' as the arms deal was to achieve 'a dominant position in the Arab world'.[49] Nasser was simply belligerent and out of his depth, independent of his worldly relations.

While the British Foreign Office and the US State Department quietly debated overthrowing Nasser,[50] JIC reports called out the

Egyptian president's lack of geopolitical good sense: His 'balancing act' between Soviet and Anglosphere assistance is unsustainable, while he shares in Arab 'bitterness' towards Israel and may become hostile any time – 'compare Mussolini and Abyssinia'. The JIC criticise his 'pragmatic' policy of seeking deeper international connections only when it benefits Egypt: By forming diplomatic ties out of 'interest', not 'principle', Nasser ignores the ethical impetus of 'be[ing] on the Western side'. Worst of all, he wants Egypt 'to stand up to the West on equal terms'.[51] Linking Nasser's shallow thinking and temper to this ambition makes clear that analysts did *not* believe Egypt could reasonably stand on an equal footing. In years to come, the JIC would continue to judge Nasser as inadequately addressing 'the problems which now confront him', his renewed relations with Britain masking stubborn 'hostil[ity] to Western interests'.[52] How this actually affected Middle East insecurity is not explained. The key is rather the assessment of Nasser's innately weak and emotional character.

The way analysts interpreted the Suez Canal's nationalisation entrenched and racialised this intelligence picture of Nasser as a man who was always misunderstanding how geopolitics works. Shortly before the event, Britain's ambassador, Humphrey Trevelyan, reported on a meeting with Egypt's president where he told Nasser to 'use his imagination' and see how Egyptian propaganda was damaging the two countries' relations. Trevelyan reports Nasser's response: that his own olive branches had only led to accusations of 'trickery'; that 'everything that he said was misinterpreted'. Moreover, Nasser presented evidence that Britain was pressuring Russia to stop arms shipments to Egypt. Trevelyan denied this to Nasser but acknowledges its truth in his report. That truth plays no role, however, in the ambassador's concluding assessment of the Colonel. Nasser thinks Britain is being 'thoroughly unreasonable in not believing what he says', pushing him into a corner where any concession would now make him appear weak. Trevelyan's recommendation? Britain should 'try again to make *him* understand *our* point of view'.[53] By ignoring Nasser's correct claim of British machinations, Trevelyan demonstrates how little 'gaining accuracy' matters in Orientalist thinking. Acknowledging Nasser's correctness might reveal something about what motivated his policy towards Britain. But it would also threaten the prop-osition that British political reasoning is superior to that of the Egyptians. Judging from his report, Trevelyan does not connive to mischaracterise Nasser. He simply cannot imagine that Nasser's complaints might invalidate Britain's position.

For the JIC, Nasser's subsequent seizure of the Canal 'revealed' him as 'a demagogue liable to be carried away by the violence of the passions he himself has whipped up'. The violence in question was seemingly the nationalisation. On this basis, the JIC warned that Nasser would make decisions not through 'a rational scrutiny of the balance of loss and gain' but simply to 'enhance his prestige'. Or at least, the committee *drafted* this warning. Their report was reworded in its final form, referring not to irrational-ity but to Nasser's 'subtlety and calculation' in foreign policy. In the draft, rationality equates to accepting Anglosphere ownership of the Canal. Rationality's absence stems from a political actor's 'emotional character' and their appeal to the 'instinct[s] [...] of the Arab mind'. This implication remains in the final report without explicitly commenting on Nasser's lack of clear-headedness.[54] Here is the process by which more explicit cultural racism gets trans-lated into intelligence assessments: Illogical emotional arrogance is traced to particular kinds of minds in one part of the world, before this claim is reworded as a tendency in people's political strategy. As we will see, a similar drafting process would link Saddam to irrationality shortly before the 2003 invasion of Iraq.

When Egypt took the Suez Canal, Ambassador Trevelyan reported that '[i]t is unlikely that we shall ever be able to trace defi-nitely the mental processes' of Nasser's decision. By shrugging his shoulders, the ambassador *gives* an analysis: of Nasser's irrational-ity (what strange mental processes!) and secrecy (impossible to trace!).[55] Towards the end of the 1950s, the CIA concurred. The US intelligence community had by now committed itself to under-standing better the 'essential motives' of nationalist leaders. In that vein, the National Estimates team were tasked with studying Nasser's 'problems, objectives and prospects' in his response to changing circumstances, *including* the Anglosphere's own 'devel-oping policies'.[56] When the team presented their conclusions, however, they emphasised Nasser's negative impact on 'the conservative and Western-aligned regimes'. This impact is unavoidable because Nasser has a 'basic belief' that both the Anglosphere and the Soviets want to 'dominate or destroy him'; it is therefore 'highly unlikely' he will abandon his suspicious hostility. Neither the validity of Nasser's suspicion nor possibilities for assuaging it are assessed.[57] In his 1959 article mentioned above, Cyrus Peake accuses analysts of being insensitive to Nasser's desire for 'world position and prestige' in response to international 'humiliation'. The Colonel wanted not simply to stay in power but to save his pride. Peake's lesson, therefore, is not strictly about acknowledging statespersons' personalities. It is actually about accepting that US intelligence officers' own 'logical and rational deductions' do not match the way people over-there see their situations. Over there, they place value on non-rational outcomes due to their engrained emotional predispositions.[58]

Into the 1960s, intelligence failure and the concept of avoiding mirror-imaging mutually reinforced one another even further. In 1964, Sherman Kent, director of the Office of National Estimates and the founder of *Studies in Intelligence*, reflected on why he and his estimators had failed to predict the Soviets' placing of nuclear weapons in Cuba two years earlier. You cannot blame analysts, says Kent, for not following the Soviet's 'inner logic'. Why not? In 'estimating how the other man will probably behave in a given situation', analysts assume that other actor is in their 'right mind' and 'not demonstrably unhinged', will have 'discussed with advisers' and put their ideas through 'scrutiny', and will be aware of their state's 'broad national interests'. Such factors 'considerably narrow' their possible behaviours. Pre-empting Robert Jervis on Saddam decades later, Kent laments that estimators cannot be expected to produce good intelligence when these factors are dampened or negated, when the other actor abandons '"normal" behaviour' to the point of 'seem[ing] [...] suicidal'. The Soviets made 'a mistake', 'a dramatically wrong decision'.[59] Four years later, Willard Matthias, of the CIA's World Situation Estimates (Chapter 1), presented his own review of previous errors. Having worked on the Board of National Estimates through the 1960s, Matthias rebuked himself for a paper which had downplayed prospects of an Arab-Israeli war and Soviet provocation in 1967. What went wrong? He and others had 'overestimated the Soviets' good sense', forgetting that the USSR's leaders are not always 'consistent'. His team had also underestimated an Israeli and Egyptian 'change of mood', these governments' newly-reduced 'threshold' for 'expos[ing] [themselves] to danger'.[60]

Peake, Kent, and Matthias, years apart, all framed their reviews around a judgemental approach to Eastern psychology, around claims that adversaries had let illogic, emotion, and regional atmosphere shape their decisions. Those flaws supposedly revealed what was distinct and innate about Middle Eastern political culture, which imposed itself on these statespersons' minds. By pointing to their colleagues' analytical oversights, that all this was unexpected, the reviewers promote *their* intellectual culture as fundamentally superior, hence why colleagues were mistaken but forgivable in assuming others' good sense. A concept of mirror-imaging that brought these elements together bubbled just below this surface. By the end of the 1960s, these intelligence scholars would have found receptive ears in the British intelligence and diplomatic communities. In 1968, embassies in Kabul, Moscow, Tehran, and Rawalpindi corresponded on whether Russia might force Afghanistan into a 'Bear Hug', into becoming a strategic Soviet outpost. During this debate, which was forwarded to British intelligence officers, the ambassador to Afghanistan speculated that perhaps 'what would appear *to us* to be compelling arguments of policy and interest *may be obscured in the minds* of the Soviet leaders by the smokescreen of Marxist/Leninist ideology'. The ambassador resigns himself to 'leave this one to the Kremlinologists'.[61] That same year, the JIC warned that 'emotional nationalism, extremism and arrogance', 'latent' in the Middle East, could prevent Arab and Iranian state leaders from recognising their 'common interest' in 'establishing a local balance of power'. British objectives within that balance are all stated explicitly – oil investment benefits, economic power via sterling, military bases – but are denied a place in analysts' account of what helps or hampers 'stability in the Gulf'.[62] The Middle East is instead judged as to whether the nation-states there 'get' how the region should work. If they do not, the problem is their non-Western history and psychology.

CULTURALLY SENSITIVE NEOCONSERVATISM

The explicit concept of a mirror-image problem certainly grew out of superpower tension – but it first emerged far from intelligence literature. Uri Bronfenbrenner, a US social psychologist who spoke fluent Russian and visited the Soviet Union for his research, uses the term in a 1961 paper on 'Soviet–American relations' to describe misperceptions by each state's citizens about those on the other side of the Iron Curtain. These 'reciprocal images' are 'distorted and irrational – a mirror image in a twisted glass'. In each country, citizens insist it is the other side who is aggressive, whose government misleads a restless populace, and whose leaders are deceitful and insane. Worse still, this distortion encourages the other to *adapt* to the image, to behave as they are treated: For instance, accusations of deception make accused statespersons suspicious and protective in future. Bronfenbrenner appeals to US elites: Break down this 'psychological barrier' of comforting myth; listen to what the Soviets say about their own societies. If not, the US will misread communism's popular appeal and lose the ideological war – a telling message at a time when Allen Dulles and his intelligence officers were grappling with exactly this issue (Chapter 1).[63] Bronfenbrenner's research was scrutinised and extended in conflict resolution research throughout the 1960s on de-escalating international tensions.[64] While some of his peers criticised what they saw as Bronfenbrenner's crude psychologising of states, others argued that the dynamic quality of mirroring, its potential to create a cycle of mutual suspicion, did indeed threaten nuclear war.[65]

De-escalation was not, to put it mildly, the direction that intelligence went with the concept. While Bronfenbrenner was sharing experiences with Soviet populations, British Foreign Office (FO) analysts were imagining the separateness of such populations. In 1960, members of the Middle East Research Department prepared a paper on the concept of the Military Regime. They had in mind the military coups which had taken place in Syria, Egypt, Iraq, and Sudan over the last ten years. Why had these happened and what did their origins say about Middle East politics? All the states mentioned above, they note, had 'import[ed]' parliamentary democracy 'from Europe', imposing a political system 'lacking roots in the traditions and convictions of the people'. These populations had no 'experience in the collective planning and conduct of the community's affairs' or in 'exert[ing] ordinary pressure on an unpopular government'. Tradition and conviction are used here to explain a deep-rooted Middle Eastern deficiency, the people's inability to fathom superior Western politics. Middle Easterners were not looking for representation; rather, a 'vocal minority' had 'emotional needs' for their government to promote 'national aspirations', which means satisfying 'emotions about Arab solidarity [and] anti-imperialism'. The FO researchers believed that these populations judged foreign policy in relation to 'national dignity' and that their governments had failed to measure up. Since the military was the only professionalised part of these states with administrative experience, it made sense that its officers would step into this legitimacy vacuum. Military Regimes, then, were the product of emotional and conservative populations who could not handle democratic development. The regimes themselves reflected that origin: Their suspicious, fearful 'obsession with British imperialism' was merely 'deeply rooted [...] old prejudice'. There was no need to take seriously the international politics of the Arab 'mob'.[66] Rather than probe Anglosphere and Arab mutual antagonisms, their reciprocal images, the British researchers conclude that the new military regimes can never reach their own level of objectivity. Regime would remain an important concept in analysis of the Middle East, right up to intelligence assessments of Saddam Hussein (Chapter 4).

After Bronfenbrenner's research was subject to years of debate, the term mirror-image entered some intelligence officers' vocabulary at the start of the 1970s. It appears in print not in reference to the Soviets but to a not-so-cold war: Vietnam. In a study highly praised by the editor of *Studies in Intelligence*, a 'post-mortem' on the US counter-insurgency, CIA agent Anthony Marc Lewis seems initially to accept Bronfenbrenner's conclusions: Analysts need 'to see "the world of the Vietnamese" as *the Vietnamese do*', to 'learn to perceive "other peoples' worlds"' without 'frequent and *unconscious* distortions' of perception. But Lewis approaches the task of understanding '*the way* [the Vietnamese] think' not by questioning the kinds of self-perception that Bronfenbrenner wanted to put into doubt – that 'We' have honest intentions and are defending ourselves against deceitful aggression.[67] Instead, Lewis takes these self-perceptions as valid, while emphasising that the Vietnamese *may not share them* in their view of Us. When the analyst hears or uses certain terms, Lewis says, they see only their own honest, benevolent understanding of their meaning, failing to realise that they may have different connotations abroad. This oversight is a 'mirror image'. Lewis interprets this problem as a naive US faith in inherently Western values: Mirror-imaging is worst when it involves terms 'which hold connotations of *our Western beliefs and values* and notably those *which Americans rank especially high*' – terms like 'national development goals', 'fair tactics', and 'democratic practices'.[68] In a review of contemporary histories of Vietnam, Dennis Duncanson, formerly of the British embassy in the country, similarly rejected applying 'our' political concepts to 'Oriental situations willy-nilly', since the 'modern, but Western, vocabulary of international politics' may mean very little to ideological Asian thinkers.[69] There is no problem, then, with intelligence's moral assumptions, say, of Western righteousness and Vietnamese dishonesty. The problem is just that, regrettably, the Vietnamese may not see it that way!

This perceived danger of mirror-imaging – that is, of assuming that others will recognise the Anglosphere's superior nobility – would soon be placed centre-stage by the historian Richard Pipes, an agency consultant in the mid-to-late 1970s who made the concept his own. Pipes' intervention came at a time of transition for Sovietology: State funding was decreasing, while academia was reeling from the public exposure of its research connections to the CIA and Department of Defence. Pipes recognised that if Russian Studies was to be renewed, it should satisfy government desires not for narrow technical expertise but for more analysis of Soviet society and culture.[70] Pipes was also part of a long 'counterrevolution', culminating in Reagan, against intellectual support for détente policy, which was founded on an idea inimical to these counterrevolutionaries: that Soviet aggression was affected by US policy gestures. Against this, Pipes' work through the 1950s and 1960s, including testimony at Senate hearings, promoted a narrative of, in his words, Russia's 'deviation from the general European pattern' of state development and political thought: While European and US society was built on historical commercial negotiation, Russia's long religious xenophobia and domestic exploitation had produced generations of insular, colonialist elites.[71]

In the summer of 1975, under the auspices of the Stanford Research Institute (SRI), Pipes led a pilot study for the US's Defence Advanced Research Projects Agency (DARPA), whose results were distributed to the CIA. The study offered a 'working hypothesis on how the USSR formulates and coordinates its foreign policy'. After a decade of Russian Studies research which had tried to demystify the Soviet Union, rejecting its totalitarian uniqueness in favour of comparative modernisation theory, Pipes and his co-authors sounded like a blast from the past – no, Russia really was unique, and it wasn't going to change anytime soon.[72] It was wrong, they said, to treat the Soviet Union as 'a mirror image of the United States', to think that the two states' nuclear strategies had naturally gravitated towards shared terrain, as if history and culture – that is, *separate* history and culture – were irrelevant.[73] Coincidentally, the SRI's major CIA contract at the time, declassified decades later, was research into remote viewing, the psychic ability to visualise objects that are hidden from view.[74] In one experiment at the Institute, the infamous Israeli spoon-bender Uri Geller responded to an unseen drawing of the devil half a mile away by drawing various Old Testament imagery (Figure 2.2).[75] In a sense, remote viewing of a hidden demon is an apt metaphor for the task that Pipes and his colleagues set for themselves. They sought, they said, to look behind the 'high degree of secrecy in the formulation of Soviet national objectives' and reveal how those objectives were prodded by 'the Russian historical legacy' and 'the Soviet political system' towards barbarism, absolute authority, and territorial expansion.[76]

In a sole-authored section of the report for DARPA, Pipes denounces the US liberal tendency to deny 'meaningful differences among human beings, whether genetic, ethnic, racial, or other', blaming this aversion on liberals' attempts to repress their guilt over their privilege within 'undeniable' global inequalities by pretending that their position was due solely to 'personal merit', not these more fundamental kinds of difference. Pipes thereby

Figure 2.2 A CIA-funded researcher draws a hidden picture of the Devil (left), which Uri Geller then responds to psychically half a mile away (right). (Stanford Research Institute, 5 August 1973)

acknowledges the hierarchy of the international system, implicitly putting it at the core of his analysis: Perhaps, he hints, the US has ended up on top due to engrained racial superiority. Pipes' narrative embraces his and the US elite's position in this hierarchy, without any fuzzy illusions as to why it is the case. He similarly dismisses the modernising ideal that 'uneven levels of [...] development' cause a 'cultural lag', and that development policy will produce people who 'behave like Americans'. Another important assumption is therefore brought into this analysis: The 'psychological makeup and aspirations' of other nations are not shaped by political context; they are a fixed part of countries' 'internal situation'. Like the CIA's William Tidwell before him, Pipes calls for 'an effort at learning and imagination' regarding 'foreign civilisations' – but it is a form of imagination based on hermetic, unequal cultures.[77] Indeed, Pipes proceeds to detail historical continuity: a seven-century lineage of Russian elites' entitled exploitation of their country; a tradition of territorial expansion to compensate for Russia's poverty; and a Soviet leadership's violent, survival-of-the-fittest peasant ancestry. This continuity has created '*a very special kind of mentality*' among Soviet leaders, one 'which stresses slyness, self-interest, reliance on force, skill in exploiting others', and 'contempt' for the weak. To ignore this character of Soviet decision-makers is to engage in what his co-authors also call 'mirror-imaging', to assume that Russians have the 'same mind' and 'same heart' as US elites.[78]

There is no mistaking here how Pipes and his colleagues base their claim of a mirror-image fallacy on the limited capacity for thought and feeling of another society, on a hereditary lineage of poor Russians whose devious, heartless nature has been shaped by their environment. Mirroring is critiqued for failing to acknowledge racial inferiority.

These ideas would soon echo in the halls of Langley, as the following year, Pipes would take part in the CIA's infamous Team B experiment. The US political scene provides crucial context here. For months, the agency's National Intelligence Estimates had been criticised by the ascending neoconservatives – figures who would later fill George Bush Jr.'s Cabinet – for underplaying Russia's violation of ballistic missile agreements. Revealingly, one member of President Gerald Ford's Foreign Intelligence Advisory Board argued that a fundamental uncertainty around weapons programmes *that might or might not exist* made it vital to try producing multiple hypotheses from limited evidence. The 'greatest value' of this effort was not any resulting 'accuracy' but rather 'call[ing] high level attention to the subject'.[79] The new director of central intelligence, George H. W. Bush, agreed to a programme whereby three groups of outside specialists would write assessments of Soviet intentions and capabilities, in competition with the CIA's own National Intelligence Estimates (NIEs) team. Pipes led Team B's assessment of Soviet strategic objectives. Their final report laid into what was described as the National Estimates Board's 'mirror-imaging' tendency: Agency officers, the report claimed, had pictured Soviet strategy 'through the prism of US assumptions about détente', wrongly concluding that the Soviets were concerned with defensive policy – a concern presumed to be held by the US – and would be satisfied with 'parity', with balancing US power.[80]

Two months later, in February 1977, the CIA's Center for the Study of Intelligence ran a seminar on 'Bias in Intelligence Analysis', where 21 officers from the agency's Intelligence Directorate discussed a bespoke paper on general errors. Prominently featured in the paper's section on analytical biases is the 'mirror-imaging' fallacy, described as 'ascribing our own motivations to the leaders of the country being analysed', 'attributing to them the same kind of logic, cultural values, and thought process that would characterise us'. The fallacy leads analysts to misread 'the things that motivate' other leaders.[81] Notice how mirroring is described here and in the Team B report: It is not about falsely assuming that the other international actor has the same thoughts and opinions as you do about a certain subject; it is about imagining how *you* would act *in their situation*, what 'would characterise' your judgement, and then naively assuming that this is how they too will act. The conceit underlying this act of imagination, the idea that gives weight to its diagnosis as mistaken by Team B, is that Anglosphere analysts can remove their own cultural blinkers and see clearly how any international actor should properly respond to any geopolitical situation. The bias being called out is not that CIA officers apply Western values to other leaders who think differently; it is that analysts assume that other leaders could ever share their own level of objectivity, their ability to perceive the appropriate way to behave and survive in the world, and thereby ignore those leaders' misperceptions about that world. Officers can, in theory, detect statespersons' partial, distorted cultural lens and its degrading influence on others' geopolitical actions. This criticism translates Pipes' racist argument about inferior cultures into the language of political science. The racialisation remains: The West has good sense and righteous principles, while the East cannot measure up.

How did the analysts writing National Intelligence Estimates react to this criticism? How did they interpret the diagnosis of mirroring and its proposed cure? In response to Team B's report, the CIA's Production Assessment and Improvement Division (PAID) looked over those NIEs from 1974 and 1975 that had assessed the political outlook of the Soviet Union.[82] Its defence was straightforward: Team B accused NIEs staff of ignoring 'soft data' on Soviet grand strategy when in fact the two groups simply had different interpretations of the same limited intelligence. As for mirror-imaging, while the criticism perhaps had some validity, the problem that PAID identified was tracing mirroring's real impact on intelligence judgements, since 'no one in the West can define the extent to which Soviet strategic policy [...] [is] determined by the Soviet "grand strategy" [...] [that] we are accused of misinterpreting'[83] PAID's Chief also argued that any mirroring was based not on 'reflections of American values and aspirations' but on 'hard evidence of Soviet hardware developments'. Yes, there had been recent indications that Soviet weapons policy emphasises 'superiority' and therefore '[differs] from current thoughts in the "West"'. But 'the Community is unable to identify an agreed Soviet *definition* of superiority or a *method* of achieving it'. The 'view of the Soviet leadership as to [the] goals and purpose' of its weapons developments remains 'the important imponderable in assessing Soviet intentions'.[84] While officers accepted the validity of a mirroring fallacy, they judged that the Soviets' unique mindset could neither be perceived by agents nor judged in terms of its impact on geopolitics. The only clear point for PAID was one that underpinned Team B's suspicions, that the true, distinct Soviet outlook remained somewhat impenetrable or secretive. Analysts thereby accepted the idea that the danger of mirroring stemmed from non-Westerners' opaqueness, despite pointing out themselves that past estimates *had been accurate* as to the Soviets' missile inferiority and appreciation of US capabilities.

Team B also prompted reflections which were echoed in wider discussion of Middle East leaders across the Anglosphere. The PAID analysts noted Pipes' criticism that the CIA gave too much weight to public speeches and official declarations of Soviet policymaking, that they ignored the domestic propaganda basis of such material. In response, the analysts reprinted the reflections of a recent NIE: Are public statements by 'lesser [Soviet] officials' merely 'reflections of pervasive ideological principle', that is, instinctive rhetoric, or do they 'also represent practical objectives'? Does Marxist-Leninism cover up policy-making or shape it? It is 'a matter of interpretation'. All the agency can do is assess what they see as 'the challenges, opportunities, and constraints operating on [the Soviets]' – in other words, apply their model of how geopolitics *should* work, which of course covered how the Anglosphere would sensibly approach those challenges and opportunities, and then ask whether the Soviets measure up by comparison. Earlier that decade, the British Ambassador to Jordan had raised the same question when reporting back to London on a conversation with Jordan's new Prime Minister Zaid al-Rifai. The latter had asserted that other Arab governments had 'two quite separate levels of policy – the Declared, and the Real', reflecting respectively 'ephemeral pressures' or 'currents of opinion' and 'the policy they would pursue if other things were equal'. The ambassador heartily agreed but worried: 'From which of these two levels of policy did action flow?'[85] The minister for the Near East and North Africa, James Craig, wrote back to lament that 'a century or more of contact with the West' had failed to change the behaviour of 'the Arabs', and that he too 'constantly find[s] it difficult to tell which is the Real and which is the Declared'. Craig blames this on Arab leaders' 'lack of moral courage' and joked that he intended one day to write an essay on 'the Arab Mentality, a study in frustration'.[86]

But it is a study a few years after Team B which puts British intelligence thinking firmly in line with the US on the danger of mirroring and that danger's cultural basis. In 1980, Britain's Co-ordinator of Intelligence, Brooks Richards, commissioned a study of the Joint Intelligence Committee's past success in detecting preparations for aggressive military operations by the USSR and other countries. The task went to Douglas Nicoll, previously the deputy director of Britain's signals intelligence organisation Government Communication Headquarters. Nicoll chose seven 'periods of crisis', stretching from the Soviet intervention in Czechoslovakia in 1968 to its intervention in Poland in 1980. The Soviets, however, were not the only protagonists: Nicoll also considered Egypt and Syria's attack on Israel from 1972–1973 and Iraq's 1980 invasion of Iran (which Chapter 3 will consider in more depth). Reviewing the JIC's documentary record on assessing statespersons' intent to prepare for war, Nicoll writes that the committee had often 'found it difficult to believe that the potential aggressor would indeed find the use of force *politically acceptable*'.[87] This is a characterisation of other leaders' moral mindsets, a judgement by Nicoll of what elites in Russia, the Middle East and East Asia could live with in terms of violence. The implication is that elites in Britain would not use such force in similar circumstances.

94

Why did the JIC have this difficulty? Not only had its Joint Intelligence Staff tended to think the Soviets care about 'world opinion', but members had also tended to assume that 'factors which would weigh heavily in the United Kingdom would be equally serious constraints' on other countries – more precisely, 'on countries ruled by one-party governments and heavily under the influence of a single leader'. Mirror-imaging for Nicoll, then, is a problem when specifically confronting autocracies: Their domestic structure insulates them from an otherwise-reasonable 'fear' of a 'military reaction', of 'super power involvement' and of 'danger to their developing economic ties' (China's 1978 invasion of Vietnam, Iraq's invasion of Iran); it also militates against them caring about world opinion (Soviets).[88]

By merely noting that the JIC had presupposed the role of these reasonable fears and constraints in each case, Nicoll does not explicitly detail the thesis that autocracies ignore these constraints; he thereby avoids having to explain its causal logic. The mere mention of autocratic structures therefore does the heavy lifting in this analysis: Autocracy, it suggests, must make leaders on the Asian continent think differently from Anglosphere elites who, by contrast, are conditioned by plural and democratic governments. Moreover, the caution against assuming that other states hold the same values as the Anglosphere, those factors that weigh heavily over here, becomes a way of calling out other states' subjectivity compared to intelligence analysts' potential objectivity: Even if 'our assessment' that a state has 'limited capability to sustain an invasion' is 'broadly accurate', 'it does not follow [...] that the potential aggressor will make the same assessment'. Finally, the problem when analysing 'a centrally-controlled, one-party State' is that they 'will normally do their best, to keep [their] build up secret' and to 'mislead the victim and others' when secrecy fails.[89] Never mind that a surprise attack by *any* state would presumably involve them using secrecy. Through this explanation, Nicoll diagnoses mirroring as a matter of underestimating Russian and Eastern insularity, recklessness, and deception.

Nicoll's diagnosis mattered, in his own view, because the internal mechanics of the states under review were what produced crisis geopolitics. '[W]ars scarcely happen by chance', states Nicoll; they happen 'because a potential aggressor plans, prepares, deploys and decides to attack'.[90] Nicoll thereby promoted an idea that the CIA had struggled with in the aftermath of Team B's assault. Echoing Pipes and his colleagues' opposition to détente, Team B accused US intelligence analysts of falsely linking Soviet military developments to US military programmes, of making the former a reaction to the latter, rather than seeing Soviet plans as coming from an internal grand strategy. Here the Chief of PAID warns against jumping to conclusions: 'This is a tough one. Clearly, in the broadest sense, there is linkage between US and Soviet military programs', even if it was hard to 'show direct linkages on program-by-program basis'. There was simply a 'disagreement' between 'reasonable men' on the issue.[91] PAID's Chief had hit on one of the most important consequences of accepting that mirror-imaging was a real problem that should be countered. This belief turned on an image of international relations as an atomised set of scheming state leaders, each with their own personal strategic preferences which blossomed internally and which leaders often wished to hide from others. The challenge of intelligence analysis is not the universal difficulty of interpreting world events and then imagining the view through others' eyes; it is now, as one commentator perceptively notes, an 'age-old problem' of 'seemingly inscrutable rivals'.[92] As subsequent chapters will demonstrate, the PAID Chief's concern seems not to have been heeded. Mirroring was conceptualised as a naive analytical approach because it failed to account for certain nations' inherited, institutionalised deceit and belligerence. The sociology of the international, of how political ideas are spread and how foreign policies influence one another, was reduced to innate cultures: of clear-sighted Western objectivity and debilitating Eastern ignorance.

INTELLIGENCE: TOO RATIONAL TO SUCCEED

Anne Hessing Kahn, the scholar who successfully got Team B's reports declassified in the early 1990s, emphasised how surprising it should be that Gerald Ford, during a presidential election, agreed to an exercise which was bound to heavily critique the CIA and his administration. 'Why in the world' did Ford agree to it? Largely,

Kahn concludes, to mollify conservative criticism of détente. Later, when Jimmy Carter won that election, the new president's officials underestimated the public resonance of Team B's report, a resonance magnified by the press stunts of outgoing CIA Director. Bush, Pipes, and others.[93] Like Dorothy in the Land of Oz, who is warned of 'lions, and tigers, and bears' lurking on the road ahead, the US and British administrations of the late 1970s and 1980s were repeatedly warned that the Russian Bear was playing a waiting game and could not be reasoned with. Key proponents of Russian historical animosity gained positions in Ronald Reagan's government, including Richard Pipes as the National Security Council's first director for Soviet affairs. William Casey's nomination for director of central intelligence in 1981 was 'like nominating Team B to head the CIA'.[94] Using the same accusation of mirror-imaging, diplomats, intelligence officers, and reviewers also claimed that the leaders of the Middle East's post-colonial states were at their core deceitful, irrational and prone to violence. Key to their charge was that these character traits emerged from within, and not through these states' international relations.

Readers who have already heard of the Team B exercise probably know how history has judged its efforts. Its alarming conclusions on Soviet bomber production, anti-ballistic missile systems, nuclear test ranges, anti-submarine systems and military texts were all either false or serious exaggerations.[95] Historian John Prados judged the report of Pipes' team to be 'nothing stunning', just 'a collection of standard cautions' with 'generous dollops of conservative presumption', whose conclusions were as 'equally unsupported by "solid information"' as the supposed CIA presumptions that it caricatured.[96] Strategic thinker Lawrence Freedman argued that while the intelligence community might not have properly appreciated the symbolic role of quantitative military arms in Soviet leaders' thinking, Team B themselves completely misunderstood the emphasis there on symbolism. '[I]n their own way', they were 'imposing an American framework', namely a frightened conservative one, on the Russians.[97] Political scientist Chalmers Johnson, who once consulted for the CIA, later called Team B 'a disaster', noting that its outside specialists vastly inflated the size of the Soviet economy because they were '[u]nable to imagine' that the

USSR, far from exceeding US military power without a sweat, was bankrupting itself via a lacklustre warfare economy.[98]

But despite these damning indictments, the concept of mirror-imaging, as a great danger to be avoided in analysis, has escaped unscathed. In fact, this idea has been heralded as a crucial contribution to the methodology of intelligence analysis. A recent well-regarded reassessment of US intelligence on the Soviet Union asserts that while Team B was proven 'more wrong than right', 'the questions it raised were more right than wrong'.[99] Most intelligence experts who refer to the concept of mirroring do not acknowledge its neoconservative origins. Its most frequently-cited outing today, in Richards J. Heuer's *Psychology of Intelligence Analysis*, includes no such reference.[100] As this chapter has shown, however, right from its origins in post-war analysis, the term mirroring was not simply a way to explain how to avoid thoughtless assumptions about states outside the Anglosphere. Rather, it was used to then describe the *internal logics* of those states. As Heuer definitively emphasises in his book, 'people in other cultures *do not* think the way we do'.[101] The unique 'non-Western' political practices and institutional structures of other states supposedly encourage mirror-imaging in intelligence agents' reports, because those practices and structures isolate autocrats from the world and cloak their intentions from analysts. They also supposedly prove *why* mirroring is bad, since it is that insularity and suspicion, with its roots in other societies' histories and long-cemented mindsets, which prevents non-Westerners from being objective. Such objectivity, of course, is presumed to be achievable for Anglosphere analysts: for that is the only way analysts could state so confidently whether another state was behaving irrationally or unreasonably in world affairs. Going on about the danger of mirroring is a way of reasserting racial belonging: Some people have shared objectivity, whereas those who live over there cannot surpass their cultural limits.

The second half of this book turns from this historical set-up – the model of a self-contained Middle East and a theory of its leaders' policy-making – to these two ideas' later entanglement in more than three decades of intelligence analysis on Saddam Hussein, his government, and the wider region. The 2003 invasion of Iraq is the key pivot in this next part of the story. It is the culmination of years of assessments of Saddam Hussein's psychology and politics; and it reverberates through intelligence reviews and analysts' subsequent struggles with Middle Eastern events up to today. Dorothy, of course, quickly learned in the Land of Oz not to put faith in the warnings of wild animals. British and US analysts, however, reflecting Tidwell's recommendation, continued to see exactly what they oh so creatively imagined.

3

Getting to know Saddam Hussein

Consider the following two events at the turn of 2020. What does each tell us about the legacy of the Iraq intelligence failure?

In the first event, General Qassem Soleimani, commander of the Iranian special operations Quds Force, is killed by a US airstrike on 3 January while travelling from Baghdad International Airport to meet the Iraqi prime minister. The strike relies on intelligence assistance from Israel and, most likely, Britain.[1] In their initial justification of the strike, US officials claim they were acting on 'advanced notice' that Soleimani was planning attacks on US personnel and civilians. When subsequent briefings offer little evidence of this 'imminent threat', the Trump administration clarifies that the strike was actually an act of deterrence against future Iranian hostilities in Iraq.[2]

In the second event, thousands of Iraqi protesters descend on the US embassy inside Baghdad's Green Zone, just days before Soleimani's assassination. Diplomats are trapped for 48 hours as demonstrators scale the embassy walls and set fire to outbuildings, before tear gas forces the protesters back. Coming in the wake of a deadly rocket attack and US airstrikes, this embassy siege is linked by journalists to the Popular Mobilisation Forces, a collective of Iraqi militias who largely pledge support for the Iranian Government. It does not take long for President Trump to accuse Iran of having orchestrated the siege.[3]

Why compare these two events? In the case of Soleimani's death, its shaky rationale seemed to echo claims 20 years previous, that Saddam Hussein had posed an imminent danger to the security of other nations. This parallel was drawn across the political spectrum: *Fox News*' Tucker Carlson denounced the 'politically tainted and suspect' intelligence agencies who had declared Soleimani a threat, accusing them of having previously 'lied about Iraq's weapons of mass destruction', while Democratic Senator Bob Menendez called for the declassification of the relevant intelligence, reasoning that '[t]he last thing we need is another weapons of mass destruction moment', when 'faulty intelligence' went unscrutinised. 'It doesn't require much squinting', declared *The Atlantic*, 'to see the ways the Iran crisis resembles the lead-up to [Iraq]': an ideological Cabinet pushing for war, using 'false justifications' from 'misconstrue[d], twist[ed], or concoct[ed] intelligence'.[4]

In-and-of-itself, this scepticism was healthy and well-justified: Classified briefings to US lawmakers contradicted the Trump administration's claims regarding Soleimani's operations; on top of this, the strike most likely broke international law.[5] Parallels, however, narrate history in ways that both make new events familiar *and* reshape the meaning of the past. Accounts of 9/11 as a 'new Pearl Harbour' allowed commentators to make sense of both domestic attacks by writing a romantic history of inevitable US triumph, while the endless comparisons between Iraq and Vietnam told a tragic tale of good intentions floundering in bloody quagmires – a tale which obscures the less honourable origins and strategy of both wars.[6] By linking the invasion of Iraq to the assassination of this Iranian general, commentators were not only criticising US actions in the here-and-now; they were also defining what had happened with the infamous intelligence on Saddam Hussein two decades earlier, as well as what lessons should be drawn from it. This, the link declared, was a repeating story of objective inaccuracy, of intelligence claims failing to measure up against the real world. Two decades ago, analysts or elected officials – which one is up for debate (see Introduction) – misreported Hussein's WMD capabilities; now, they were doing the same with the Quds Forces' plans for violence.

No such link to past mistakes was made with the US embassy protest. In fact, in this case, intelligence analysts believed they had the inside scoop. A senior Pentagon official confidently stated that unlike recent Iraqi protests *against* Iranian influence, which was an 'organic uprising', the embassy siege protesters had been 'directly influenced, orchestrated, prodded by the Iranians'. The official did concede that it might have been a 'mix' – say, '900 idiots, and 10 instigators'.[7] Such an assessment chimed with leaked Iranian intelligence documents on the country's 'vast web of influence in Iraq', with Iranian spies reported to have 'co-opt[ed] the country's leaders' and 'infiltrate[d] every aspect of Iraq's political, economic, and religious life' during the 2010s, so as 'to maintain Iraq as a pliable client state'. Constituting 'an extraordinary glimpse inside the secretive Iranian regime', these documents were purported to show 'how Iran, at nearly every turn, ha[d] outmanoeuvred the United States in the contest for influence'. And at the centre was the 'unique role' of Soleimani, whose Quds Force 'determined Iran's policies' regarding Iraq. Soleimani, 'more than anyone else' had used 'the dark arts of espionage and covert military action' to support 'political factions loyal to Tehran'.[8] Those same dark arts had allowed the Iranian general to manage proxy wars 'in Iraq, Syria, Lebanon and Yemen', as he 'Built a Shiite Axis of Power in Mideast'.[9]

While this story acknowledges a kind of policy failure – of US strategy scuppered by Iran's hidden hand – it sticks to a narrow, well-worn script on Middle Eastern power politics, one that had long contributed to avowedly successful policy-making. An opaque, autocratic Middle Eastern Government, bent on nothing less than regional domination, using subterfuge to achieve its aims – no one questioned the assumptions, significance or implications of this tale. In fact, as this chapter will argue, the same story was woven through the long history of intelligence assessments on Saddam Hussein and Iraq. Yet this providence in intelligence reporting went unacknowledged. Saddam was instead written into the story of Soleimani's death as an earlier example of what the Quds Force leader now represented: part of a generation of mutually suspicious statesmen 'shaped by the brutal war between Iran and Iraq in the 1980s', before joining 'a long line of slain tyrants' whose cultivated image of 'invincibility' came crashing down.[10] The Middle East, in this further re-framing of history, is simply cursed with a lineage of deceitful expansionists.

But this latest telling left out an important question: Why was Iran trying to gain power now, in this manner, at the very real risk of US counter-subversion? 'Malignant intent' is not an answer, since it does not account for circumstances: Why at this moment and through these means, especially under the shadow of 'punishing

US sanctions', not to mention President Trump's threat to 'hold Iran responsible' for the embassy siege.[11] Asking these questions begins to uncover just how much political context is obscured when you jump from describing a deceptive, manipulative autocracy to assuming a nefarious, belligerent intent abroad. In their revelation of the leaked intelligence documents, the state-sceptical US outlet *The Intercept* tried to nuance its eye-catching headlines, describing how Iran was 'grappling with many of the same challenges faced by American occupying forces' before them.[12] It surely stings, though, that their reporting was cited by arch-neoconservative John Bolton, Iraq War architect and one-time national security adviser to Trump, as justification for legally designating Iran's Revolutionary Guard Corps a terrorist organisation and giving up on Iraq's government.[13]

Subsequent studies of the leaked documents have formed a different conclusion: While Iran's then-President Hassan Rouhani was promoting Iraq as an arbitrator of regional summits in order to improve regional links with Saudi Arabia and counter-balance crippling US sanctions, the Quds Force discounted the chance of any regional alliances and therefore undermined such diplomacy through its covert actions, actions which actually fostered unrest inside Iran.[14] The Quds' attitude came after years of Soleimani reaching out to the US administration in occupied Iraq, as Iran's armed influence in the country shifted and ISIS challenged both Iranian and US control.[15] By the end of 2019, it was widely reported that Soleimani was being criticised by both colleagues and citizens for violent crackdowns and the slow erosion of Iran's regional legitimacy.[16] As for protests in Iraq, while US officials emphasised the anti-Iranian bent of massive protests at the end of 2019, protesters themselves criticised the US and Iran's 'alignment' in together making Iraq 'a failed and weak state', and demanded both 'the expulsion of the American military' and 'the expulsion of Iranian influence'.[17] In 2021, the US National Intelligence Council warned that 'ongoing internal conflicts' in Middle East states were bolstering '[p]roxy conflicts' involving Iran along with 'sectarian rivalries', and bemoaned that in Iraq, '[f]ears of civil war' were 'losing their deterrence power' against public protest. This narrative erases Iraqi protesters' mass opposition to Iraq's political system, which divides public offices and resources along religious sect lines and fuels corrupt patronage networks – a system institutionalised by the United States during their occupation of the country.[18]

But this international context to Iraq's protests and Iran's foreign policy deliberations has not entered the debate on the reality and significance of Iran's leaked documents and the accusations of political manipulation. A *New York Times* article sums up this paucity of thinking: As they put it, Iraq's compromised government opposed US policy on Iran, with its security forces even abetting pro-Iranian militias, '[d]espite a 16-year American effort to establish a government friendlier to Western interests'.[19] The moral of the story is clear: Well-intentioned Anglosphere policy-makers have simply failed to overcome Iraqi intransigence or to foresee the extent of Iranian duplicity. With Iraq's population reduced to idiotic dupes and Iran presented as the duplicitous foil to a valiant West, Soleimani's story became a racialised narrative, where some nations and governments fail to grasp what is good for the region. When it comes to intelligence, it seems, only certain lessons are allowed to be learned.

MAKING *WHICH* MISTAKE ALL OVER AGAIN?

This chapter examines how the narrative of intelligence failure as a failure to measure the true awesome power of deceptive Middle Eastern regimes found its apotheosis in the figure of Saddam Hussein. The chapter explores how Anglosphere intelligence constructed a narrow model of one man's psyche and intellect, so that questions of how Iraq's international relations influenced its leader's perceptions and intent became impossible to ask. As discussed in the Introduction, by circling around the issue of capabilities – did he have WMD – critics of the Iraq invasion have been caught in a bind. If the main issue is empiricism, then any critique needs to establish why intelligence ended up inaccurate and how it could have been otherwise. Defenders can respond with appeals to that real world out there: 'You don't have proof that reports were manipulated'; 'besides, it was impossible to prove that Saddam *didn't* have the weapons'. So little has actually been resolved in the public debate around the Iraq intelligence because of this smoking gun conundrum.

Using the previous chapters' explanation of post-war Anglo-sphere intelligence – as an emergency intellectual response to anti-colonialism – we can begin to piece together the way that analysis of Middle Eastern autocracies has been rigged in advance, by a narrow accepted wisdom of what intelligence does, for whom, and what we can expect from it. Previous chapters have traced how intelligence agencies interpreted the dramatic changes of the twentieth century as evidence of new independent governments' and populations' hermetic, inflexible cultural approaches to world politics. This interpretation racialised these societies as lacking the intellectual and emotional capacity to navigate the world stage, and therefore tenuously preserved a belief in international inequalities – with the US and allied states at the top – as the most reasonable and rational 'balance of power' in this post-colonial world.

Saddam Hussein's emergence on the world stage could not have come at a better time for agencies to further develop this thesis. When Saddam became president of Iraq in 1979, the country was not high up on the list of intelligence priorities.[20] What was being written, however, set a trend in analysis that would only intensify over the next 20 years. US and British agents were tasked with dissecting Saddam's policy-making, in order to determine his political calculus and its implications for their own countries' strategies. Analysts used the intellectual tools they had at their disposal: an understanding of the Middle East's geopolitics and of non-white Asian and Arab states' uniqueness. This use legitimised Anglosphere dominance, at the inadvertent cost of obscuring the international sociology of this new world.

Three themes stand out in this story of getting to know Saddam from the 1970s to the turn of the millennium, which together turn the established story of the Iraq intelligence failure on its head. First, Iraq's threat was always understood to be not about evolving *capabilities* but about the historical, acculturated *mindset* of its leader, a mindset of belligerence and expansionism. Second, gaps in intelligence *proved* this man's culturally-entrenched deception and paranoia. Finally, decades of evidence that Anglosphere policy was reinforcing Saddam's preference for violence could not be computed, since this proposition would challenge analysts' model of a post-colonial power balance; the evidence was translated instead as proof of Saddam's pathology and unpredictability. Underlying all of this was a belief – sometimes coded, sometimes explicit – in Saddam's psychological and cultural irrationality, that a man like him was inherently incapable of reading international relations intelligently in the way that Anglosphere analysts could.

As this and the following chapter will argue, it is this long-term profiling of Saddam Hussein's personality and politics that, by the early 2000s, hemmed analysts into the judgement that political brokerage with Iraq's head of state was impossible and that force was a valid, indeed the only viable, policy towards him. More than simply favouring realist power politics over a liberal diplomatic alternative, intelligence analysts drastically reduced their own potential to comprehend *why* Saddam was acting the way he was and how their own states' policy actions were influencing his thinking. As with the Baghdad embassy siege two decades later, these questions of why and how challenged a certain idea of how geopolitics worked; as a result, I argue, it simply did not make sense to analysts to ask them. Besides, the ultimate evidence of Saddam's irrationality was his refusal to abide by 'reasonable' Anglosphere policy objectives. Given this thoroughly racialised and colonial mode of thinking, where bad geopolitical decisions are the product of innately inferior cultural thought and feelings, the present chapter concludes that the problem with the Iraq intelligence is not what agencies got wrong about weapons stocks. The problem is what these agencies, and almost everyone still debating their results, believe they got right about Saddam.

THE (NON-)POLITICS OF IRAQ

Saddam Hussein was in Anglosphere intelligence's sights for more than four decades. However, he first entered them not in his own right but through the lens of a post-colonial Middle East. This entrance is important: Saddam's early profiling, despite being marginal, established an easy-to-follow framework for interpreting his later rise to power. As Saddam's position propelled him up intelligence priorities, he and Iraq would come to represent the enduring legacy of the modes of analysis detailed so far in this book.

In July 1958, in yet another intelligence surprise,[21] a coup by Iraqi military officers overthrew the country's Hashemite monarchy. This not only weakened a US regional alliance against Arab nationalist and communist influence, but also renewed the Iraqi threat to occupy Kuwait, a vital source of British oil operations and sterling reserves.[22] The US National Security Council (NSC) debated supporting armed opponents of new Prime Minister Abd al-Karim Qasim, especially once Qasim tore up a longstanding security pact and nationalised Iraq's oil. CIA head Allen Dulles insisted that NSC members 'could not sit by and let the situation in Iraq deteriorate further'.[23] Some US policy-makers and CIA officers were desperate enough to draw up plans for covert action and to promote a rapprochement with Egypt's Nasser, who was himself funding armed subversion against this revolutionary rival.[24] Britain, by contrast, tried to gain Qasim's favour as a way of securing longstanding oil, sterling, and anti-Nasser objectives. Within two years, however, Britain's hopeful supply of arms and support for Qasim against internal coups turned into a pessimistic preference for regime change.[25] Tellingly, the more Qasim dismissed Anglosphere oil and basing agreements as imperial hangovers, the more intelligence analysts psychologised him as a deluded idiot, 'a neurotic and unstable individual' who was 'verging on madness'.[26] Then in February 1963, soldiers with the Pan-Arab Ba'ath Party captured and killed Qasim before carrying out mass executions of opponents and genocide against Iraq's Kurdish minority. This violence was handsomely supported by Washington, while British intelligence analysts calmly mulled over whether it was better to arm the new government and gain influence, or to starve it of assistance so that it would remain stuck in its long, bloody counter-insurgency in Kurdistan.[27] Although the Ba'athists lasted less than nine months before being deposed by pro-Nasserites, their leaders would mount another successful coup d'état in July 1968. This second period of rule would last until March 2003.

Having joined Iraq's branch of the Ba'ath Party in his early twenties, Saddam Hussein took part in an October 1959 assassination attempt on General Qasim, possibly with CIA support, before fleeing to Egypt.[28] Returning to Iraq in 1963, Saddam's increasing role in the Ba'athists by 1968 made him a figure worthy of attention. Ba'athist Iraq was one of the many Middle Eastern governments placed within the 'Regime' category (see Chapter 2). For the US State Department's Bureau of Intelligence and Research, this categorisation demanded clarity: to understand '[t]he Present [post-1968] Ba'athi Regime', you have to know 'who speaks with authority *for* the regime'.[29] The problem for analysts was that the volatile Iraqi political scene teemed with conflict on that very issue. Understanding the country's geopolitical direction became a matter of mapping this internal struggle for state power. Following the changing fortunes of factions was now shorthand for intelligence expertise on this country's strategy. By summing up Iraq's politics as 'a faltering regime' trying to distract from its own instability, Bureau reporting created a narrow intelligence narrative where Party Secretary General Saddam played a supporting role. Saddam was first described as the leader of one contending faction, a 'prominent figure' with 'a personal following of his own'. He was defined by his chances of political survival and his shared desire for power.[30] The CIA later explained these internal struggles for power through racialisation. The Iraqi Government's 'pattern of domination' towards potential sources of opposition is not just about shoring up 'current party loyalties' but is 'a reflection of traditional Iraqi politics', which involves 'making political alliances among family, clan and village networks'.[31] If the Ba'athists could be summed up by their insecure squabbling, then that behaviour was rooted in the country's ancient cultural make-up.

From the late 1960s to the mid-1970s, power struggles between paranoids was presented as the main indicator of Iraq's geopolitical strategising. In regular 'tentative' assessments of the Persian Gulf's future, Britain's Joint Intelligence Committee (JIC) examined the growing trend of revolutionary organisations in terms of the instability of the states supporting and opposing them. In Iraq, one such supporter, the country's social conditions and political currents are summed up as 'internal troubles'. Addressing these troubles is less about politics than about whether the Ba'athists have 'absolute control of the armed forces' and can overcome their own inner 'tensions'. When Saddam Hussein is mentioned, it is to measure his wavering 'authority and popularity' in that struggle; policy moves are judged in terms of how they may 'refurbish his image'. The JIC do not actually explain how all this bears on 'the ambitions of Iraq' or 'the struggle between traditionalist régimes and the proponents of radical change'. It all simply sets the scene – Iraq is unstable and Saddam is 'Iraq's strong man'.[32] When the JIC *do* try to explain this causality, they see Iraq's instability as reflecting its leaders' limited statesmanship: Being 'preoccupied with their internal political problems', Iraq's government will have 'little time for coherent thought or action' on foreign policy.[33] Britain's ambassador in Kuwait, writing to Middle East Department Head and future JIC Chief Patrick Wright, was more blunt: Although feeling 'not particularly well qualified to pontificate about the interplay of personalities in Baghdad', he suggests that 'rivalries in Baghdad are far more concerned with the struggle for power than with differences of opinion about the policies to be followed'.[34] The CIA agreed: Regular government and military purges 'revealed' to analysts 'the ascendency of personalities' under the Ba'athists and 'the lack of any real issues in defining either political actions or actors'.[35] This was a political movement with no politics, a government defined by opaque rivalries. Power struggles were used by intelligence officers to explain both Iraq's strategic future and the personalities of its leaders.

But power struggles wouldn't give intelligence agents enough material to sketch Ba'athist Iraq's emerging role in Middle Eastern geopolitics, nor Saddam and others' impact on Anglosphere interests. Analysts would need details of these new leaders' foreign policy views and ambitions. Unfortunately, they had few sources to go on. In response to Israel's attacks on Egypt, Syria and Jordan in June 1967, Iraq had cut off diplomatic relations with the United States. Notwithstanding CIA spies that remained in the country, this left the US reliant on the Belgian diplomatic mission for reports on Ba'athist policy-making.[36] The British Government, meanwhile, had announced it was withdrawing its military forces from the Arabian Peninsula, which a JIC Working Party acknowledged would impact intelligence priorities and capabilities.[37] As this withdrawal wound up, Iraq cut off diplomatic relations with Britain too. None of these changes, however, stopped analysts from turning their own speculations into baseline data. Beginning with their equilibrium model of Middle East geopolitics and their idea of avoiding the mirror-image fallacy, analysts in the 1970s sought out the 'essence' of the new Iraqi Government, the underlying logic that shaped its leaders' actions in its own, distinct way. What made Iraq and Saddam Hussein tick?

From their distant observing position, analysts had three kinds of intelligence to go on. First, paradoxically, was their lack of access. The inability to see the inner workings of Iraq's government became a quality *of* that government. British analysts had defined the Ba'athists by deception since 1963. Without first-hand intelligence insight into this first Ba'athist Government, the JIC worked on the basis of what it called 'the basic Iraqi belief' in absorbing Kuwait, a belief which 'long predates the [previous] Qasim regime'. The present Iraqi Government therefore 'must have had in mind' the 'increased opportunities for subversion' to this end. Historical Iraqi desires prove the Ba'athists' deceit.[38] The Cabinet and Foreign Office agreed: While only renewed air reconnaissance would determine the truth of 'alarmist bazaar rumours', this new Ba'athist Government was nevertheless 'conspiratorial by nature', making it 'naive to take their protestations of friendship for Kuwait at face value'.[39] Into the post-1968 administration, Britain's chargé d'affaires in Iraq summed up Iraqi politics as 'intimidation of a suffocating *and smog-like kind*', with Ba'athist '[i]ntelligence penetration of every limb of the body politic' and 'covert troublemaking in the Persian Gulf States'.[40] A CIA study defined 'the predominant political forces in the country' as an insular administration focused on repression and its violent rivalries – although 'limited' information stopped analysts from 'elucidat[ing] much more on Iraqi political dynamics'. Iraqi elites have 'mysterious [...] motivation[s]', while Presidents Bakr and Vice Chairman Saddam are suspicious and closed-minded, their 'consolidation of power' making them 'no more [...] responsive than before'.[41] Secrecy was taken as a defining point of Iraq's politics and was in turn translated as insularity and irrationality – in effect, 'those inward-looking Iraqis won't respond to the demands of our interests'.

Analysts linked this insularity to Iraq's unworldliness: As the CIA assessed, '[s]uccessive coups and purges' had rid the state of administrative employees who had 'some experience of the outside world'.[42] Provincialism was seen not as a policy challenge for Bakr and Saddam to confront but as an engrained habit that distinguished Iraq from a normal state. Britain's Middle East intelligence experts lamented that Iraq's leaders '[do] not seem able to make up [their] mind' about recognising Kuwait's sovereignty, to 'swallow the pill' that was militarily and politically sensible; then again, in the British Ambassador's eyes, 'the present [Iraqi] Government', not being well-travelled, 'are very ignorant about Kuwait'.[43] Among British observers, their own equilibrium model of the Middle East prevented similar ignorance: As they saw it, Iraq–Kuwait relations normally 'follow[ed] a traditional pattern' and would hopefully 'revert to a more normal, dormant state', once the players become sensible.[44] 'Expertise' was defined within the context of this equilibrium model. To practice good governance meant adhering to current international inequalities: So, Britain's ambassador describes a 'tug-of-war' in Iraq of 'the technicians and the realists' versus 'the doctrinaire extremists', with the latter 'preferring [ideological] logic to commonsense' on Israel's occupation of Palestine.[45] For the CIA, the country's 'lack of direction' stemmed from the fact that its 'lower middle class' civil servants 'lack[ed] political training and experience' – that is, they had not been internationally socialised in the proper way.[46] It went without saying, of course, that Anglosphere analysts considered themselves expert enough to judge such experience and proper behaviour. But the implication that unworldliness fostered uniquely Iraqi behaviour could lead analysts astray. Much is made of Saddam and co.'s suspicious outlook, that they 'regard all diplomats with suspicion and watch them closely [...] especially the Communists' with their 'dirty tricks'. The Ba'athists, after all, are 'particularly jumpy'.[47] Does Britain not similarly regard Soviet diplomats this way? If so, does this shared suspicion really reveal much about Iraq's unique inexperience?

The second piece of intelligence for officers to go on was that Iraq's governing party was most definitely Ba'athist. But here lay another problem. To assess the Ba'ath Party's outlook on foreign affairs risked confronting Ba'athism's criticisms of colonial powers and allied states for their roles in Middle Eastern politics. The intelligence model of the Middle East as an equilibrium to be inter-vened in could be threatened by arguments of the Anglosphere's negative ongoing presence. Luckily for analysts, their focus on the insular life of states in a supposedly self-contained region, part of their attempt to avoid mirror-imaging, made it easy to dismiss Ba'athist philosophy. An important example was Kuwait. By the early 1970s, it was enough for Britain's Joint Intelligence Staff to note that 'many Iraqis still hanker after the recovery of what they regard as Iraq's lost province' to forgo any consideration of Ba'athist ideology and a policy response to it. This included forgoing how the Ba'athist 'tempt[ation]' for Kuwait's 'oil wealth' might compare to Britain's own 'important economic interests' there. No, Iraq's foreign policy simply reflected 'the less reasoned attitudes of the more militant Arab States' contra Kuwait who, by 'assist[ing] the pursuit of British objectives', was by definition 'a moderate skaikhly régime'.[48] The CIA, meanwhile, dismissed the Ba'ath Party's political platform as 'an involved, if somewhat vague, left-wing socio-political philosophy' masking the revolutionaries' real politics: an Iraqi 'tradition' of militarised violence and a desire for a regional expansion of influence. Saddam Hussein, 'a shrewd, ruthless operator', shared in this shallowness; his only policy differ-ences with others were around levels of 'aggress[ion] [...] against the Kurds'.[49] Britain's ambassador to Iraq went further, stating that '[w]e all know that the intellectual content of Ba'athism is tiny', its literature 'congealed porridge'.[50]

Fair or not to Ba'athist writers, this dismissal of the Iraqi elite's political outlook meant that Iraq's mid-1970s 'ambitions as a champion of the developing countries and a leader of the Non-Aligned Movement', as Britain's ambassador put it in reports to London, did not need to be explained through international currents of thought or political aspirations vis-à-vis the US and Britain – you did not need to explore their desire for 'what they call an equal relationship'. Ostensibly sitting outside regional politics looking in, analysts such as the ambassador instead noted the 'disastrous' policy decisions by which the Ba'athists had 'isolated [themselves] in the Arab world'. Iraq was not shaped by the world; it had simply 'reverted to type'.[51] In 1971, Britain's ambassador to Bahrain cited 'experience *over nearly 30 years*' – that is, well beyond the Ba'athists' time – to assert that 'Iraqi foreign policy is never positive except for mischief', 'mean[ing] in practice that *we have to ignore* Iraqi "aspirations"', including what the ambassador admitted was the 'legitimate Iraqi interest' in Gulf trading routes.[52] According to the British embassy, the Ba'athists had little understanding of interests anyway: By 'promot[ing] revolution in eastern Arabia', Iraq's government is pursuing 'what they regard as *their* interests' against 'what we and our Iranian and other allies know to be *ours*'.[53] Their policy is based on illogical reasoning; Britain's, on accurate appraisals of geopolitics.

Race – specifically, an assumption of engrained limits to Ba'athist clear thinking and emotional control – lies as the unspoken foundation for this distinction between Iraq and Anglosphere politics. Not only do analysts explain the Bakr Government's 'quarrelsome', 'troublemaking' attitude through a historical Iraqi preference for violence and a paternalistic regret that Iraq continues to unfairly disparage 'the imperialist West'.[54] Not only are Iraq's actions framed by the 'taunts and prophecies of doom' from fellow 'revolutionary Arabs', along with their 'curious' allies of 'outlandish layabouts' in the Middle East and Africa.[55] Reports also judge the Ba'athist Government by vastly different standards than they do Britain and the United States, on the implicit grounds that only one side sees the world accurately. While Iraq is disparaged as 'full of sound and fury' but ultimately 'treating [...] the rest of the world in practical ways', Britain's incessant attempts to further open up Iraq's 'valuable market for us', a market whose 'potential is vast' according to Britain's ambassador, are not seen as undermining the British Government's indignant noise and anger over Iraq.[56] Diplomats assert that Iraq only 'suspects' Britain's intentions, whereas Britain 'are *right* to believe' that the Ba'athists are 'in no sense genuine friends of the West'. Those same diplomats' common refrain that Britain is not yet 'reaping the harvest' of Iraq's growing wealth, while 'our competitors' are 'reap[ing] the reward', is not seen as evidence that Britain's friendship credentials might also be genuinely suspect.[57] The politics of Iraq's government was also consistently dismissed by the JIC as puerile pride: Being unable to 'afford wholly to neglect Arab nationalism', the Ba'athists support revolutionary uprisings elsewhere that 'vie with one another' to prove their 'defiance'. The committee's own worry that such groups could potentially '[claim] that it was their activities which had driven out the British' from the Persian Gulf is not judged to be similarly shallow or a display of proud self-regard.[58]

The reduction of Ba'athist foreign policy to shallow belligerence also made all this intelligence analysis, on the face of it, a lot less useful to policy-makers. To the extent that Ba'ath Party leaders were avowedly 'hostile to all sheiks, sultans, and shahs' in the Gulf, it was clear that they would want to influence regional politics in a different direction. But just as CIA and State Department analysts collapsed Iraqi actors' political ends into their most visible means – their philosophies into their squabbles for state control – so too did they reduce Iraq's geopolitical objectives to 'expand[ing] [Iraq's] present role in' and 'exert[ing] a major influence on future Gulf politics.'[59] The JIC agreed on this point: Iraq's foreign policy could be summed up as a 'vehemently anti-Western [...] stand taken by successive Iraqi governments since 1958' and unspecified 'ambitions in the [Gulf] area.'[60] Iraq's support for 'popular war[s] of liberation' in Palestine and elsewhere is better understood, say the committee, as an attempt to take on the 'leadership of the Arab world'; its actions to that end are based not 'on realistic calcula-tions' but on 'limitless' levels of 'self-delusion'. The problem is that regardless of the truth of Ba'athist actors' presumed megaloma-nia, such extrapolations by intelligence analysts say nothing about what Bakr and Saddam's desired expanded role in the Gulf would look like or how Iraq might use its 'increas[ed] [...] influence in the Arab world'.[61] Expansionism on Iraq's part begins to appear in intelligence texts as an unelaborated end-in-itself.

Third, to build up a picture of Iraq, intelligence analysts drew on their long-developing idea of an ancestral-religious divide in the Middle East, between a conservative Islamism and a revolu-tionary Arabism. Underneath this image was a racial judgement of regressive Arab culture in the Persian Gulf. In a 1968 report on revolutionary movements in the Gulf, the JIC describes 'oil lorries driving past bedouin and their camels' by way of demonstrating the 'incongruous' co-existence of 'the modern and the ancient' in the region. Any revolutionary ideology, they say, therefore operates through the 'Arab trait' of 'coffee house [...] airing of grievances', producing merely divided movements and 'communal disturbances' which are, the committee notes approvingly, easily repressed. '[M]odernity' is desired by 'only a minority' – in fact, many revolutionary insurgencies are actually 'reactionary rather than progressive', seeking to preserve the 'essentially tribal structures of Gulf society'.[62] The image of modernity's incompatibility with Arab tradition solidifies a colonial and racial definition of the Arab psyche, as unable to adapt to political trends brought on by the region's opening-up to the world. The oil lorries are disturbing the coffee houses. Self-avowedly anti-monarchist governments such as Iraq's are therefore not only disingenuous; they are feared and disapproved of by a common Arab traditionalism on all sides. Ironically, this reading creates a contradiction picked up on by other analysts: If these Gulf revolutionary movements were conservative, how could they be threatening the spread of Pan-Arabism?[63] But towards the turn of the 1970s, this kind of political inquiry gave way to analysts' judgement that it was states like Iraq that were upsetting the natural order of things, by supporting unpopular minority revolutionaries, while it was conservative monarchies, including Iran, that '[o]bjectively speaking' should recognise their sensible 'common interest in stability in the Gulf'.[64] Religion, race, and Regime type overlapped one another as part of the JIC's explanation of political tensions.

With this framework of a regional tradition-modern antagonism, intelligence analysts could now easily explain Iraqi politics. For the CIA, the country's fundamental 'disunity and instability' comes down to 'fragment[ation] among ethnic and religious communities' who have 'limited sense of national identity'. Iraqis are 'in the first instance an Arab, Kurd [...] Sunni, Shiah'. 'Baath ideology or Arab socialism' have not overcome the 'traditional practices' of 'a backward society' which define 'the reality of the country'.[65] This assessment predicts the more recent image of Iraqi society as having always been defined by violent sect affiliation, summed up as 'sectarianism'. In fact, this idea of Iraq's politics came out of modern Iraqi history. Ba'athist authorities linked citizenship to stories of sect identity as they juggled ways of demonising Iran in the 1980s and insinuating a kind of bloodline treachery across generations of political dissidents.[66] In the view of Anglosphere intelligence, however, ancestry and sect were already key to under-standing the society.

The idea of traditionalism was extended to foreign policy. Con-servative 'Iranian nationalism' is judged to *de facto* threaten Iraq's 'concept' of the 'Arab nature of the Gulf'. As the US's Bureau of Intelligence and Research saw it, this rivalry constitutes the two states' 'competition for leadership in the Gulf'.[67] The JIC reduced Iraqi foreign policy to the 'long tradition' of this rivalry: 'Hostility to, and rivalry with, Iran are the mainspring of Iraq's Gulf policies'; actual current policy disputes or ideological divides on monar-chism only 'exacerbate' a timeless antagonism.[68] Analysts thereby established a regional-cultural underpinning to Iraq's expansion-ism, further diluting any trace of contextual political motivations – including the US's aim, as Henry Kissinger outlined it in 1972, to encourage Iran 'to assume the main responsibility for the security of the entire Gulf area', not to mention extensive British oil and military contracts with Iran's Shah.[69] Such context did not matter; the stage had already been set. Closed-minded, paranoid expan-sionism was a model of Iraq's government that intelligence agents could work with. Historical sectarianism only further confirmed to them that these political dynamics were hermetically sealed within and essential to an Iraqi and Arab disposition.

SADDAM THE STATESMAN

These building-blocks of ideas – from insularity to expansionism to historical Arab antagonism – shaped the Anglosphere's early intelligence assessments of Saddam Hussein by racialising his psy-chology and diminishing the scope of interest in his politics and their international dynamics. In policy-making terms, the structure provided by these ideas made certain ways of approaching Saddam – like using violence as a signal to him – seem plausible and others – like relinquishing power and demilitarising the region – seem ridiculous. This happened decades before Saddam was targeted by Bush and Blair for overthrow, establishing enduring narrow boundaries of acceptable thinking about his Ba'athist Government, which would speak to both hawkish and doveish readers of the intelligence reports.

This reduction in acceptable thinking took place throughout intelligence assessments of the 1970s. In May 1972, as he prepared for a presidential trip to Iran, Richard Nixon was given a briefing on 'Iraqi politics in perspective'. The briefing did not mince its words. Iraq's '[c]hronic instability' and 'extremist nationalism bordering on the xenophobic' had made it 'the most unreliable and least realistic of Mid-East states', that is, for US strategic purposes. This poor governance stemmed from a 'legacy' of 'ethnic and religious' divisions, which British colonialism had previously solved 'only [through] harsh and imposed rule'. It was therefore natural that Iraq's post-independence leadership had 'evolved with the same militaristic mentality and inability to resolve internal divisiveness except through force', along with 'an unusually intense hatred for foreign [...] influence'. The echoes of reports that assessed countries during their decolonisation are striking – once again, there is no present politics, only historical emotion. This hate-filled leadership includes Saddam Hussein, 'virtual king of the Iraqi security apparatus'.[70] Two things are significant here. First, Saddam's political outlook is determined and defined by Iraq's historical xenophobic and militaristic environment. Second, this briefing's sociological explanation for Iraq's present state is international but only up to a point. Analysts assert British colonialism's imprint on Middle Eastern politics but this imprint has a finality to it. There is no further foreign influence on the behaviour of Saddam and the post-independence elite. Iraq's vacillating policy positions and contemporary isolation have internal sources only. Anyone reading this paper would conclude that Iraq's international relations stopped evolving around the 1930s. Needless to say, much which was discussed earlier in this chapter is conveniently left out as a result.

Britain's diplomats in the region in the 1970s, meanwhile, were watching Saddam Hussein's machinations inside the Ba'ath Party for evidence of how his mind worked. Though he had 'established himself as [a] leading Party theorist in the background', he now 'delivers homilies on political philosophy which are impenetrable'.[71] Sovietology-style sifting through speeches and reshuffles for proof of policy plans was the norm. Indeed, those analysing Iraq do sometimes notice 'the tendency in our reporting', as the ambassador to Iraq puts it in 1976, 'to make too much of small things' due to secrecy, 'as in this case, the speeches of Saddam Hussain'. Glimpses of policy might be fooling diplomats into looking for a 'clearly defined' Iraqi policy and 'consistency in Iraqi actions' where none exists. In the ambassador's view, then, government secrecy and dense discussions might actually be evidence of incompetence, that the Iraqi state is not thinking and expressing very much about foreign policy at all. After all, Iraq's leaders have had 'little exposure to normal political and diplomatic processes'. In that climate, Saddam's own thought process is more likely '"intuitive" rather than "deductive"' – he will be incapable of logical reasoning. Despite his own caution, the ambassador bases this claim, once again, on Saddam's speeches: The latter does not make arguments 'logically' but 'repeat[s] point[s] which [appear] to him self-evident'. '[H]is policy is a result of feeling rather than thought' which 'sometimes leads him astray', to commit to actions that '[leave] no room for manoeuvre'.[72] Framed by the wider belief in Iraq's vacuous political culture, this assessment of Saddam takes the man's long-winded style and inwardness as evidence of a limited psyche. Like other Middle Eastern statesmen, he just cannot think and feel properly.

Other than speeches, analysts followed Saddam's involvement in the Ba'ath Party's bloody internal struggles. The assassination of General Hardan al-Tikriti in 1971, for instance, was quickly traced to 'master-mind' Saddam, whose probable role in lulling Hardan into a false sense of security was judged '[v]ery Iraqi, & very probable'.[73] Hardan had in fact been seeking to reopen diplomatic relations with the Anglosphere through oil company contacts. His efforts were rebuffed by the US State Department and CIA figures, who doubted the Ba'athists' staying power and level-headedness. Harden subsequently fell out of favour in government.[74] But for analysts invested in the idea of a traditional and separate Middle East equilibrium, where people think totally differently, Hardan's assassination remained an internal affair – very Iraqi indeed.

The CIA's Office of Political Research (OPR) further expands on their analysis in a 1976 report on 'Iraq Under Baath Rule'. After eight years, with Iraq now seeming to have a 'relatively stable regime', what was shaping the 'operating assumptions of its Ba'ath leadership in its decision-making processes'? Although they admittedly '[lack] sufficient and accurate documentation' due to diplomatic troubles, and while 'some aspects remain obscure', the OPR attempt to answer this question.[75] To their mind, under the facade of socialist 'party tenets', a 'traditional and cautious set of assumptions' guide to Iraq's leadership, centred around 'the unity and stability of the state, the maintenance of the national self-inter-est, and the survival of the regime'. When it comes to foreign policy, '[r]elations with the outside world are determined by internal necessity, by the need for political stability'.[76] Such an assessment tells the reader little about what Iraq's geopolitics might look like. 'National self-interest' might be served in very different ways. Nor on its own terms does it mark Iraq out as particularly unusual: What government would not, on balance, be in favour of its state's stability or its own longevity? But by singling out these principles as if singularly Iraqi, being integral to Ba'ath ideology, this assessment justifies scrutinising internal party dynamics, which themselves are enmeshed in 'Sunni Arab dominance' and 'dependence on family and clan loyalty', in order to assess survival prospects.[77] CIA analysts therefore quickly zoom in on Saddam Hussein's history of power plays in this context (Figure 3.1). Being by experience 'the conspirator' and 'essentially an opportunist, not an ideologue', Saddam does not construct policy in this analysis but merely 'isolate[s] and eliminate[s] dissident person and factions', 'consol-idate[s] [his] power over the military', is 'maintained in power' via his 'control of the party'.[78]

Analysts' intelligence image of Saddam, which frames his thought within party, clan and sect rivalries, is cripplingly weak in explanatory terms. It cannot assess how ongoing foreign relations might be influencing the deputy's political outlook and deci-sion-making. Whether or not a state's foreign policy is designed to improve personal status or preserve group power, its particu-lar international focus, along with what leaders perceive to be its potential and options, will be shaped by factors beyond that internal motivation. Oil nationalisation, the response to the 1974 Kurdish revolt, and the 1975 Algiers accord with Iran – analysts describe each event blow-by-blow but then reduce their politics to how they 'strengthened the regime' and altered 'the prestige of

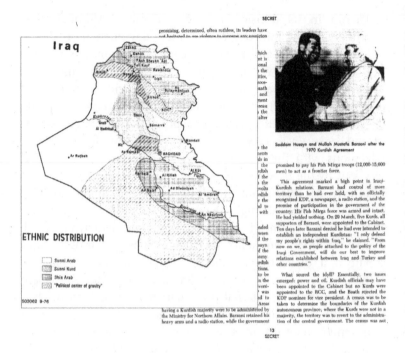

Figure 3.1 The CIA framed Saddam Hussein's policy-making within Iraq's racial-religious divides. A map of Iraq links 'political [centres] of gravity' to ideas of sect and ancestral groups, while Saddam is portrayed on the facing page taking charge of the country's relations on that basis. (CIA, 'Iraq Under Baath Rule', November 1976: pp. 12–13)

the deputy'.[79] When the CIA report reaches Iraq's international relations and lists 'certain Iraqi strategic goals', such as 'balancing a pro-American Iran' and opposing 'any militarisation of the region', including 'new American bases' around the Indian Ocean, OPR analysts lack the intellectual tools to *explain* these policy preferences. Asking why these are Saddam's priorities and how he thinks he can attain them would mean examining the effect of Iraq's international relations on leaders' outlooks. For example, how has Iraq's recent 'isolation from the West and the Arab world' affected the elite's concept of regional status and its possibilities?[80] And how has covert US support for the recent Kurdish uprising affected Saddam's view of a US military presence?[81] Analysts eventually mention what they call Saddam's 'non-aligned and anti-imperialist' world-view for Iraq, his hope that the country will 'become one of the Arab world's largest oil producers' and 'resume its place as [...] a participant in the shaping of Arab and Gulf affairs'. They do so only in passing, however, since to acknowledge this world-view presupposes that actors *other* than US policy-makers, including Saddam or indeed any self-described anti-imperialist, can judge the ideal future geopolitics of the region. It is easier to pin Iraq's 'shifts in foreign policy' on 'the need to establish [internal] legitimacy' across bloodline and religious groups.[82]

Meanwhile, in a report from Baghdad on Iraq's 'positive neutrality and non-alignment', Britain's ambassador gave his own assessment of Saddam's foreign policy. The ambassador finds both parts of Iraq's policy proposition puzzling. How can the country claim to pursue this kind of neutrality when its government so often sides with the Soviets and '"national liberation" movements', in 'Vietnam, Angola, southern Africa, or whatever', in ways 'consistently inimical to Western interests'? The ambassador reads the Non-Aligned Movement as accepting that the world is 'otherwise divided [...] into East and West' and therefore argues that for them to be consistent, they must avoid antagonism towards either side's policies. This surely cannot involve opposition to 'Western imperialists' and 'even the active obstruction of their policies'![83] And as for Saddam's desire that Iraq be 'a leading member' of the Non-Aligned Movement, how could his desire, which he 'claims to found [...] on principle', possibly square with the specifically *Arab* quality of Saddam's Ba'athist revolution? Most likely, the ambassador assures himself, the inexperienced Ba'athist leaders have not had time to make their 'comparatively underdeveloped' ideas more consistent.[84] Britain's Middle East Department wrote back that the Foreign Office's own researchers had agreed – Iraq is, after all, 'a strange country where even the strangest explanations of events cannot *a priori* be ruled out'.[85] In both Britain and the US, then, intelligence on Saddam sacrificed better insight into his political thinking by asserting that his dense, confusing foreign policy reflected the innate traditionalism and inconsistency of Iraqi political culture.

Saddam's own inexperience and need to learn on the job is a frequent refrain. A brief British personality profile of Saddam says he 'lack[s] the President [Bakr's] knack of winning respect and loyalty'. His 'considerable skill' lies instead in 'imposing his will'.[86] But for British diplomats and intelligence analysts, there were signs that Saddam had been forced by what they saw as the Middle East's equilibrium to adjust to reality. The JIC characterised Saddam's moves in the mid-1970s to reach a settlement with the Anglosphere companies who had lost out through nationalisation as a positive, a sensible response to 'public dissatisfaction' with the economy. His personal 'fence-mending' diplomacy with Egypt and Syria were judged similarly.[87] For the diplomatic community, Saddam was being compelled to practice more sensible governance, since he and party colleagues '*must see*' how they were being 'held back' by their ideology. If Saddam 'can manage to educate the hard nuts' in the party on 'the realities of political life', then analysts would judge that 'he is doing well'.[88]

By prioritising their model of how Middle Eastern geopolitics normally worked towards stability – that is, in the Anglosphere's favour – analysts cannot discern the possible effects of Iraq's ongoing international relations on Saddam's reasoning and actions. When lamenting the Ba'ath Party's preference for internal repression and external belligerence, there is no mention of the US's extensive military support for the party's ill-fated first government, nor British analysts' sanguine assessment of providing such support. The CIA blame Saddam's 'political behaviour' in power on his lack of 'real administrative or governmental experience'.[89] Again, the US's push in the early 1960s for the Ba'athists to overthrow Qasim does not come up. And when Britain's Middle East Department laments that Iraq necessarily 'had to join one of the recognised international clubs' in order to survive in the Middle East, and that siding with her 'neighbours of the Third World' was 'the only realistic choice', this lament does not affect whether analysts would judge Saddam's foreign policy as geopolitically sensible.[90] The simple reason for this is that Saddam's world-view and decision-making are understood as reflections of Iraq's historical internal politics. Diplomatic paranoia, meddling in other countries' affairs, worries about prestige – these dynamics may well take place in other states, even the US and Britain, but they say nothing about *those* states' racial belonging, about their inexperience or narrow-mindedness. In Iraq and Saddam, however, those same dynamics are proof that Arab societies are utterly unlike and inferior to the West.

JUDGING THE TACTICIAN, PSYCHOLOGISING THE WARLORD

In 1976, Saddam was given the role of general of the Iraqi armed forces. In July 1979, having pushed President al-Bakr to resign, he assumed the Presidency. Not coincidentally, just one month earlier, the US-backed Shah Mohammad Reza Pahlavi was overthrown and Iran became an Islamic Republic under Ayatollah Khomeini. Khomeini had for many years sought refuge in Iraq and made connections with Shi'i political opposition in the country; Iraqi Shia demonstrations before and after Iran's revolution may have tempted Saddam to speed up his succession of the more cautious Bakr.[91] Iran certainly came to dominate the deliberations of the Iraqi Government, as border skirmishes, inflammatory rhetoric, assassination attempts, and a breakdown in diplomatic accords shifted Saddam's thinking towards this anti-Ba'athist clerical state.[92] In September 1980, Iraqi forces crossed the Iranian border and began what would become an eight-year war – the first of three this president would ultimately fight.

Iraq's invasion took US Government officials and intelligence agents by surprise. Increasing tensions had been noted but analysts were either focused on other events in the Persian Gulf or unconvinced that the two sides would escalate their skirmishes.[93] In the UK, the JIC did not foresee either Iraq's aggression or the military build-up, in part because of the country's low ranking in intelligence priorities.[94] The spectre of intelligence failure, of two unwanted surprises in Iran's revolution and Iraq's war, once again threatens to delimit the kind of questions we should ask about these events.[95] While there has been plenty of attention given to what outside states knew of Saddam's military plans, of equal importance is how the war shaped US and British assessments of the new president.

Analysts' conclusions were wrapped up in ideas of the rationality of war and the cultural blinkers of Middle Eastern leaders. As open conflict along the Iran–Iraq border increased through September, a US inter-agency briefing explained that, in the past, '[b]oth Baghdad and Tehran have been constrained from initiating a major conflict' by 'the threat of superpower intervention', oil installation vulnerabilities and domestic repercussions. Now, however, 'Iraq's willingness' to seize disputed territory might end up altering 'either side's perception of the constraints'.[96] The ambiguity here is interesting: Did analysts think that this changed perception would be an astute response, or a miscalculation? CIA officers clarified a few days later: Iraq's actions did not reflect a 'preconceived plan', perhaps not even 'a clear definition of its objectives' – which, confusingly, are nonetheless described as 'to redress border grievances'. What the invasion did reflect was that Iraqi decision-makers 'appear to have miscalculated Iran's will to resist'.[97]

The implications for the intelligence picture of Saddam were written within a month: The new president was clearly 'risk[ing]' his previous 'progress' in dealing with Iraq's 'weaknesses', namely domestic instability and international reputation, by prosecuting 'a war that he probably cannot win in any decisive military way'.[98] A Special National Intelligence Estimate went further: Anything less than victory would lead Iraqis to blame Saddam for 'miscalculating Iran's potential and military reaction and for embroiling Iraq in a protracted war that it could not win'.[99] Analysts were no longer learning in real-time of Saddam's miscalculation; it had become a foregone conclusion. The moral of these assessments was clear: Saddam Hussein was a poor strategist and a poor reader of international relations, prone to cascading suspicions and vengefulness.[100] It was UK intelligence which linked this explicitly to the mirroring problem. In the 1982 internal study discussed in Chapter 2, former Government Communication Headquarters Deputy Director Doug Nicoll writes that the JIC's 'correct assessment' of Iraq's limited military capabilities had been assumed 'likely to constrain Saddam Hussein from invading Iran', which it obviously did not. The lesson for analysts? '[I]t does not follow […] that an aggressor will make the same assessment [as us], or […] that he will draw the same conclusions from it'.[101]

Claiming that Saddam was jeopardising his recent 'progress' with this war put rather a different spin on Iraq's policy-making than earlier assessments. A desire for greater foreign influence used to be seen as a threatening marker of Ba'athist revolutionary fervour or historical anti-Persian hysteria; now it was an objectively rational policy move being squandered by Saddam's militarism. This switch caught US agents in an analytical circle. Iraq's long push towards greater regional status risked being stymied by Saddam's invasion, an opportunistic attempt to 'precipitat[e] the overthrow of the Khomeini regime'. But at the same time, Saddam's own recent positive efforts towards modernising Iraq's politics had been waylaid by what was actually *only the most recent manifestation* of a historical enmity and competition for regional dominance'.[102] Saddam's decision-making and agency were left unclear. Was this war Saddam's way of pursuing regional domination, or had he decided upon the invasion by different criteria? Was it a mark of his influence as a new unstable element in Middle Eastern affairs, or a reflection of historical continuity, Iraq being Iraq? In this analysis, Saddam's actions became overdetermined by ideas of Iraq's belligerence. It made it sound like Saddam's antagonism was inevitable – a tragic undoing of his unexplained moves in the opposite direction.

The only consistent point that prevents this circle from collapsing is Saddam's irrationality, be it due to sectarian Middle Eastern tradition or his own uncontrolled psyche. Analysts' focus therefore remains on Saddam and his power relations, within a fundamentally 'non-Western' context of Iraqi politics and society. No one asks, with an international eye, why Iraq's government might desire regional influence and how this war might relate to that thinking. Its 'leadership ambitions in the Arab and non-aligned worlds' are simply taken as a given insofar as they 'will continue to foster policies irritating to Western and moderate Arab interests, especially once the war with Iran ends'.[103] Left unspoken is that this irritation will continue because it is endemic in Iraq's politics, not because it has any dynamic relation with how Anglosphere interests are pursued. In fact, during the Iran–Iraq War, that pursuit included first the US providing the Iraqi side with battlefield intelligence, finance, and equipment, then the US and Israel secretly providing military equipment to Iran, in a convoluted effort to increase Anglosphere influence in the Gulf vis-à-vis the Soviet Union (Figure 3.2). The revelation of this duplicity only inflated Saddam Hussein's suspicion of US motives and image of his regional significance.[104] In Britain, the government decided to honour a minority of its pre-1979 military contracts with Iran, while widely reported Iranian arms brokering and transfers, carried out in London offices, were largely downplayed by a Foreign Office which wanted to improve diplomatic and commercial relations.[105] But intelligence analysts, with their trust in their own knowledge of Middle Eastern geopolitics and their commitment to discover the foreign essence of Arab decision-making, did not factor these policies into their analysis. For them, they now not only had the Ba'athist president's bloody rise to power as evidence of his culturally determined psyche; they also had his irrational aggression abroad.

Iraq's invasion of Kuwait in 1990 and the Gulf War that followed saw a blossoming of analytical theories around Saddam Hussein, of how he operated and what kind of threat he posed to 'the Western world'. Saddam's mindset had become a key frame for public debate on Iraqi geopolitics through the 1980s. Iraq's 'cult of personality' of 'monarchic pretensions', with Saddam's image 'omnipresent

Figure 3.2 Iranian soldiers use a BGM-71 TOW anti-aircraft missile during the Iran–Iraq War. These missiles were sold to Iran by both Israel and, through the NSC and CIA, the United States. (Sajed.ir via Wikimedia.)

and far distant, on every shop window, on every office wall', was thematic in press coverage, a symbol of the president's political domination. Also common was his deceit, with promises of liberal reforms betrayed by clear evidence of vast human rights abuses. Finally, commentators bluntly summed up Iraq's governance: The Ba'ath Party was a 'rubber stamp' for Saddam's will, 'since Saddam Hussein is the regime'.[106]

This regal-despot frame fitted neatly when Kuwait was invaded in August 1990. The invasion prompted the press to bemoan yet another intelligence failure: Both the CIA and the Foreign Office's much-touted 'elite 'camel corps' of Arab specialists' were accused of being 'particularly inept at judging the psychology of the Iraqi regime'.[107] Even as the madman label was rejected as 'betray[ing] a lack of understanding', Saddam's violence was a prompt for frantic discussions of 'the Middle East mindset in general and Hussein in particular'. Maybe he wasn't 'a mad Arab warrior', but how was he opaquely deciding foreign strategy? What kind of man was the US and Britain facing, diplomatically and perhaps soon militarily? Analysts, reported the *New York Times*, agreed Saddam had 'miscalculated badly' but were 'at a Loss Trying to Predict [his] Next Move'.[108]

And so, as all the public demonisation raised the value of knowledge of Saddam's inner workings, intelligence analysis entered the limelight via anointed experts on 'personality analysis at a distance'. Profilers appeared on *Good Morning America* to discuss how Saddam was 'sane and rational, but also a fanatic who is determined and stubborn'. Former British intelligence officers were quoted in the press explaining the impenetrable family- and village-based decision-making of Arab states. The CIA director himself publicly rebuffed US Senate criticisms that his agency lacked the presence of mind and the Arabic expertise to fully process Saddam's thinking.[109] Most notably, Jerrold Post, the former director and founder of the CIA's own psychological-personality centre, testified to Congressional hearings shortly before coalition forces began bombing Iraqi troops that Saddam had demonstrated a 'lifelong pattern' of actions in pursuit of 'messianic ambitions'.[110] Saddam was no madman but a 'malignant narcissist' with dreams of historical grandeur. Post's explanation of this messianism was an uncle's incitement in teenage Saddam of nationalist anti-Western-ness, 'tales of [past Arab] heroism' that led the future president to be 'consumed by dreams of glory'.[111]

There is much riding on this story of Saddam's psyche. If Saddam believes 'destiny has inscribed his name' as the 'supreme Arab nationalist leader' of his times, then '[n]othing must be permitted' to block his 'messianic path'. Only a military threat will deter him; the 'unified civilised world' must use 'the language of power', '[t]he only language Saddam Hussein understands'.[112] As with past intel-ligence assessments of Iraq's elite, this personal narrative allowed Ba'athist anti-imperialism to be dismissed as an ideological fig-leaf for xenophobic expansionism, but also as the emotional angst of a teenage runaway.

However, it is unclear just how much of Saddam's strategy all of this explains. While emphasising Saddam's steadfastness, how he 'struggle[s] all the harder' to reach his goals when met with resistance, Post clarifies that Saddam will 'revers[e] his course' if 'circumstances demonstrate that he miscalculated'. Post calls this Saddam's 'revolutionary opportunism'. Presented as nuance, this reading undermines the relevance of Saddam's life story. Post gives foreign policy examples where Saddam's revolutionary pragma-tism won out, 'despite his lifelong hatred of the Persians' or in a 'revers[al] [of] his earlier militant aggression'.[113] Each time, the explanatory variable is Saddam's will to survive and to ensure the status of Iraq. Arab parochialism and violent heroism, however much a part of his psyche, are therefore less crucial to explain-ing Saddam's policy choices than his ongoing assessment of his government's international security. Once read on its own terms, this analysis is neither remarkable nor unique: Saddam remains in power because he has 'a pattern of reversing his course when he has miscalculated'; he does not want to pick a fight where 'Iraq will be grievously damaged and his stature [...] destroyed'.[114] These are fairly generalisable characteristics of average state leadership, as pointed out at the time in a critical response by Najib Ghadbian.[115]

What Post's narrative does is drape an assessment of Saddam's strategic conservatism – that he 'has no wish to be a martyr, and survival is his number one priority' – in a racialisation of his psy-chology, that a culture of Arab anti-Western hatred determines

Saddam's psyche.[116] 'Revolutionary opportunism' might be a label for unremarkable policy-making, but it makes clear that those policies' roots are unique, namely Saddam's inferior ability to think objectively. Post displays a mocking tone when describing Saddam's belief that '[o]nly by courageously confronting imperialist powers could Arab nationalism be freed from Western shackles'. Saddam's Ba'athism is linked to a 'worldview [which] is narrow and distorted', making him 'politically out of touch with reality'. Having 'scant experience outside of the Arab world' – echoing previous assessments of Iraq's elite – is now defined as being part of Saddam's malignant narcissism. So too are his Pan-Arab messianism and anti-Western paranoia.[117] The combined effect of this personality profiling is to turn acknowledged questions of politics into cultural characteristics of psyche. Anti-imperialist nationalism becomes an 'ambition for unlimited power'; lack of worldliness becomes a personal preference; and belief and ability in instrumental force becomes 'unconstrained aggression'.[118] Saddam's own image of geopolitics, the factor that makes policy options appear more or less useful to him, is reduced to an Arab messiah complex. But unless one diagnoses psychotic delusion at this point, messianism cannot explain how Saddam's perceptions of a regional power balance and of Anglosphere threats, the conditions for his actions, have been reinforced over time.

By the time he gave this Congressional testimony, Post had been out of the CIA for four years. His former colleagues, however, were not far from his own thinking. That same month, the agency's director led a Special National Intelligence Estimate on Saddam's mindset (Figure 3.3). The US's various agencies were concerned that Saddam was misreading the international scene and misinterpreting the intentions and resolve of the George H. W. Bush administration. Saddam, they all agreed, remained unconvinced that the US would launch a military offensive in response to his continued occupation of Kuwait. To different degrees, they believed it would be difficult to change his view.[119] Yet the objective signals to him were, they asserted, clear: 'At the moment [...] he continues to question US resolve, *despite* the increase in US forces in Saudi Arabia'. The recent UN resolution approving military action is also mentioned. Misreading these signals, Saddam was illogically building up his forces in Kuwait and looking diplomatically to legitimise the occupation.[120] This is very much the deluded, inexperienced statesman of Post's and others' past analyses.

But there is a colonial underpinning to this estimate's logic that severely diminishes its usefulness for shaping policy. While Saddam's predicted actions are traced to his long-term goals of

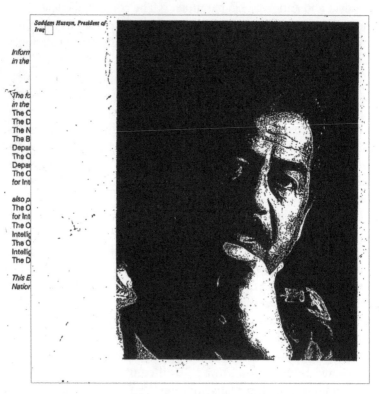

Figure 3.3   This December 1990 Special National Intelligence Estimate visualised the challenge of deciphering non-US minds. A pensive Saddam looks back at the reader, teasing a cryptic thought process within. (This is unfortunately the best-quality digital version of the file that the CIA have made available.) (CIA, 'Iraq's Saddam Husayn: The Next Six Weeks', December 1990: pp. i–ii)

'surviving' and 'exert[ing] Arab leadership and intimidat[ion]', the possibility of a US military response has no such conditional causes. Like an act of God, it simply will happen. The conundrum that analysts set themselves is 'whether Saddam understands his own vulnerabilities and sees them as foreclosing his ability to win or even survive a war with the United States'. There is no question here of Saddam deterring the US, nor consideration of whether a war would foreclose future diplomacy or even induce further Iraqi aggression. The Special National Intelligence Estimate describes Saddam as suspicious that President Bush's offer of diplomatic talks is a deceptive act of 'going through the motions'. Given the coalition military build-ups in Saudi Arabia throughout late 1990 and their own emphasis on the US's resolve, would analysts say that Saddam was wilfully misreading things here as well?[121] Without considering an attack by a multi-national force as a conditional variable in a dynamic situation, or as something whose consequences might be altered by other factors, analysts can only read Saddam as either delusional or an idiot.

The most convoluted assessment in this vein was over the very possibility of Saddam withdrawing Iraqi troops from Kuwait, this being the objective of recent United Nations Resolutions and, giving the benefit of the doubt, presumably a key Anglosphere policy aim. Having acknowledged Saddam's long-term goals, the director of central intelligence judges that 'a partial or total withdrawal from Kuwait' might become '[Saddam's] principal weapon against the coalition'. What form would this weapon take? If Saddam became 'convinced' that 'a devastating war' was in the offing, he would withdraw to prevent it. He might also retreat if he thought it would mean 'significant political or territorial advantages'. In other words, Saddam would withdraw Iraqi troops if he saw purposeful, existential incentives to do so. Pulling out of Kuwait is characterised as a 'ploy' and 'the most effective Iraqi option for disrupting the coalition' – that is, the coalition to push Iraq out of Kuwait.[122] The issue, then, is not whether Saddam now complies with coalition demands; it is that he is by definition dishonourable in his objective of disrupting the Anglosphere's transparent, honest policing of the Middle East. How he acts in future, including backing down, cannot change this assessment of his character and its essential threat.

The supposed danger of Iraq's withdrawal similarly animated British intelligence. Documented discussion between analysts and politicians reveals that the problem, as they saw it, was not the occupation but Saddam's psyche. Both Margaret Thatcher's and George Bush's administrations saw the overthrow of Saddam as a desirable outcome of any intervention, if it could be induced internally by coalition forces *pushing* Iraq out of Kuwait.[123] One of the people assessing this was Percy Cradock. Over a decade before British intelligence was charged with politicisation over Iraq, Cradock was both a foreign policy adviser to Thatcher and the Chairman of the JIC, ostensibly two 'very different job[s]'.[124] In many ways 'the archetypal Foreign Office mandarin', having gone from chief of the Assessments Staff to ambassador to Peking and chief negotiator on Hong Kong, Cradock was proposed to head the committee because of his 'penetrating and original mind, being someone who knows the Middle East' and 'is used to looking at problems world-wide'.[125]

In mid-December, Cradock laid out the 'dangerous implications' of an Iraqi withdrawal from Kuwait before any coalition military intervention. There would be a 'great boost to Saddam's prestige' for having 'survived confrontation with the United States'. Like US analysts, Cradock noted that any withdrawal would also accent 'the fragility of the coalition' against Iraq. The key question was how to 'make the best of a bad job', that is, 'the recovery of Kuwait but the survival of Saddam'.[126] In fact, this shared US–British fear that Iraq would withdraw *before* it irrationally tested their resolve had some justification. Starting the same month as Iraq's invasion, Saddam Hussein made repeated offers of grounds for negotiation towards a political settlement. Key to his first proposal was that Iraq's withdrawal from Kuwait be linked to Israel's withdrawal from occupied Palestinian territories, in accordance with existing UN Resolutions. When the US did not take this up, Saddam then offered Iraq's withdrawal in return for the lifting of sanctions and control of an oil field that extended two miles into Kuwait over a disputed border. In January 1991, Iraq compromised further, offering withdrawal in return for a commitment to solving the Israel–Palestine situation and the withdrawal of the amassed coalition troops. Iraq's proposal was described by a State Department official as a 'serious pre-negotiation position'. All offers were rejected outright by the Bush administration.[127] Cradock's dangerous implications were seemingly too overwhelming for the diplomatic achievement of withdrawal to be an option.

The intelligence profile of Saddam that lay behind this policy-making demonstrates just how much the Anglosphere image of the post-colonial world was risking further violence. Following a JIC meeting, Cradock himself reported to Thatcher that although Saddam's war objective was to recoup the sharply diminished oil revenues, which Iraq blamed on Kuwait, 'success in this venture, already virtually certain, *will only feed the appetite for more* [...] The Iraqis have territorial ambitions'.[128] Any negotiations would be used by Saddam to '[string] things out' and avoid war, prolonging his more essential threat. In Cradock's eyes, therefore, 'the less said to the Iraqis [...] the better'.[129] According to the British Embassy in Washington DC, Atlantic colleagues' shared 'diagnosis' was of the 'difficulty for us *to get through to* [*Saddam*] the determination and unity of the international coalition', to get him to realise 'the real possibility' of a military response. 'If he were a rational man he would realise already how much sanctions were hurting his country [...] The trouble was of course that, so far at least, *Hussein did not seem disposed to be rational*'.[130] Saddam's intransigence was evidence of his blind miscalculation, his inability to read the international scene, and to compute clear messages. This made the question of how international relations might invite him to pursue one or another policy irrelevant.

De-escalating the situation by letting him back down gracefully, moreover, was a negative outcome. As the JIC Chairman recommended, 'in order to maximise the chances of [Saddam's] overthrow' if Iraq withdrew, it was 'essential to deny him any face-savers or diplomatic prizes', which would boost Saddam's 'prestige' among Arabs, a 'dangerous [implication] for the area'. Saddam had to be positioned as 'a defeated figure'. Prime Minister Thatcher agreed: Ideally, Saddam should be forced 'to face his people as a beaten leader'.[131] Any dangers to regional security that may come with domestically and internationally humiliating Saddam are not considered. British intelligence, then, were also reading the situation through colonial eyes. Saddam's thinking was tainted by old Iraqi ambition and Arab status-seeking. This explained his irrational rejection of British objectives for the region, for which he had to be punished.

THINKING IT OVER BETWEEN THE GULF WARS

Among the 'enormous miscalculations [...] at the root of the Persian Gulf crisis', announced the *New York Times* in September 1990, the 'most glaring' was 'Saddam Hussein's rash assumption that the world would do little or nothing if Iraq devoured Kuwait'.[132] Indeed, the idea that Iraq's invasion of Kuwait had been a strategic surprise, a failure of Anglosphere intelligence, morphed fairly quickly into a discussion of first Saddam's mindset and then Saddam's own mistake. When their judgement that Saddam was bluffing was disproven, officials emphasised that this actually demonstrated an error of judgement on the part of Saddam. The same Arab state contacts who had wrongly reassured British intelligence on Saddam's motives now assured the JIC Chairman that Saddam 'had grossly underestimated international reaction to his invasion of Kuwait', both from the Anglosphere and regional governments. Thatcher's private secretary, C. D. Powell, who had followed JIC assessments throughout the invasion, reported years later that the 'intelligence failures' were Saddam's, since he had acted despite the 'common knowledge' that Thatcher and President Bush would be meeting on the very day of the invasion.[133]

In the months and years following Operation Desert Storm, Intelligence and Strategic Studies scholars developed their own theoretical framework for understanding Saddam's mistake. Coming after the fall of the Berlin Wall, the Gulf War paralleled analysts' and scholars' interest in forecasting the post-Cold War intelligence landscape. What new challenges awaited Anglosphere agencies? How would attempts to interpret the world be different? Saddam's actions appeared to provide answers. Writing in the CIA's in-house journal, James J. Wirtz warned US analysts in this apparently multi-polar world to expect more 'reckless gambles' by adversaries. Surprise attacks would appeal to weaker 'Third World' nations, Wirtz argued, as a way to gain the upper hand; but they carried the risk of wasting resources on secret plans that fail to elicit the relative gains or cowed opponent that was desired.[134] At first, Wirtz appears to deduce this from a strategic logic: Weaker actors will inevitably find surprise attractive but will structurally be more vulnerable to its downsides. But Wirtz clarifies that such miscalculation becomes likely 'when statesmen and officers from divergent cultural backgrounds [...] become embroiled in a conflict'.[135] 'Third World policy-makers', lacking 'large intelligence organisations' would 'project their individual biases' on others. With Kuwait, Saddam Hussein had let his 'extremely ethnocentric view of the world' blind him to the US's post-Cold War assertiveness. By deceiving his regional neighbours, he had accidentally 'reduced' their 'traditional Arab reluctance' to US intervention.[136] Weakness may generally predispose statesmen to surprise attacks, but Saddam's deadly 'myopia' actually reflected a 'cultural gulf'.[137]

What the intelligence literature of the time demonstrates is that Iraq's invasion and the Gulf War allowed the concept of the mirror-imaging problem to evolve for a post-Cold War world. Mirror-imaging was now not just due to the opacity and secrecy of foreign 'Regimes'. It was also a habit *reflected* in the insular policy-making of those very same states, as their way of compensating for their inferior intelligence apparatuses. The implication is that a well-resourced and well-advised administration would not project provincial values abroad – an idea somewhat frayed by President Bush Sr's own insistence, against his advisers' judgement, that Saddam Hussein was the devil incarnate, a figure similar to the one drawn by psychic researchers at Stanford two decades earlier (Chapter 2).[138] In the UK, the determination to uncover the inferior psychology of Eastern states was reinvigorated by internal reviews of intelligence's contribution to the Gulf War. A review of Operation Granby by Air Chief Marshal David Parry-Evans lamented that 'the "intentions" of a dictatorship are extremely difficult to discern'. A Defence Committee report concluded that analysts had wrongly assumed clear-sightedness, humility and a desire to protect Iraq's population on Saddam's part. Analysts' mistake was in thinking that Saddam understood the consequences of his actions the way that Britain obviously would have understood them in his place.[139]

This extension of the mirror-image concept took historical assessments of Iraq's Ba'athist insularity, those judgements in the 1970s and 1980s of vacant revolutionaries who lacked worldliness, as the basis for an image of Saddam Hussein as inherently threatening. This was a thin racial profile presented as cultural sensitivity. The focus on decrypting Saddam's psychology led analysts away from considering how the international scene itself conditioned any threats. As Wirtz makes clear, Saddam's miscalculations were so important because they represented '[a] challenge to the Bush administration's vision of a "New World Order"'; anticipating others' mistakes would be crucial if the US was going to increase its 'involvement' in 'Third World military contingencies'.[140] As we will see, this way of explaining intelligence failure's importance would only get stronger in the fallout of the Iraq War.

Looking at it from the perspective of those Middle Eastern states that were supposed to be bad at intelligence analysis, their own intelligence nemesis was therefore not the US and Britain's alien, intrinsic way of thinking. Their intelligence target was really an aspiring interventionist hegemon, the only post-Cold War superpower. Judging such a target arguably takes more than acknowledging different cultures of thought. For instance, Wirtz faults Saddam's use of the Vietnam War as an analogy to predict US behaviour, as did Strategic Studies Scholar Norman Cigar in a similar post-mortem of Iraq's 'underestimation of US national will'.[141] Yet the substance of that analogy – that the US would recoil from a potentially unwinnable and high-casualty quagmire – was correct: The Bush administration chose not to push its ground forces into Baghdad for fear of what Bush precisely called 'another Vietnam'.[142] What Saddam miscalculated was the US and UK's willingness to punish Iraq's government through massive aerial bombardment and then continued sanctions, or as Prime Minister Thatcher put it to Bush, to 'fit the politics to the military requirement', in order to secure '[t]he whole reputation of the US and the UK' and gain what the JIC Chairman later called 'great prizes in terms of the future international order'.[143] British intelligence scholars parsed Iraq's underestimation of Anglosphere punishment merely as Saddam's naivety and his neglect of air power.[144]

Bush and Thatcher's adamant decision that Iraq not be offered a way to withdraw with some status intact was passed over by baffled regret that Saddam had 'fail[ed] to seize the various face-saving formulas offered to him during the crisis to withdraw from Kuwait'. This line comes from a joint study, written by biographer-at-a-distance Efraim Karsh and future Chilcot Inquiry member Lawrence Freedman. In a reversal of the CIA's concern with Saddam's suspiciousness, the same study faulted Saddam for incorrectly assuming that 'President Bush's [...] offer of direct talks' reflected the US's 'readiness to reach a compromise'; as a result of this geopolitical bad sense, Saddam had decided 'not to pre-empt by attacking coalition forces in Saudi Arabia', a fatal measure of restraint on his part which undermined his military position'.[145] Presumably, a further reflection of Saddam's bad sense before the US attack was his successive offers of negotiations towards a political settlement. Karsh discusses these diplomatic openings in his 1991 co-authored political biography of Saddam. Karsh does not consider them as a basis for negotiations but simply concludes that had Saddam's proposals 'been accepted, let alone implemented, it would have represented a shining achievement for Saddam' and made him 'the undisputed Arab leader', since 'his sweeping demands articulated the cherished hopes of the majority of people in the Arab World'. On this basis, Karsh says, it was '[n]ot surprising' that Saddam's offer was 'dismissed by the West'.[146]

What the Gulf War allowed for, then, was a revanchist intelligence agenda. Any doubts over the work of intelligence analysis being able to adapt to a world without a dominant, well-studied antagonist could be assuaged. The post-colonial model of a self-contained Middle East and the commitment to avoiding mirror-imaging were backed up with renewed confidence, since they explained not just how the world is supposed to work but why Arab dictators persistently refused to accept it. Saddam Hussein's actions reflected a culturally-embedded, illogical aggression. Through the rest of the 1990s, intelligence analysts echoed this appraisal of Iraq's leader. US intelligence officials tasked with 'psychoanalyz[ing] [Saddam's] behaviour' were described in the mid-1990s as suffering through 'a maddening exercise', their efforts 'frustrated' by Saddam's 'utter unpredictability', 'his actions seem[ing] to defy logic'.[147] In Britain,

Percy Cradock drew on the Iraq experience to conclude that gauging the intentions of autocratic leaders was well-informed guesswork, relying either on faulty mirroring or on trying to estimate the 'different calculus' of the leader.[148] And in an analysis lauded in Intelligence Studies for 'get[ting] almost all of the big questions right', Colonel John Hughes-Wilson, recently retired from the British Army's Intelligence Corps, pointed to Saddam's upbringing among Iraq's 'mafia-like warlords' as having shaped the president's 'psychology, cruelty, and the true nature of his regime', all potent intelligence material. '*By any objective criteria*', the Colonel insists, 'the Iraqi leader [in summer 1990] was looking like a loose cannon […] unpredictable and dangerous'.[149]

Chilcot's Iraq Inquiry covers the UK's pre-2000 intelligence material on Iraq as follows: There was an 'ingrained belief' in JIC assessments that Saddam Hussein was 'determined to preserve and if possible enhance [Iraq's] [WMD] capabilities' and was 'pursuing an active policy of deception'. Indeed, it was Iraq's potential retention of WMD programmes from the 1980s that was 'the fundamental tenet of UK policy towards Iraq' by 1991.[150] When discussing the JIC's earlier judgements, Chilcot drew heavily on the Butler Report, which looked back to the 1990s to try to detect any 'systemic issues' in the 'intelligence process'. To the extent that Butler and his colleagues covered intelligence on 'the strategic intent of the Iraqi regime', this was a discussion of Saddam's assessed attempts to pursue WMD programmes; Butler highlighted the way that limited information was translated into broad estimates 'at [the] upper end worst case', an analytical tendency 'exacerbated by Iraqi […] deception'.[151]

What neither report does is consider how this limited intelligence would have been contextualised by this point in Iraq's relationship with the Anglosphere, that is, how intelligence analysts would have been encouraged by their past knowledge to interpret this trickle of new information. This is key to answering the question: Why go from a dearth of concrete data on capabilities to a worst-case scenario? The intelligence analyses of the previous two decades suggest the following points:

- Iraq's Ba'athist elite were judged to be closed-minded expansionists, shaped by traditional backstabbing and devoid of real ideology. It therefore made sense that there would be no limit to their military desires, and there was no need to address their vacuous political stands;
- Saddam Hussein's psyche was the product of violent Arab xenophobia. His challenge to Anglosphere proposals for the Middle East reflected his uncontrolled cultural vindictiveness and personal delusion, making any arguments from an anti-imperialist perspective irrelevant;
- Saddam was also irrational and unpredictable. He could not understand international relations and could not be trusted to do what geopolitical reality was obviously asking of him. He therefore could not be reasoned with and was a threat to (Our model of) stability.

This is the context in which the later crucial intelligence assessments from 2000 to 2003, leading up to the Iraq War, need to be understood. Even before 9/11 changed the 'calculus of risk', as Chilcot reported,[152] US and British intelligence had made any de-escalation of the threat and use of force in the Middle East conditional not on US and UK actions but on the racialised thoughts and feelings of Iraq's leader. The crucial intelligence reports declassified by Chilcot's Inquiry build upon this assessment.

4

'They buried things in the sand': The threat of Iraq and the secret of race

It is worth paying attention when former spies talk about how they themselves understand their role in the world. During John Chilcot's official inquiry into the Iraq War, a number of members of the intelligence community were called before the inquiry's members for witness hearings. One British intelligence officer, referred to only as 'SIS4' (SIS being the Secret Intelligence Service, or MI6), appeared as a witness to discuss, as one inquiry panel member put it, 'what we knew about Iraq' – that is, 'the Government's pre-conflict knowledge of life in Iraq under Saddam', including 'political dynamics' in the country.[1] While the press picked up on this officer's testimony about discussions for regime change in Iraq as early as 2001,[2] it is clear from his released testimony that SIS4 wanted to discuss other things. 'I would like to say one or two words', says SIS4 at the end of their second evidence session, 'just to put my mind at rest before leaving you': 'I think my old Service [MI6], across the years, the Cold War and working all round the world, had developed a very good sense of the signs of the times and *what really matters in the world*'.[3] On the face of it, this comment could refer either to what matters for intelligence analysis or to what matters in geopolitics. From their wider testimony, SIS4 meant both. They discuss the Ba'athists' secretive structure of 'blood relationships', the political geography of the country over time, and 'the deep emotions, the longer wavelength trends that underlie the life of a country'. It was these things, SIS4 suggests, that a good intelligence agent would be interested in; but their underestimation by government meant the latter had only a 'very, very superficial' knowledge of Iraq.[4] SIS4 does a good job of summarising the social and cultural scope of intelligence analysis in the decades before the 2003 invasion, the analyst's and diplomat's 'deep sense of the region' that sadly witnessed a 'falloff' into the 2000s, as the British Government began favouring technical data on WMD. But SIS4's examples of where to get that deep sense are instructive too. Among the 'fundamental texts' that they remember recommending were 'the 1946/7, I think, Admiralty Naval Intelligence Handbook of Iraq. A magnificent volume like that (indicates size). The real thing'.[5]

SIS4's reflections give us pause for thought as to how intelligence analysts saw their expertise on Iraq, along with how their view fed into their written assessments of Saddam's threat. First, analysts like SIS4 had formed a social and cultural appreciation of Iraq that not only explained why the country was a 'hard target' in intelligence terms – its autocratic secrecy, its ever-shifting power balances – but was also used by officers to explain the Iraqi Government's foreign policy. Even if the Blair administration's knowledge was superficial, SIS4 insists that intelligence analysts like themselves 'had a great love of Iraq and background on Iraq'. They were interested in Iraq's underlying historical and emotional currents, those 'wavelength trends', because SIS4 and others believed that those currents imposed 'limitations [...] on the choices available to the [Iraqi] regime'. And second, analysts' appreciation of these influences on Iraq's politics was formed over a long historical period. A handbook from the mid-1940s could impart fundamental knowledge for today. SIS4 recounts, with satisfaction, that the Ministry of Defence 'had been bulk buying' the Admiralty Handbook before the invasion.[6]

SIS4 was actually referring to a 1944 volume on Iraq and the Persian Gulf, part of a 58-volume series combining geography, economics, and sociology, which were commissioned during the Second World War by Naval Intelligence and written by Oxbridge academics. The handbooks on the Middle East included significant contributions from a former Anglo-Persian Oil Company researcher.[7] It is 'extremely difficult', begins the Iraq handbook, 'to probe beneath the surface of events in Iraq' owing to the country's engrained popular secrecy. Nevertheless, Iraq's 'international importance' comes down to 'the recent discovery of oil', while its peoples have just enough 'belief, ethic and custom' for 'a crude basis of relations with a man's neighbour and his Deity'.[8] Later in the book, a discussion of 'racial types' is followed by measurements and photographs of Iraqi 'physical characteristics', emphasising the handbook's recent colonial heritage. The handbook's comments on Iraqi 'Mental and Moral Characteristics' mix Protestant judgements of laziness with suspicion of Arab treachery towards white Europeans. Iraqi political machinations are likened to the Irish, pointing to the handbook's contemporary colonial setting: Iraq in 1944 was being occupied by British forces, just a decade after Iraqi independence and two decades after the Irish War of Independence. A discussion of 'Life in the Towns' continues this undercurrent of colonial anxiety, emphasising the importance of coffee- and tea-houses 'where all who can afford to be idle spend the day "talking gossip and plotting against the government"'.[9]

SIS4's testimony only further demonstrates that intelligence analysts draw on ideas about the world from years, even decades, of developing assessments; those ideas can echo and evolve through the work lives of subsequent generations of analysts. The Ba'athist Government of Iraq, with Saddam Hussein at its helm, was not a new subject when the 11 September 2001 terrorist attacks 'changed everything'. Anglosphere intelligence analysis of the Middle East was a form of expertise that had accumulated and shape-shifted since even before the Ba'athists first came to power in the 1960s. Intelligence expertise was not static – ideas changed as events provoked surprise and disbelief. But these ideas' beginnings in a post-colonial model of how Middle East geopolitics was supposed to work, and in a theory of the dangers of assuming other states' similar rationality, set them and the analysts who followed them down a narrow path of compartmentalising and racially essentialising the region and Iraq. This path offered little scope for self-reflection, except for the endless worry that the region's normal workings were being violated and faulty mirror-imaging was behind every intelligence failure.

This direction of travel in intelligence on Iraq brings us to the assessment period covered by Chilcot's Inquiry and forces us to consider whether one major criticism of the intelligence – that it failed to consider social and cultural context – is actually highly misleading. That context is there, peeking out behind Joint Intelligence Committee (JIC) statements on Saddam Hussein's mindset in the new millennium and reflected extensively in the testimonies of analysts who appeared before the inquiry. Even right before the invasion, though, that intelligence path was not unavoidable. There were opportunities for reconsidering assumptions about Saddam. The chapter therefore examines how those opportunities were interpreted and squandered by those tasked with explaining Middle Eastern geopolitics to the British Government. This examination demonstrates that cultural racism continued to shape analysts' work even into the 2000s. Iraq and Saddam were presented as threatening on the grounds of the former's emotional anti-Western culture and the latter's inherently limited ability to think through his actions and overcome his longstanding feelings. Because these qualities were thought to be essential to Iraqi politics, contradictory evidence that might have revealed the negative influence of the Anglosphere on Saddam's behaviour could not be computed. It is in this way that possible avenues for de-escalating the situation right up until the invasion were shut down in intelligence analysts' output.

And as for the question of how we gauge the policy consequences of this intelligence analysis from 2000 to 2003, consider briefly the fate of SIS4. The anonymous secret service officer was later named in the press as Mark Allen, 'easily identified' through his testimony 'by his witty style and Latin quips'.[10] In the early 2000s, Allen was MI6's director for counter-proliferation and counter-terrorism. He was, by his account, no fan of the looming attack on Iraq – '[t]hose of us who had been around [...] knew perfectly well what a disaster for countless people a war was going to be'[11] – and so left government shortly after the invasion, only to join British Petroleum, helping them to negotiate a £15 billion oil drilling contract with Libya's Muammar Gaddafi. Years later, when Libya's government was also overthrown, Libyan documents would reveal that Allen, in one of his last MI6 duties, had discussed the rendition of two Libyan opposition figures, Abdel Hakim Belhaj and Sami al-Saadi, who had fled abroad with their families. In a letter to Gaddafi's intelligence chief, Allen described Belhaj's rendition, which had been planned by MI6 and the CIA, 'the least we could do for you and for Libya to demonstrate the remarkable relationship we have built over the years'. Once Belhaj was released in 2010, after his torture in a Tripoli jail and interrogation by British intelligence officers, he sued Allen to force a government admission. In 2016, the Crown Prosecution Service (CPS) backed away from pursuing a case against Allen, saying it was 'unclear' whether he personally had shaped Libyan policy-making on the renditions, even though the Met had told the CPS that there were grounds for prosecution.[12]

I detail this because a professed 'great love' of a region or a people by no means rules out your complicity in those people's suffering. Nor, as Allen's career shift shows, does that great love necessarily need to challenge the belief that ex-colonial states and their business associates still know best how to distribute Middle Eastern wealth and power. Those attending the JIC – which included Allen – were producing and circulating intelligence knowledge within the context of that overall outlook on the world. The present chapter demonstrates the impact of that context.

MISSILES AND MINDSETS: HOW THE JIC DETERMINED 'THREAT'

Much of the post-Chilcot political commentary emphasises a shift in intelligence reporting from the 1990s into the 2000s. The inquiry itself frames this intelligence history within policy-makers' conviction that Saddam still had chemical and biological capabilities after the Gulf War, then within their increased interest in proliferation after 9/11. So while JIC assessments in 2000 placed equal weight on countries other than Iraq as potential WMD threats, by late 2002, assessments focused on Iraq's many hypothetical uses of chemical and biological agents.[13] Reviewing Chilcot, intelligence scholars Judith Betts and Mark Pythian argue that 9/11 'transformed threat perceptions [of Iraq]', eventually leading to unjustifiably firm conclusions in JIC assessments that were then never re-evaluated.[14] In their overview of JIC history, Richard Aldrich, Rory Cormac, and Michael Goodman place this within a decade-long act of overcompensation. Having 'downplayed Saddam's capabilities' before the Gulf War and then been embarrassed by UN inspections, the

Joint Intelligence Staff became prone to 'overcorrection in the early 2000s' – '[t]hey did not want to be wrong twice'.[15]

Risk-aversion and bruised pride, though, do not explain unacknowledged continuities with all the reporting on Iraq from the 1960s to 1990s discussed in the previous chapter. Again and again in the years before the invasion, analysts viewed Iraq's policy-making through the lens of Saddam Hussein as psychologically primed to be a belligerent, unreasonable expansionist. When this image appeared in assessments, it reflected historical assumptions of the Ba'athists' political emptiness, of the Iraqi elite's unworldliness, and of Saddam's violent delusions of Arab heroism. Analysts made sense of Iraq's capabilities *within the context* of this image of Saddam – that is, they argued that Iraq's potential weapons stocks were *on this basis* dangerous.

JIC reports from before the 9/11 attacks, declassified for Chilcot's Inquiry, reveal the importance of this continuity, even compared to that game-changing event. An April 2000 assessment of Iraq's chemical and biological weapons (CBW) capabilities begins by acknowledging that Iraq's 'doctrine for offensive chemical and biological warfare remains unclear'.[16] But this admission of ignorance is quickly passed over with reference to past history as a guide, times when '[w]e know that Iraq has used chemical weapons', before the report turns to what Iraq 'could be modifying', reported actions that 'could be associated' with weapons programmes, and things that if completed 'would help any revival' of those programmes.[17] Hypotheticals are left to speak for themselves as evidence of potential threat. While a May 2001 assessment admits that '[l]ittle of the intelligence' is 'sufficiently clear to identify the exact status and ultimate objectives of [Iraq's WMD] programmes', it goes on to discuss what Iraq 'could be investigating' in terms of uranium enrichment, what it 'could produce [...]' within weeks of a decision to do so', and what its missiles 'could deliver' in terms of warheads. By saying its 'knowledge of [WMD and missile] developments [...] is patchy', the report abnegates responsibility for its hypothetical claims. The report makes these hypotheticals relevant by stating them. Most importantly, the JIC describes capabilities in a way that implies an unspoken intent: '[T]hese capabilities represent the most immediate Iraqi WMD threat'.[18] Beyond past history, the context of that threat – to whom? To what end? – is left unexplained.

So what fills in the context of that threat? Across these early assessments, the answer is Saddam Hussein's personality. Iraq's geopolitical objectives and potential use of WMD were explained not through Iraqi policy-making in response to the international situation, but through Saddam's inflexible psychology. A November 2000 JIC assessment states that while '[w]e have little direct intelligence on Saddam's thinking [redacted]', Saddam has 'good reason to remain intransigent' on UN inspections, will be 'content to drag out any decision', and will only co-operate on inspections 'if it could be portrayed as a victory'. The report's description of Saddam as stalling, unmoving, and zero-sum frames his strategic objectives, which only appear later on: 'he wants to halt the erosion of Iraqi's military capability and rebuild it', which means getting sanctions lifted; '[h]e wants [...] rehabilitation in the Arab and international community'; and he has 'ambitions to rebuild weapons of mass destruction programmes'.[19] As the report portrays them, these desires and ambitions have no origin point in a political situation, no motivation outside of themselves. Nor does the JIC connect these objectives to what they acknowledge as Saddam's fear of ongoing 'attempts to overthrow [him]', to his 'belie[f]' that the US will not lift sanctions 'while he remained in power' and his desire for 'an end to US policies to topple the Iraqi government'.[20] The implication that Saddam's actions are partly shaped by his perception of existential threat to his government is overrun by the much more explicit description of Saddam as intransigent and seeking victory. This puts front-and-centre not Saddam's possible political assessment of threat but his supposed psychological drive for domination.

This analysis of Iraq's WMD potential was contextualised in 2000 by assessments of Saddam's internal power base, which again echo historical judgements of his violence and lack of politics (Figure 4.1). An assessment in May sums up 'Saddam's regime' in terms of how Saddam maintains his 'mastery', his reliance on 'patronage and fear', as '[h]e manipulates and terrorises, punishes and rewards' to dismantle any potential rivals. He 'can rely on traditional Sunni fears of the majority Shia population' to gain 'support for ruthless suppression.'[21] An assessment of the no-fly zones (NFZ) around Iraq in December opens by discussing Saddam's vicious mercilessness: 'When he perceives a challenge, he meets it ruthlessly and systematically', and his persecution of Iraq's Kurdish and Shia populations, motivated by the '[e]thnic and religious' suspicions of the 'Arab Sunnis', can be 'constrained but not

Figure 4.1 A 2000 JIC assessment of Saddam's hold on power provides a prominent photograph of the man. Discussion of his birthday celebrations frames the image as revealing Saddam's vain self-approval. The same photo later appeared on the cover of a British Defence Intelligence Service report in March 2002 on 'Removing Saddam'.

prevented'. The NFZs 'have a considerable symbolic and psycho-logical impact' on Saddam, 'complicat[ing] [his] calculations'. Any future military operations 'are likely to be brutal [...] to boost his strong man image'.[22] Again, international politics are reduced to Saddam's racialised psyche.

Elsewhere, JIC analysts framed Saddam's behaviour within popular Middle Eastern attitudes that are racialised as irrational prejudices. Saddam's foreign policy was dismissed in one paper as him being 'quick to act' in merely 'exploiting' Israel–Palestine violence to 'revive [...] his popularity on the Arab street'. His efforts to 'rebuild relations with his neighbours' is *de facto* negative for regional stability because it risks overcoming sanctions against Iraq. Neighbouring states meanwhile 'face pressure' to improve relations with Iraq because of 'popular sympathy for the Iraqi people', 'sympathetic Arab brotherhood' and 'perceived bias' by the Anglosphere on Israel and 'double standards on UN Resolu-tions'.[23] As officials watched the potential for military intervention in Iraq increase, this problem of Arab solidarity only became more vivid. An April 2002 assessment of Iraq's regional relations encap-sulates Saddam's foreign policy as based on manipulation, using 'economic leverage' and 'propaganda' to 'boost [Saddam's] popu-larity', and as therefore not what a 'normal' state would do. Iraq's success, meanwhile, comes from sympathy 'on the Arab street' for Iraq's position on Palestine and 'strong anti-US sentiment' in 'the Arab world', which is 'unlikely' to 'dissipate quickly'.[24] Both here and in the 2000 report, the idea of 'the Arab street' collapses race and place into one, projecting an atmosphere of popular sentiment in the region that dictates Arab people's easily incited feelings and prevents rational thinking.

The racialised component of this analysis is clearest when the JIC assess the sanctions imposed on Iraq following its invasion of Kuwait. During the 1990s, the UN and US trade embargoes prevented billions of dollar worth of supplies from entering Iraq, decimating the country's infrastructure at the same time that it was levelled by US bombing. Wages collapsed, child malnutri-tion reached the hundreds of thousands, clean water supplies were reduced, cholera and malaria re-emerged, and the health system was set back, in the World Health Organisation's words, 'by at least fifty years'.[25] This social decimation was well-known to US and British policy-makers. But for the JIC, it is 'Saddam' who 'needs the Iraqi people to suffer to underpin his campaign against sanctions', negating sanctions' prime role in that suffering.[26] A follow-up report pins any possible sanctions criticism on 'popular Arab opinion [being] susceptible to [Saddam's] propaganda'. Popular politics, then, is not just conditioned by unmanageable currents of emotion but by weak minds. The prefix 'Arab' invites a racial reading of this limited capacity for thought. The JIC are content, however, to advise the British Government on how to 'shift the political debate away from the humanitarian issue' by readjusting sanctions, to win over regional states' 'political perceptions' and to 'help to rebuild UK public support for our policy'.[27] None of these are described as manipulative propaganda efforts, nor are they traced to the British Government's essential vindictiveness.

Saddam's unwavering aggression finally comes down to his emotional refusal to accept Britain and the US's better sense in running the region. Saddam was judged likely to use his chemical and biological weapons only 'in extremis, in order to try to preserve his regime *or as a final gesture of defiance*'.[28] Talk of defiant gestures puts what is an unremarkable observation – that a state would use deadly force if threatened with external destruction – in terms that suggest a psychological refusal to adhere to justified pressure. A November 2001 assessment of Iraq's terrorist links, requested by the Foreign Office, acknowledges that any potential relationship with al-Qaeda's Osama bin Laden was held back by 'mutual distrust'. But the report's supposition of Saddam's post-9/11 thinking is clear: While Saddam will have 'ruled out [terrorism abroad] for the time being' and is 'currently constrained', 'he hates the US and UK, and Kuwait and Saudi Arabia for their continued support to the West'. Thus Saddam's 'threat to Western and Gulf interests remains credible', including the chance that he would use terrorism to 'exact revenge on his enemies'.[29] This idea of Saddam's underlying hatred circulated in the context of intelligence analyses made over decades, papers asserting that Iraq's Ba'athists were unable to understand the world because of their volatile emotions and political immaturity. Putting Saddam's vengefulness front-and-centre would have fitted perfectly within this racial story of why Iraq acted the way it did. Anglosphere states might disapprove of their adversaries' policies. But Middle Eastern states are motivated by hatred.

Chilcot's report makes no comment on this language, noting instead the minutes of a JIC meeting which concluded that this report was 'significant' and that 'it would be important to get its judgements and nuances right', given debates about 'what might or might not be done next in the campaign against terrorism'.[30] It is worth considering whether intelligence analysts would describe British policy-makers' views of Saddam in similar emotional terms. More urgently, it is worth assessing how useful these judgements and nuances are as analysis: By the JIC's own admission, Iraqi state terrorism is only now a possibility because of the increased impetus for 'a major US attack against Iraq', including 'a longer campaign aimed at regime change', which 'could alter Saddam's calculations' about terrorism's risk.[31] Saddam's hatred and vengefulness, however, are given no such motivating factors. They explain themselves.

IRRATIONAL EAST, OBJECTIVE WEST

In a situation where tensions between Iraq, the US, and Britain were increasing, where tolerance of the possibility of WMD programmes was considered no longer politically viable, intelligence analysts could have asked *why* Saddam Hussein might maintain the kind of emotional, aggressive mindset that they ascribe to him. How had his strategy of gaining dominance in the Middle East developed? What was influencing the tactics that analysts believed Saddam saw as necessary or sufficient to reach that dominance, including pursuing chemical, biological, and nuclear programmes? But in the British intelligence assessments that built up in 2002, analysis of Iraq was committed to the model of the Middle East as a self-contained equilibrium. Saddam was trying to upset its dynamics, while constraints on his policy-making coming from actors outside the region were described like acts of God or nature, unquestionable and irrelevant to analysis. In their attempts to avoid mirror-imaging, intelligence analysts developed a crucial proposition: By deciding to carry out actions that the US and Britain saw as grounds for threatening to overthrow him, Saddam was simply being irrational, and that was all the more reason to get rid of him as a threat. Historical judgements of Saddam's lack of geopolitical skill and the Ba'athists' vacuousness bolstered this idea, while gaps in intelligence on Saddam could even be used as evidence of this irrationality.

In February 2002, the JIC put Saddam Hussein 'Under the Spotlight'. Their report aimed to assess Saddam's 'threat perceptions and internal position', including 'what he is doing to try and avoid the internal and international threats he faces'. Those international threats were principally '[t]he US reaction to 11 September', which 'has been a jolt to Saddam's position', including President Bush's 'labelling Iraq as part of an "Axis of Evil"', which 'will have reinforced his concern'. Saddam 'is undoubtedly concerned about potential US military support to his internal enemies' – which of course had happened before. But by being described as threats that Saddam faces, these US actions are made to already-exist like the rest of the international system, not needing explanation and not being amenable to any influence by British policy-makers. Saddam is therefore only judged in terms of whether he gives in to US and other pressure. Saddam himself 'recognises that the greatest risk' is that his weapons programmes and non-compliance with inspections and sanctions 'may be used to justify a US attack to overthrow him'. Yet in the report's view, he continues to follow these paths: His international re-engagement is only 'a nominal policy' combined with 'a diplomatic charm offensive'. Any negotiations are merely 'tactical move[s] to buy time'. In other words, Saddam is knowingly risking giving the US their justification. So how do the JIC explain this irrationality? What is the underlying strategy? Saddam is stubborn, not wanting to make 'an admission of defeat'. Descriptions of his politics go only as far as 'Internal security', the ways he 'concentrate[s] [power]' among his 'Sunni majority', reinforcing the idea that his mindset is primarily conditioned by affiliation to one religious sect and violence against all others. There is no motivation given for his 'long-term strategy' of avoiding UN inspections and overcoming sanctions. Saddam's irrational responsibility for risking international violence is finally made clear by his emotions: If he cannot deter regime change, 'he would go down fighting'.[32]

In this February report, a model of an insulated Middle East and a wariness of mirror-imaging discourage intelligence analysts from thinking about Saddam's international perceptions and their influence on his actions. Saddam becomes intrinsically, stubbornly adversarial in this narrative because there is no opposite international adversary being portrayed and analysed on similar terms. In fact, this predisposition in analysis got stronger. Chilcot's Inquiry report quotes the minutes of a JIC meeting about this report. Members apparently agreed that the assessment should 'put [...] to one side' what Chilcot sums up as 'the issue of Iraq's interpretation of US policy', on the grounds that such policy was, in members' words, 'itself developing' and was not yet 'clear'. Instead, the assessment 'needed to say a bit more *about Iraq's aspirations* and potential in terms of Weapons of Mass Destruction', since this was 'an important area for policy discussions with the US'.[33] And so Iraq's view of the Anglosphere seemed not to bear on Saddam's ultimate objectives. This analytical blind spot continued. An October 2002 assessment of how Iraq would deal with the return of UN inspectors emphasises Saddam's 'determin[ation] to retain [WMD] which he considers to be a key part of Iraq's regional political and military power'. Again, there is no effort to examine why he thinks this and how he imagines that regional power. Only at the report's end does it note 'the changed political context', namely 'the clear determination of the US to bring about regime change'. That fixation on overthrowing Saddam is euphemistically commended for hopefully 'encourag[ing] a greater intelligence flow'.[34]

Other intelligence documents released by Chilcot demonstrate that the historical assessments of Saddam and Iraq's Ba'ath Party were continuing to reinforce this active disinterest in the leader's political views of the Anglosphere. As detailed in the Iraq Inquiry, in November 2002, Tony Blair spoke with President Bush about the need to 'imply' to Saddam, 'without spelling it out', that 'there would still be action' against him regardless of the UN. Blair understood the importance of 'pressure and humiliation' to make the Iraqi Government 'crumble'. With all this in mind, he suggested that a 'psychological profile [of Saddam] would be useful'. Downing Street then commissioned this profile from the intelligence services, which was based on Defence Intelligence Staff work back in 2001. The profile was sent by MI6 to JIC Chair John Scarlett as a draft for his Assessments Staff to consult, and was viewed by Blair's chief of staff and his foreign policy advisor.[35]

The report is a classic case of personality profiling at-a-distance. Its significance lies in how it juggles evidence of Saddam changing in response to the outside world with an assessment of his immutable, illogical mindset. The latter idea comes from the long-established intelligence history. Saddam – 'whose name', the report notes, means *the fighter who stands steadfast*' – is described as someone whose abusive childhood pushed him into the arms of a hateful ideological uncle, causing Saddam to be 'steeped in Arab history and Ba'athist ideology'. This material matches the profile made by former CIA officer Jerrold Post in the 1990s (Chapter 3). He became 'a leading Party theorist', had two convoluted marriages – the relevance of this is not explained – and gained 'little experience of political life outside of the Arab world'. This regional and family framing makes Saddam's hateful ideology appear peculiarly Arab. In terms of 'Perception of Threat', the profile argues that this life story has produced someone 'by no means irrational, but [...] contemptuous and aggressive', with 'an intense distrust' stemming from his uncle's 'antipathy towards certain foreigners'. These attitudes, and his supposed 'desire to [...] expand his power', are far more prominent in the report than the profile's late acknowledgement that he 'is not aiming to gain extra power or resources'. These attributes also frame discussion of foreign policy: Saddam can only see 'the Western world as a harassing, imperialist superpower', though to the profile's amusement he 'does not personally reject Western culture within his own lifestyle'. As the report explains – in the same section on Saddam's threat-perception – the man 'has a penchant for branded, Western style clothing and watches Hollywood films'.[36] Given the emphasis on his upbringing, two-faced anti-Western hatred ends up appearing fundamental to Saddam's culturally conditioned psyche. This emphasis on cultural hypocrisy resembles Allen Dulles' comments decades earlier on English language use by the Non-Aligned Movement (Chapter 1).

This character study of Saddam resonates with decades-past intelligence assessments of what makes him tick as a person. It traces his foreign policy thought process to his long-established paranoid psychological disposition towards the outside world, a limited ability to think and feel, which the report links to an emotional, unreasonable Arab cultural suspicion and hatred. But the profile also tries to cover Saddam's 'Political Behaviour and Motivation', a move which risks contradicting mere psychological paranoia and hypocrisy. Saddam has three motivating factors: 'personal survival, survival of his regime, and an Iraqi-led Arab unity'. Moreover, these motivations are 'interdependent', so that he sees his own survival as necessary for the 'dream' of 'Arab solidarity', with Iraq as 'the major player in the Arab world'. These political ambitions, while doubtless boosting his own 'exalted self-concept', attach more complex conditions to Saddam's aggression and distrust. These ambitions, rather than Saddam's emotional instincts, would have to be shaping his foreign policy outlook – the report tries to square these two aspects by saying that '[h]is aggressive drive is *instrumental* in pursuing his *goals*'. In the context of these motivations, anti-Western hatred is also more complicated: Saddam sees 'the political world as highly anarchic and threatening', implying that he thinks any claims of geopolitical stability cannot be relied upon. The Anglosphere, as part of this anarchic world, is threatening *to his goals*, and he believes that 'no matter what course of action he chooses he will be subject to further harassment and sanctions by the West'.[37]

In policy terms, this suggests a need for outside states, perhaps led by actors *other* than the US and Britain, to guarantee that any disarmament action will be responded to positively, and that Iraq's desire for regional status is legitimate, rather than use these as justification to continue harassment, or to press for Saddam's resignation. But these political implications are not pursued – the profile has already established its psychological picture. Consequently, Saddam's belief in a threatening world and the Anglosphere's duplicity within it is explained away as delusion: Given his 'deeply entrenched belief[s]', 'it is not difficult for him to find', i.e. invent, 'a persuasive chain of evidence' to back up his beliefs.[38] A British policy-maker presented with this psychological profile would be strongly encouraged to see Saddam's views on international politics not as arguments that need countering but as a reflection of immovable cultural limits on Saddam's ability to think straight.

Within this frame of analysis, where the JIC and Defence Intelligence Service (DIS) dismiss Saddam's policy-making as a product of entrenched delusions about the world out there, gaps in British intelligence-gathering could be transformed into evidence not just of Saddam hiding things but of his unpredictable political psychology. The JIC defined this unpredictability not as a variable in a complex situation but as a personality trait of Saddam's. In an August 2002 report requested by the Ministry of Defence on Saddam's 'options [...] to deter, avert or limit [...] a US-led attack', the JIC begins by warning of 'significant potential for Saddam to miscalculate, either by escalating a crisis at an early stage, or by making concessions too late in the day to be acceptable'. The reasons why early escalation would be a miscalculation or late concessions could not be accepted are not elaborated. The report simply states that '[i]n the past, Saddam has shown an ability to be innovative and spring surprises; we should expect him to demonstrate this again.[39] Through these words, miscalculation becomes part of Saddam's tactical capabilities. The November 2001 assessment of Iraqi terrorism similarly warned that Saddam had 'miscalculated in the past' and 'could again misread the response his actions would attract'. This potential is explained by Saddam's hatred.[40] Finally, unpredictability could simply turn intelligence gaps into threats: A September 2002 assessment of Iraqi WMD 'doctrine' cautions that '[i]ntelligence remains limited *and Saddam's own unpredictability* complicates judgements about Iraqi use of these weapons'. There is no way that this can be read as suggesting the possibility of *less* threat from Saddam. Indeed, the paper notes that while there is 'no intelligence to indicate' some courses of action, 'we cannot rule out the possibility' of them.[41]

In a 4 September 2002 JIC meeting, while discussing a draft of the paper just mentioned, committee members and Assessment Staffers made explicit that their assessment of Saddam relied on a racialised understanding of his irrationality. Attended by JIC Chairman John Scarlett, Head of Assessment Staff Julian Miller, and a handful of Assessment Staff, among others, the meeting considered the draft as their third agenda point. The meeting minutes do not specify who said what but states that 'the following main points were made'. The first point was that the paper 'would help to underline' to ministers and officials 'the importance and seriousness of the threat Iraq posed with [CBW]'. The reality of that threat seems taken-as-given by this point. Members agreed that '[t]he fact that Saddam Hussein possessed these capabilities, and that he showed every sign of being prepared to use them, was significant'. When the meeting identifies three ways Saddam might use these weapons, they do not explain in what scenarios these would take place. 'Threat' has no context. But members instead emphasised '[a]nother important message' which they believed 'needed to be brought out more clearly' in the draft. This was that Saddam would not be deterred from using CBW if his government was under 'threat of extinction'. The minutes then note: 'Readers of the paper needed to be reminded of Saddam's unpredictability, and of the fact that his thought processes did not work *in a recognisably Western, rational and logical way*'.[42]

This statement traces Saddam's inferior thought processes to his cultural, even civilisational difference, as if his limited reasoning was an inevitable feature of his psyche. It also casts out these bad psychological qualities from the Anglosphere – only those over there, those without Western minds, are irrational and illogical. By raising this important message during the discussion of how to explain Saddam's threat, committee members make clear that Saddam's thought process was part of the explanation for that threat. This is a rare but significant case where analysts concisely summarised their racialised view of Saddam. Chilcot, in his inquiry report, does not comment on it.[43] No one in the meeting is recorded as objecting. Scarlett recommends that the paper be 'revised to reflect the committee's discussion'.[44]

The final version of the draft that this meeting discussed, an assessment of 9 September 2002 on Iraq's potential scenarios for using CBW, can be read in light of these minutes. Its opening claim that 'Saddam's own unpredictability complicates judgements about Iraqi use of these weapons' most likely has the racialised underpinning about a non-Western mind raised in the meeting five days earlier – he is unpredictable *from our perspective*, because of his difference.[45] So too the report's comments on Saddam's values. Saddam, we are told, 'attaches great importance to having CBW' since it allows him 'to dominate his neighbours and deter his enemies *who he considers are unimpressed* by his weakened conventional military capability'. This statement appears just above the now-infamous claim about munitions being ready to fire within 45 minutes.[46] With no explanation of what domination means, what it would look like, the report's idea that Middle Eastern states are swayed primarily by displays of military power frames Saddam's strategic objectives as little more than showing off. Even more confusingly, this appears in the section summing up Iraq's capabilities, *before* the section on Iraq's 'Intentions for Use'. That latter section assumes a rather conventional and unremarkable reason for most likely use, 'to defend the regime from attack'. But by this point, the report has already painted its image of Saddam: He has an intrinsic and immutable desire to dominate, a desire which is shaped by the unique, non-Western relations of 'Arab countries'.[47] It would have seemed hard, from reading this report, to reason with a political actor consumed by a culturally unique and irrational status symbolism. This conclusion is merely a more subtle form of the racialised concern raised in the earlier meeting.

Both the Butler Report and the Chilcot Inquiry noted that this 9 September assessment 'relied heavily on inferences made by the JIC' and that '[i]ts tone [...] reflected a significant change from previous JIC judgements on Iraqi possession of chemical and biological weapons'.[48] Neither, however, consider either the decades-long history of judgements of Saddam Hussein's limited psychological capacity or the explicit statements to that effect in the 4 September meeting. During his testimony to Chilcot, Julian Miller of the Assessment Staff described that meeting's discussion as 'one that gelled with the very firm view amongst the community about both the possession and the readiness to use, on Saddam's part, these weapons'. Referring to this 'discussion in the JIC' as having produced 'a very firm expression' of their judgements on 'intent', he calls the post-meeting period 'the moment which sticks with me as being quite an important one'. The views on Saddam's willingness to use his weapons 'was the view that was shared around the JIC table' and the key thing that the committee believed 'ministers should read from their intelligence committee' at that time.[49]

THE MANY MEANINGS OF REGIME

When the JIC and its Assessment Staff were not putting Saddam's engrained irrationality in such bold terms, they were explaining the uniqueness of Iraq's policy-making during the increased tensions of 2001–2002 through an ever-shifty concept: the Regime (Chapter 2). Judging from how frequently the term pops up in assessments, the JIC were convinced that Iraq's Regime status was an important part of assessing its threat. This is despite the consistent failure to coherently define the term and its analytic value. In December 2001, MI6 head Richard Dearlove sent Tony Blair's office a requested assessment by SIS4, aka Mark Allen of MI6's counter-terrorism division.[50] Allen frames the challenge of overthrowing Saddam in terms of Iraq being 'a centralised state' led by '[t]he Tikritis' with 'formidable' defences. Key for Allen is the inner psychology of this and neighbouring states: While Iraq was 'a revolutionary regime which resonate[s] with the Street under conservative regimes', the aim of Allen's proposed 'Iraqi agenda' – covert support for a coup – would be to bring about 'climatic change in the psychology of regimes in the region'.[51] Regime, then, refers to tribal, autocratic states, often at odds with their own populations. They can have distinct ideological hues, but ultimately they operate on psychology; the only way to deal with them is by frightening them.

A July 2002 assessment of Iraq's 'Regime Cohesion' gives this country's regime its own identity: Its '[s]ecurity' is 'the overriding principle determining the regime's structure and actions', 'subordinat[ing]' any other interest, 'whether ideological, economic or political'.[52] This again dismisses interest in foreign policy motivations that 'staying in power' cannot by itself explain. But despite this emphasis, the regime itself appears to be different things: Sometimes it is a personified actor that 'takes few chances with military loyalty'; at other times, it is a structure that others join or leave, with actors like the military or 'the top few' being 'insiders' among its 'hierarchy'; and other times still, it is a possession of Saddam's, 'his regime', which 'feel[s] the pressure' alongside him. The regime may even be Saddam himself: 'The Iraqi regime is defined by Saddam Husain [sic]', such that while one minute in the report '[t]he regime relies on a mix of patronage and extreme fear to motivate its supporters at all levels', another minute '*Saddam relies* on a mix of patronage and extreme fear *to retain power*'.[53] A further assessment in November goes further: popular dissatisfaction is described as 'signs of strain *within* the regime', 'regime breakdown' means the loss of military 'loyalty', and the regime is 'aware' of and 'knows' about these problems within itself![54] Lack of coherence does not matter; for the purposes of these reports, the Regime category works to define Iraq's *uniqueness*. This is '[t]he Iraqi regime', dominated by 'a large and proven security apparatus [...] drawn from [Saddam's] own Tikriti tribe', whose '[b]lood ties' are 'no guarantee of harmony' and which endures through members' 'loyalties' or 'allegiance'.[55] What gives Regime as a category an explanatory veneer here is this talk of tribal power politics: The regime must be a coherent entity because it is based on a single social group. In the same way, Iraqi politics is racialised, reduced to Tikritis' narrow interest in alliances and betrayals.

Tellingly, the Regime category was fitted into analysts' longstanding image of Middle Eastern geopolitics, so that the question of people's 'loyalty' to the regime could only be seen as a binary question: Either you are for the regime or you are in principle supportive of a US-led military intervention. At a July 2002 meeting, the JIC discussed the first paper on regime cohesion discussed above, 'an important paper with a specific focus' which 'would be of interest to ministers'. Members agreed that the paper needed to analyse 'in more detail the nature of Saddam's support', because policy-makers would want to know 'the point at which self-interested loyalty for Saddam might turn into disillusionment, fragility and fragmentation'. After all, operations in Afghanistan had proved that 'generating expectations and influencing people's perceptions' could 'effect real and rapid change'.[56] The politics of Iraqis' connections to Saddam's rule, including the political values they may attach to state survival or disintegration, to type of polity and to a country's independence or occupation, are reduced to one issue:

Loyalty to Saddam or implicit support for what Britain decides to do about Iraq.

Finally, Regime as an ever-changing concept would stand in for an explanation of Saddam's irrationality. In August 2002, John Scarlett sent Tony Blair 'classified reading material on Iraq', including a paper by the Defence Intelligence Service on potential US routes to remove Saddam and the latter's likely responses. The Iraq Inquiry, which says that Blair read the paper, describes it as 'provid[ing] insights' into judgements made by the JIC in their 'Saddam Under the Spotlight' paper.[57] The paper describes 'Regime security' as 'the central organising principle and chief activity of the Iraqi state'. The regime is therefore first a matter of Iraq's 'formal security structure' of 'concentric and mutually suspicious organisations' filtered through 'the Sunni tribal network'. The patronage given to tribes means that 'Saddam, for all his revolutionary pretensions, represents a rather conservative tradition in modern Iraqi politics – Sunni hegemony'.[58] The DIS thereby define Saddam's politics by the narrow community and sect affiliations of Iraq's government, along with insincerity. Their judgement echoes the 1960 paper discussed in Chapter 2 on Middle Eastern Regimes' conservative traditionalism. But since the DIS conclude that Saddam 'feel[s] diplomatically exposed' and 'would eventually permit' inspections if he thought it would prevent 'a US attack aimed at overthrowing him', these discriminatory, autocratic bases of power do not actually explain anything about his decision-making or thought process. They do, however, frame his willingness 'to take a risk, erring towards an assumption [...] that the West will not sustain an attack' within this deep tribal-religious hierarchy. It is as if Saddam were cocooned by his protective Sunni tribal links from a fact that DIS analysts take for granted – that 'Iraq was moving into US sights'.[59]

Three months later, the DIS' psychological profile of Saddam would explain in its 'Key Points' section that the Iraqi leader's 'strong nationalism [...] comes from his narrow and distorted view of the world which in turn largely stems from his limited experience' of world politics. Not only were his politics a product of geopolitical innocence, but he 'filter[s] information to support his beliefs', backed up by advisers who do not challenge his ideas.

This 'perpetuat[es]' his 'deeply entrenched belief that the intention of outsiders is unjust'. Saddam also 'isolate[s] his country from Western influence', controlling 'the myth' of 'the "West"'. And so Saddam's ignorant righteousness towards the Anglosphere becomes a product of deliberate 'cultural isolation'. There is no grappling here with the disparity of cultural influence – Britain does not exactly invite 'Iraqi influence' or challenge its myths about the country, in part because it feels no pressure to respond to any such influence. But only in Iraq is this judged to produce 'conspiracy theories' that echo the 'personal mindsets' of the elite.[60]

Both DIS papers were sent to Scarlett and the JIC's Assessments Staff, and indeed resonated with their thinking.[61] In July 2001, the committee claimed that the 'secure position of 'the regime' in Iraq meant 'Saddam through overconfidence is prone to miscalculation'.[62] By the end of 2002, the committee linked the scale of this threat to the regime as well. While Saddam is likely to 'avoid extreme actions', 'there is still considerable scope for Saddam to miscalculate, react unpredictably and surprise us'. Why? The only explanation given was that '[h]is total control means that Iraqi policy could change substantially with little warning'.[63] It was Saddam's all-powerful position in the regime hierarchy that could lead him to make errors. Iraq's unique state structure invited irrationality – at least, irrationality from the perspective of those who wanted predictable compliance.

In their witness hearings during the Iraq Inquiry, intelligence officers went even further in grounding Saddam's irrationality in something unique about Iraq. SIS4/Allen says that intelligence judgements on Iraq's WMD threat stemmed not just from intelligence on 'very, very small' WMD items but from a 'broad impression' of Iraq's 'danger to the world [...] *given the nature of the regime*'. Allen explains his informal papers of late 2001 as an attempt to 'bring out [for policy-makers] [...] something about the nature of Iraq as a country and as a Ba'athist state'. This Ba'athist nature is important because it explains for Allen an essential difference in political maturity between Iraq and liberal democratic states. Like his colleagues in that September 2002 JIC meeting, Allen is more explicit about the racial nature of this difference. The Ba'athists, he says, 'were culturally Sunni, genealogically Sunni', although lots of

Sunnis in Iraq 'would have liked Iraq to be run differently'. After a redacted paragraph, he argues that it was not 'plausible to transfer an adversarial, party political, representational political system to Iraq'. Citing a historiographical text about the Mesopotamians which talked of the 'diffusion' of 'civilisation', Allen concludes that 'the difficult place which is Iraq' has 'never had stable political geography' and could not have been 'fitted out with Republican, Democrat, Lib Dem identities'. Something about Iraq's turbulent history and biological/religious make-up made its politics wholly unlike analysts' own cultures. The ideas of civilisation had not reached Iraq's shores.[64] Allen's explanation of Iraq is an exemplary case of colonial race-thinking: A distinct political environment had shaped a society whose culture limited their capacity for forms of political thought that are considered superior and uniquely Western. Allen does not consider whether a freer, politically plural Iraq could involve something *other* than the representational party system endorsed by him.

In his testimony to the inquiry, John Scarlett gives his own reading. He says that '[a]ll totalitarian states are difficult almost by definition as intelligence targets and that's one of the reasons they are totalitarian states', with their 'tightly controlled [...] environment', 'strong security agencies', and 'climate of intimidation'. But Scarlett then goes on to refer to this as a 'totalitarian *society*', which 'by its nature [...] generates, deliberately or not, obfuscation and uncertain[t]y', where even senior military officers are unsure 'who knows what about what'. This, Scarlett argues, is quite different from '*normal countries and societies* which are relatively open or completely open'.[65] Scarlett not only explains the lack of definitive information on Iraq's foreign policy through its Regime quality, but also puts Iraq in the category of the non-normal state on that basis. He may well be right about the difficulties of gaining direct intelligence from such a state. But this focus puts the burden of responsibility for the foreign policy of Iraq on the abnormal governing structure of that state. Britain and the US, the normal states – whose populations do not exactly have greater influence over their leaders' strategic WMD use – are not part of the equation.

This lets Scarlett make his primary defence in his testimony: intelligence's difficulty in gaining 'insight into Saddam's state of mind'. Scarlett maintains that the JIC correctly understood the importance Saddam placed on CBW 'as an integral part of his power structure and his influence'. But '[t]he problem was' that 'this was a highly autocratic state, where almost everybody revolved around the person, the thinking, *the behaviour and whims* of the leader'. This meant 'what was going on in his mind [...] was critical, and that was *very difficult to fathom*'. Scarlett then goes on to imagine senior Ba'athists' similar uncertainty on this issue of Saddam's thinking.[66] This might at first sound like a neutral disclaimer, that intelligence-gathering simply faced tough odds. But the material discussed above, along with Scarlett's reference to Saddam's behaviour and whims, suggests he meant something else: that Saddam was unfathomable because of his flippant and obscure psyche, existing in an abnormal society and reinforced by his position in his regime. Scarlett's statement of a hard intelligence target is also a judgement of totalitarian irrationality.

BLINDED BY THE ANALYSTS' LIGHT

There were opportunities for British intelligence analysts to reconsider the political motivations of Saddam Hussein's actions between 2002 and early 2003. Their analysis so far had pinned Saddam's actions on an emotional, sectarian psyche, produced by Arab culture and reinforced by an insular, distorting state structure. Past history was referenced only to emphasise his lack of good geopolitical sense and sadistic preferences. But moments when their intelligence assessments point to something else, when it appears that Saddam's thought process and perceived options are being influenced by Anglosphere actions, provided cause for re-evaluation. Analysts did sometimes recognise the significance of these considerations. Why, then, did they not pursue them and analyse whether US and British actions were increasing the chances of Iraq's aggression? Assessments at the time and witness hearings during Chilcot suggest that analysts could not compute the possibility of a negative Anglosphere role in their much-valued Middle East equilibrium. Instead, their fear of mirror-imaging pushed them back towards their racialised image of what had always made Saddam's limited personality a threat.

There had been hints that something more complicated was going on than Saddam's intrinsic irrationality. In August 2002, the JIC was asked by the Ministry of Defence (MoD) to assess Saddam's diplomatic and military options in response to any US intervention, 'how he is likely to weigh the balance of risks and potential benefits of each course of action and how his analysis may change' over time. It begins with the uncontroversial judgement that the more likely an invasion became, the more Saddam would consider responses that carried risks. Another unsurprising conclusion was that he would 'avoid giving the US a pretext to attack'. Once again, though, there was 'significant potential for Saddam to miscalculate' by escalating the situation too early. But halfway through this report, this possibility is portrayed rather differently. Saddam in fact 'might see some benefit in engineering a 'mini-crisis' before coalition forces were fully prepared', in order to provoke 'an early and less decisive attack'. Even 'an extreme course of action at an earlier stage' might 'provide sufficient advantages, through disrupting US plans'.[67] By the end of the report, it is unclear whether the JIC still see the possibility of Saddam lashing out at a build-up of coalition forces as a sign of his inability to properly read his geopolitical situation or as a logical tactic.

The MoD asked for a further paper on Iraq's military options in December. Here, the JIC professes superior knowledge of geopolitics: 'Saddam knows', i.e. recognises, what analysts reassure the reader to be a fact, 'that an Iraqi military victory over a US-led coalition is implausible'. A short paragraph on 'Saddam's calculation if it comes to war' portrays him as being cornered into desperation: 'If attacked', he would 'protest his willingness to co-operate', then 'use [chemical and biological weapons (CBW)], in order to undermine the coalition's will to continue', and 'in the last resort', 'seek to inflict the maximum possible damage on his enemies'.[68] There is no discussion of whether, if Saddam knows he cannot win militarily and is trying to avoid an invasion, the Anglosphere should respond in a conciliatory way to Iraq's current gestures, so as to increase the chances for de-escalation. The invasion is an unexamined background assumption that cannot be altered. No link is made between that assumption and Saddam's emotional disposition, what analysts call the certainty that he would be 'motivated by revenge'. And so when the committee conclude disapprovingly that Saddam could not be 'deterred' from using CBW if faced with 'military defeat and being removed from power', the blame is on his emotions, not the brittle diplomatic position of threatening to or actually invading a country while forbidding the other side's use of force. The JIC also repeat their earlier comment about the benefit to Saddam of a mini-crisis.[69] Again, it is unclear by the end of the report if the Joint Intelligence Staff think that Saddam's diplomatic and military considerations are a reasonable response to threats or reflections of a larger psychological unsteadiness.

It certainly becomes clear for analysts by early 2003. Following the negotiation of the UN Security Council Resolution 1441, which imposed what Chilcot calls ambiguous disarmament obligations on Iraq and vague conditions for military intervention, the Iraqi Government submitted a required declaration of its WMD programmes.[70] British policy-makers including Blair and Foreign Secretary Jack Straw saw this declaration as 'patently false' and argued that '[i]f Saddam persists in this obvious falsehood, it will become clear that he has rejected the pathway to peace'.[71] At the same time, British intelligence gained second-hand knowledge from those near to Iraq's elite that Saddam had ordered his officials to give inspectors 'no grounds for claiming that inspections were being obstructed'. This was interpreted differently by the Assessments Staff, as Saddam being 'confident the inspectors would not find anything'.[72] An initial JIC meeting to discuss Iraq's declaration concluded that it was 'surprisingly bad' and that its sections, which had not yet been translated from Arabic were 'unlikely to contain the missing information' they believed was required.[73] As Chilcot highlighted, the JIC's subsequent assessment of the declaration used the British Government's own public dossier on Iraq, released in September 2002, as a baseline by which to judge Iraq's compliance, which was 'not [the] purpose' of the United Nations Security Council Resolution (UNSCR) 1441 – it was 'not [for] the UK to define the bar for Iraq'.[74]

But there is another part of this assessment worth mentioning. The assessment finishes by saying that while Iraq's declaration 'makes no attempt to answer' points in the September dossier, '[t]he Iraqis may feel they dealt with these points in their previous rebuttal of the Dossier'.[75] So while the Iraqi failure to answer Britain's questions sets up Saddam's government as deceitful and ill-intentioned from the get-go, the JIC acknowledge that, deceitful or not, Iraq may have a different perception of what it needs to do to convince Britain and others. What started out looking like defiance may in fact be a new attempt at de-escalation. Pursuing this possibility would have represented a way of avoiding intelligence officers' and policy-makers' fear of mirror-imaging, of thinking that others share their values, without the racial implication that others have defective engrained ways of thinking. Perhaps Iraq's political elite is reading the international situation as well as Britain or the US and is trying to navigate it soberly.

The JIC, however, quickly read different implications from Iraq's diplomacy for their judgements of Saddam's psyche. Scarlett wrote to Julian Miller of the Assessments Staff at the start of 2003 emphasising the need to analyse 'what will Saddam do now or next?', since '[t]he answer to this might allow us to retest the standing judgements' on the stability of Iraq's government and the attitudes of regional states.[76] Three reports followed which confronted the possibility that Saddam was being pushed toward aggression by external pressure. On 13 January 2003, the same day that Tony Blair publicly argued that it was important to set an example for other so-called rogue states and to consider 'whether it is necessary to change the regime in Iraq in order to disarm them', Julian Miller sent JIC members a note produced by the Assessments Staff, to be discussed at a JIC meeting two days later.[77] Although Miller's letter and attached note were declassified and released by Chilcot, the Iraq Inquiry report makes no reference to their contents.

Miller intended the note as a sounding board for discussion rather than a draft JIC paper, and indeed the note's scope is unusually thematic: a list of Saddam's 'errors of judgement […] during the current crisis' and 'areas for potential future mistakes'. These errors come down to Saddam's misunderstanding of geopolitics and self-aggrandising paranoia. He has 'failed to appreciate the scope for the US and its allies to shape the course of international debate'; he has 'weakened [Iraq's] position' in relation to UNSCR 1441; and he has 'misjudged' diplomatic gestures to Kuwait. Saddam makes these sorts of errors because he 'overestimate[s] Iraq's ability' and 'read[s] too much' into certain developments. Miller concludes that it is this blinkered view of the world which constitutes Saddam's threat: In future, the Iraqi leader could 'misjudge US and international resolve' and commit military actions that 'bring upon Iraq the attack Saddam is seeking to avoid'.[78]

This was the ultimate sign of Saddam's irrationality: By his unwarranted faith in Iraq's international abilities and his lack of geopolitical savvy, he was risking the very regime change that he so desperately wanted to prevent. Miller's Assessments Staff note was followed by a JIC assessment two weeks later which tried 'to look at current developments in Iraq *from the point of view* of the Iraqi regime, particularly Saddam Hussein'. This was the first time since 2000 that the committee had formally attempted to put themselves in Saddam's shoes. In fact, the assessment interpreted Saddam's way of thinking *through* his relationship with the regime. The paper's 'Key Judgements' on page 1 establish that Saddam 'has not lost control' and 'continues to maintain regime cohesion, primarily through intimidation'. This discussion of Saddam's Regime-position frames the discussion on page 2, 'Reading the Outside World'. Here, the committee argue that Saddam and his officials may not have 'fully grasped the severity of the military attack they face', that in fact 'Saddam is misreading the international scene' by 'overestimat[ing]' both the political barriers to coalition military action and his own ability to corral 'Arab and international support'.[79] Saddam's irrationality looks here like a product of his position: cut off from that outside world, gaining only a distorted view from inside based on his self-reinforcing delusions. The unique cohesion of the Iraq Regime stymied the kind of objectivity that JIC analysts implicitly attributed to themselves.

In evidence to the Iraq Inquiry, another anonymous MI6 officer corroborated this way of judging Saddam's actions. 'SIS1', as best as can be read from their heavily-redacted inquiry testimony, had some responsibility for counter-proliferation in the service. SIS1's staff, in their own words, had '[d]aily' dialogue with the JIC's Assessments Staff. When asked about whether intelligence on 'Saddam's strategy for dealing with inspections' strengthened the conviction that 'there was really something to hide there', SIS1 insists that 'they looked guilty as hell', 'they' presumably referring to Iraq's political elite. SIS1 then frames this issue of perception management, of how Iraq looked to the world, as 'a sort of spectacular miscalculation, and I think it's partly because of their paranoia about being open to hostile scrutiny, and partly because they had stuff to hide, but not necessarily what the inspectors were looking for', things like 'military secrets'. Iraq's government, then, misunderstood how to deal with its international situation because of the regime's paranoia. This miscalculation, according to SIS1, 'form[ed] part of a consistent picture' for analysts, 'allowing for the fact that there was a certain assumption in the first place' that Iraq had WMD to hide.[80]

In that January 2003 JIC assessment on the Iraqi point of view, a later section on 'Saddam's Mindset' builds on those qualities later reported by SIS1 to argue that Saddam's distorted perception risks emotional aggression: If he still 'fail[s] to realise' the situation, the eventual harsh impact of reality will 'provoke murderous rage' and a 'fear' of 'humiliation'. The JIC's last-minute attempt to explain how the world looks from Saddam's point of view ends up turning into a negative judgement of Saddam's bad geopolitical sense, a bad sense brought on by his own emotions and autocratic blind-spots. Nowhere do the JIC address the 'US determination to deal decisively with him' *as a variable* in its own right, as something that could prompt changes in Saddam's perceptions – say, his perception of the sincerity of diplomatic offers or of the feasibility of his own objectives – and as something whose wisdom itself could be judged in terms of its effects on the likelihood of a regional escalation of violence.[81]

Because Iraq is read as a unique Regime-state, and Saddam as murderous, the US and Britain must be able to see *and act* rationally by contrast. That is how analysts know Saddam is making mistakes, and why coalition military action is not up for analysis. The problem is in Saddam's head. Even without referring to Sunni tribalism or Arab emotions – although those ideas filled the papers that surrounded this one – this JIC assessment interprets Iraq's actions as a product of a so-called 'non-Western' form of governance and a delusional psyche that could never understand how the world works. This interpretation fitted neatly within other assessments over years of Iraq's racial difference. For this reason, the report's claim that there is 'no sign' that 'Saddam is unstable or losing the capacity to make rational tactical decisions' reads as pessimistic rather than hopeful. For Saddam may have the stability and rationality required, in analysts' view, for him to 'play' the 'strong cards' that '[h]e may well believe that he has'. But analysts disagree that he actually has strong cards – he is always wrong about international politics![82] By trying to avoid anything which resembles mirror-imaging, and by therefore reducing Saddam's political judgement to a narrow emotional ignorance propelled by an insular government, the JIC establish Saddam as irrational in a way that Britain and the US cannot be by definition. Intelligence analysts' open society, to use John Scarlett's words, sees clearly the facts of the world.

Finally, when the above JIC assessment was released and submitted to Prime Minister Blair, Scarlett himself wrote an accompanying minute. While the JIC paper to his mind focused on 'Saddam's continuing control inside the country', Scarlett explains that he wants to 'add some personal observations on the overall intelligence picture, which I have been studying now for nearly a year'. That overall picture turns out to involve, as Chilcot later puts it, 'Saddam Hussein's mindset and likely actions'.[83] Here, the historical judgement of Saddam's inherent psychological limits and shallow political objectives makes sense of Scarlett's conclusions. Scarlett begins: 'I have not seen a single reference [in intelligence reports] to Saddam even considering the renunciation of WMD to save his regime (and probably his own life)'. Indeed, 'the Iraqi leader has followed essentially the same strategy and tactics as during the 1990s'. This is the same stubborn and irrational man that intelligence had been assessing for decades. That background makes sense of what Scarlett's testimony to the Iraq Inquiry would later suggest: that absent 'a contrary flow of reporting', intelligence on Saddam was not seen as needing a 'challenge'.[84]

But the implications that Scarlett sees in Saddam's behaviour are something new and significant. Saddam's decision not to reveal even some of his WMD, as Scarlett judges him to have decided, came from the fact that doing so 'would have been a big risk', potentially 'opening up lines of [UN] investigation to what was still being concealed'. A 'flat denial' was therefore '[f]rom Saddam's point of view [...] *probably the right decision*'.[85] Scarlett gives Saddam some tactical rationality here: If Iraq's leader wanted to keep the weapons, it made sense not to give any hint of their existence. Yet this is the exact opposite of Julian Miller's conclusion in his note earlier that month, that Iraq's decision to issue a full denial was evidence of Saddam *mis*handling the situation, by removing his 'credibility' in front of inspectors and reinforcing that he has 'no long-term contingency plan' on how to approach the UN.[86] Scarlett is instead suggesting that Saddam *correctly* saw the usefulness of a full denial. Scarlett also says that any 'genuine [...] renunciation' of WMD by Saddam is actually impossible. It is '*simply too dangerous*' for Saddam, since it 'would remove the one weapon of last resort with which Saddam can threaten his population and neighbours'. It would 'send a signal of weakness to both [groups]', with 'possibly unmanageable consequences (for him)'.[87]

What to make of Scarlett's reading of Iraqi geopolitics? So late into the debate and planning for the invasion of Iraq, this is a rare attempt to consider how international relations are shaping Saddam's outlook and decision-making. Scarlett colours this consideration with yet more imagery of a self-contained and unique Middle East system – one where states either threaten their neighbours or face annihilation – and so does not analyse other ways that states might interact and negotiate. But Scarlett's conclusion represents a glimpse at Saddam's *motivations*: He fears losing regional power-credibility. As such, Scarlett's comments hint at the possibility that the US and Britain's resolve, their determination to face down Saddam, is putting the latter in a lose-lose dilemma: Either give up credibility and risk downfall, or be overthrown by outside forces. An intelligence analyst like Scarlett is presented here with an opportunity, an opening to assess what geopolitical perceptions are leading Saddam to think he needs to preserve regional credibility, primarily through WMD, and what the US and Britain could do to first *reduce* his feeling of being trapped and then try to *affect* his geopolitical calculus and perception of necessity.

What happened instead is revealing. Scarlett turns from Saddam's motivations to the question of how Iraq is managing to maintain this presumed tactic of concealment. Rather than follow the line briefly raised in the JIC assessment of Iraq's declaration – that Saddam may have been trying to convince the world and thereby de-escalate tensions rather than defy it – or the line in the Assessments Staff intelligence which suggested that Saddam did *not* want to provoke inspectors' ire, Scarlett expresses surprise that Saddam and his advisers are so 'confident that concealment would work'. 'Oddly', Saddam's elite 'have not appeared worried by the obvious risk of leaks from the thousands of people aware of this concealment activity'. Scarlett is more interested in Iraq's elite social ties than its foreign policy motivations. His explanation for Saddam's confidence only further confirms the singular nature of this Regime-state: 'They have relied on the brutal discipline of the regime' and 'extreme intimidation' to prevent any leaks; after all, '[t]his is the nature of this kind of totalitarian regime. "You never know who is listening", however safe it might appear'.[88]

Not only is a lack of intelligence once again translated into evidence of the distinctive interior roots of the Iraqi state's actions – something backed up by Scarlett's assertion that the JIC's list of Iraq's potential actions are not speculative because 'Saddam is ruthless and, if necessary, will try anything'. More crucially, the possibility that the US and Britain have been *increasing* the chances of Iraqi aggression is papered over and can be dismissed. Saddam's actions instead look more like the result of stubbornness and arrogance, acted out through brutal regime discipline, and a reflection of poor international instincts. Indeed, the rest of Scarlett's minute discusses 'Saddam's Hold on Power', his use of 'fear' over 'love' or 'loyal[ty] in the unselfish sense of the term'. 'No cracks must show, even to your closest advisers *and indeed we have no evidence of any wavering on Saddam's part*'. Scarlett concludes that Saddam is 'not irrational' to think he is not yet 'finally doomed', given his military options inside Iraq. But 'he has not had many choices' so far, '[g]iven his fundamental objectives'. Like Miller, Scarlett sees Saddam as tactically astute but strategically lacking, ensnared by his foolish psychological desire for power.[89]

If that was not enough, in their inquiry hearings testimony, Scarlett and other analysts elaborated on the importance they attached to avoiding a mirror image of Saddam at this time. Following up the issue of Iraq being a hard intelligence target – where the leader's mind is so difficult to fathom, as Scarlett put it minutes earlier – Chilcot suggests to Scarlett that 'Saddam was playing a two-card trick game, wasn't he?' As Chilcot sees it, Saddam wanted to 'get out from under sanctions' and so had to feign compliance with UNSCR 1441 and inspections. But on the other hand, 'he needed to project in the region and to the neighbours the fact that he was *the great hero* and the possessor of *these magical weapons* that gave him status'. Chilcot draws on imagery that was appearing in JIC assessments of decades past – Saddam seeing himself as the heroic leader of Arab liberation – and projects irrationality on to Saddam, that he ascribed something inexplicable or supernatural to WMD that he desperately wanted to capture. The psychological effect of this weaponry magic is reduced to Iraq's neighbours, to the Middle East region. Asked by Chilcot if the JIC were aware of this two-way game, Scarlett replies that it is 'a very interesting point' and reflects Saddam's 'paradox or ambiguity', something 'which maybe is in *the nature of a regime like his* and a system like his'. Saddam's rationality was overrun by this nature: He found it 'difficult [...] to put all his focus' on getting sanctions lifted 'because he felt he needed to project power and intimidation [...] in the region, particularly [...] in relation to Iran'. No one at the inquiry hearing finds it questionable that Chilcot and Scarlett would talk about international relations in terms of impressionable Middle Eastern minds and a natural irrationality in particular states. Scarlett only regrets that the JIC did not 'confront' this paradox and 'discuss' it. The comments are allowed to characterise Saddam's government and radically separate his decision-making process. Scarlett's brief reference to Saddam 'watching the Iranian nuclear programme', by contrast, is not explored further.[90]

Another witness explicitly cited the idea of a mirror-imaging danger to make their point. In November 2009 the inquiry held a joint witness hearing with William Ehrman and Tim Dowse. During the run-up to the invasion, Ehrman had been director general of defence and intelligence in the Foreign Office, while Dowse had been head of the FO's Counter-Proliferation Department. The two give a long run-down of how Iraq was perceived as a threat in terms of WMD strategy and proliferation, that Iraq was unique because of 'Saddam's history of aggression against his neighbours, against his own people'. One inquiry member, Lawrence Freedman, pushes back and suggests 'there was a defensive case [...] taking into account Iran' and 'Israel'. Freedman also asks about the difference between non-compliance with UN Resolutions and actually being threatening'. The two witnesses again lean on Iraq's 'long history', 'the whole experience of the 1990s', as demonstrating a 'potential threat' of Iraq hiding any rearmaments. Freedman suggests that it would have been sensible for Iraq to only pursue CBW, since they could be produced quickly, without Iraq needing to hold on to incriminating 'stocks that might cause you embarrassment'. Perhaps this is what Iraq actually did? In response, Dowse cautions that 'there is a danger in assessment [sic] of intelligence – and, of course, this is primarily an issue for the Joint Intelligence Committee rather than the Foreign Office itself – but a danger in mirror-imaging'. As Dowse sees it, '[j]ust because we wouldn't do it that way, doesn't mean that somebody else would not do it that way'. What was Dowse's evidence in this case? 'The Iraqis did quite a lot of things that seemed to us to be irrational, but, by their lights, presumably it was not'. As an example, '[t]hey buried things in the sand, entire aircraft, which was not something that would seem a particularly rational thing to us, but they did it'.[91]

Dowse was referring to news in August 2003 that coalition forces had dug up Soviet-made Iraqi jets around an air base near Falluja, partly-stripped then buried underneath soil and camouflage netting, presumably intended to be dug up had Saddam survived military action (Figure 4.2).[92] Of course, the example of buried aircraft bears very little on the question of whether Iraq would have retained incriminating WMD material. It is also interesting to compare Iraq's burials with Britain's decisions to abandon military equipment for private companies to then sell off, such as a tent village in Afghanistan in 2014.[93] But the point in Dowse's words is clear: As JIC members had put it, Saddam and the Iraqi Government did not think in a logical, Western way. We in the clear-thinking British political elite would not do such things, so they in Iraq must be irrational, and this must apply to their thinking more generally. They must lack the capacity for good policy-making and geopolitical thinking. We could even use this essential difference to get over problems in intelligence. Dowse later confirms that his team's assessment of Iraq's non-defensive intentions for WMD came from 'Saddam's past form', which included his invasions of Iran and Kuwait, 'both of which *by normal standards* one would regard as rather irrational acts *in view of the consequences* they brought to Iraq'.[94] As Dowse testifies, then, Saddam's previous misreading of an objective, unchangeable world, read as reflections of his poor mind, had been part of analysts' thinking in the run-up to the invasion.

Figure 4.2 Buried fighter jets, like this MiG-25R, at al-Taqqadum airbase were referred to by US Defence Secretary Donald Rumsfeld as a 'classic example' of the challenge in finding Saddam's WMD. (US Air Force/Master Sgt T. Collins)

Finally, Chilcot himself reiterates the point about Saddam's mindset, noting the challenge of 'interpreting Saddam's own behaviour and the behaviour of the clique around him at the top of the regime'. Not only did he have 'a nationalist drive' but also 'by our standards, a kind of irrationality that comes up now and again'. Chilcot asks if analysts like Ehrman tried to therefore 'peer behind the curtain into the mind of the regime of Saddam'. Ehrman responds that 'I think maybe we are going to come on to intelligence gaps, or gaps in our general knowledge'. Dowse concurs, that when trying to analyse 'the political context in terms of the nature of the Iraqi regime', 'really you are trying to say what's in the mind of one man and that's the most difficult thing of all'.[95] Difficult, yes, but like decades of reporting on Iraq and the Middle East, a difficulty in analysis was turned into evidence of defective politics and inferior psyches.

CONCLUSION

Following the Gulf War, an anonymous British intelligence officer was quoted arguing that Saddam's invasion of Kuwait should have seemed obvious beforehand to the JIC and others. After all, 'Saddam was a good old-fashioned Arab dictator. Everyone knew what he was and what he was capable of'. The officer lists Saddam's character traits – 'devious, untrustworthy, greedy, ambitious and scared shitless of being toppled [...] paranoic and desperate' – before noting that Iraq's rich vulnerable neighbour was 'stick[ing] two fingers up and tell[ing] him to push off'. What else was going to happen? Did any analyst seriously believe that 'a psychotic dictator with 5,000 tanks is going to sit back' and do nothing? This was 'a simple intelligence matter of capabilities and intentions, *and knowing your man*. In the circumstances, *what else was Saddam Hussein to do?*'.[96]

What else was he to do? On the face of it this question seems self-explanatory. Consider all the intelligence assessments reviewed in this chapter, which interpret Saddam's foreign policy in terms of the man himself being untrustworthy, emotional, and deluded, someone prone to committing violence based on a misreading of what was happening in the world and how he would be treated in response. To ask this question therefore points to Saddam's invasion of Kuwait as an inevitable consequence of his political psychology, shaped by cultural conditions – after all, he was an old-fashioned Arab dictator. But what if you read the anonymous officer's question as one about circumstance? What if Saddam's perceptions were important, yes, but in terms of how they respond to what they see as much as how they try to impose ideas based on what they feel? This question encourages us to look at the geopolitical situation Saddam was in at that moment – this could include the decline of his political legitimacy, or the financial losses incurred from a decade of war with Iran. Iraq's autocratic state structure certainly allowed one man to push for such a momentous decision as an invasion, but does the uniqueness of Iraq's state primarily explain that actual decision-making process?

I have tried to show in this chapter how British intelligence analysis of Iraq from 2000 to 2003 built on past assessments of the Ba'ath elite as lacking any politics worth addressing, of Saddam as moulded permanently by delusional Arab xenophobia, and of the Iraqi state as conditioning distorted perceptions and irrational geo-political strategy. When the Bush and Blair administrations came into office and began shaping a doctrine of international inter-vention, and when the 11 September 2001 attacks led to a more gung-ho political atmosphere, intelligence analysis was drawn on by policy-makers as a way to make sense of what Britain and the US were up against, of who Saddam Hussein was and how Iraq's own policy-making worked. The analysis that British decision-makers received on these two topics did little or nothing to challenge any pre-conceptions about Saddam's inherent threat or the wisdom of a coalition invasion in terms of producing 'stability' in the Middle East. The intelligence model of that region as self-contained and requiring intervention to be stabilised contributed to this failure, as did an analytical culture which allowed the need to identify other societies' cognitive and emotional limits to pre-empt and cut off any attempt at international sociology, an attempt to examine how one state or society's political dynamics influence another's. As Scarlett put it to the inquiry, fathoming Saddam was simply very difficult – of that, more than anything else, analysts were deadly certain.

Conclusion: Libya, the Arab Spring, and the success of intelligence failure

What has been happening in the intelligence world since Iraq was declared a disaster of inaccurate assessments? What role have the ideas of a mirror-image problem and a Middle Eastern equilibrium been playing as Britain and the US get involved in yet more regional developments? And how should we think about intelligence's political role if we want to break its contribution to the kind of social violence suffered by Iraq from 2003 to today?

THE THREAT OF ECCENTRICITY: FROM IRAQ TO LIBYA

A good place to look after Saddam's downfall for the continuing role of intelligence's post-colonial racial thinking is in the 2011 Libyan intervention. Since Muammar Gaddafi had divested the country's small stockpile of chemical weapons at the end of 2003, relations between Libya and the Anglosphere had improved immensely, particularly on so-called counter-terrorism co-operation. On Gaddafi's part, having pursued WMD as 'a shield against the application of US power' from the late 1980s, he shifted in the 1990s to back-channel dealings on potential disarmament, which came to a head shortly before the invasion of Iraq.[1] As for Britain, it had severed diplomatic relations in 1984 amid Libya's targeting of dissidents and support for the IRA; it then pushed through UN sanctions for Libya's accused role in the 1988 Lockerbie air-plane bombing. Britain restarted diplomatic relations shortly before 9/11, whose condemnation by Gaddafi allowed for improved EU relations and intelligence co-operation.[2] Indeed, witness the Libyan security force's relations with Mark Allen/SIS4, as discussed in the previous chapter. This turnaround was rewarded with meetings between Tony Blair, Gaddafi, and representatives of General

Dynamics and British Petroleum, leading to an oil exploration agreement and a military equipment contract worth hundreds of millions of pounds.[3] Of course, the uprising against Gaddafi in 2011 undid this militarist and lucrative relationship. In the context of the Arab Spring, demonstrations in February developed into an armed uprising that took control of a large part of Libya, before pro-government forces launched a counter-offensive in March. UN Security Council 1973 authorised a no-fly zone over Libya and 'all necessary measures' to defend 'civilian-populated areas'. This was quickly used as a pretext for a NATO intervention on the side of the uprising, with airstrikes accompanied by special forces operations and intelligence agency advisers, along with arms transfers that themselves violated UN Resolutions. In October, Gaddafi was captured and killed, and Libya was declared liberated.[4]

NATO's intervention was fiercely justified by its proponents on the grounds that Gaddafi was planning to massacre civilians in towns re-taken by his forces. Gaddafi's mindset was a key part of US and British analysis right through the post-9/11 period, to the limited extent that analysts' views have been disclosed – there has not, as yet, been a Chilcot-style inquiry into the Libya intervention. Diplomatic relations with Gaddafi may have warmed during the 2000s, but intelligence assessments of the man had not. Intelligence scholar Christopher Andrew reports that SIS officers who were sent to Libya in 2003 to discuss its disarmament offer found Gaddafi illogical, 'rambling', and blindly absorbed in his own monologues. 'There was no dialogue' with him, said one officer. Subsequent meetings were described second-hand by CIA Director George Tenet as erratic, with Gaddafi reportedly giving 'a loud and colourful diatribe, slamming the West' one minute before exchanging pleasantries with Anglosphere intelligence officers the next.[5] Despite Gaddafi having broached his own disarmament, intelligence officers portray the action as having been completed despite his personality.

Later assessments from the US embassy in Tripoli, released by Wikileaks, stuck to the intelligence script for the Arab world, characterising Gaddafi as incoherent and lacking real politics, and Libyans themselves as easily manipulated and ignorant. When Gaddafi's policy-making process, sarcastically dubbed the 'Vision

Thing', became more public and debate-driven in late 2008, this was read as 'political theatre' designed to make a 'largely conservative, risk-averse Libyan public' feel content with the status quo. Incidentally, this strategy was supposed to allow Gaddafi to block privatisation measures, referred to neutrally by the embassy as a type of 'political reform' that would inevitably follow from 'Libya's economic opening' to the world.[6] The embassy's analysis was more interested in such reforms, which would allow yet more US capital to enter the country, than in improved living conditions, which had motivated recent popular protests.[7] Paradoxically, the embassy assessed that when Gaddafi was not playing up to a conservative public, he was cultivating revolutionary international politics within them. Through the 2000s, Gaddafi sought to portray himself as an African political leader rather than an Arab one. The embassy assessed that his 2007 call for a Muslim North African political union 'strike[s] a chord with his audience and the broader Libyan population' – not the 'better-educated', who know that the ideas of this 'lunatic' have no 'chain of logic', but the 'less worldly segments of Libyan society', those who do not understand international relations but who are worried about 'sectarian turmoil in Iraq'. Once again, Gaddafi's 'latest ramblings' are dismissed as status-seeking and 'personal antipathy towards Arab leaders'. His ramblings' content – that the Arab League was being pressured by the US, that inter-sect violence had been fostered by the Anglosphere – are passed over as his usual rants about 'colonialist plot[s]'.[8] In this way, US diplomats translate Gaddafi's and Libyans' political concerns into proof of their Muslim geopolitical ignorance. The US's then-current strategy of arming both Sunni and Shia militant groups against one another in Iraq, which had effectively segregated Baghdad by this point, is not brought up in the report.[9]

Instead of addressing Libya's political outlook, the embassy continued to emphasise Gaddafi's and Libya's own social isolation from the world, that the Libyans had not been properly socialised for the twenty-first century. In 2009, a US investment consultant who met Gaddafi a number of times offered his thoughts to the embassy, who saw them as significant primarily because he described the leader as 'paranoid about those around him', as well as being pleased to have finally expressed his 'feelings' during his recent UN General Assembly 'performance'.[10] Reports of Gaddafi's 'personality quirks' during a trip to the US that same year – his apparent fear of flying over water and his love of flamenco – were heralded as 'rare insights' that confirmed US diplomats' view of him as 'mercurial and eccentric'. Though this report warned against reading 'instability' into Gaddafi's personality, how exactly these insights helped to understand his 'motives and interests' is not made clear.[11] Earlier, during an embassy meeting with a Libyan Government development adviser, the latter balanced Libya's success as 'a catalyst for anti-imperialism' against its 'absolute fail[ure]' to 'address the concerns (education, employment) of Libyan youth'. In the embassy's sum-up of the meeting, however, the advisers' thoughts reveal that Gaddafi's ideological 'thought' has 'left many Libyans ill-equipped to participate in the broader world from which they have been isolated for so long'. Libya's concerns that their relationship with the US is 'overly focused on security' may have some truth, but those concerns really 'reflect the inevitable *growing pains of a society* and body politic struggling to come to grips with *its place in the world*'.[12] That place, which Libya must adapt to, is below those outside states which get to decide the counter-terrorism priorities of the region.

The above demonstrates that Gaddafi was being analysed through an anti-mirroring logic, whereby his behaviour and policy actions stemmed from something radically different to professed Anglosphere norms of geopolitics and rationality. It was this mindset of Gaddafi's that drove Libyan foreign policy, except when he was thankfully forced to accede to the neutral standards of the world out there, on issues from economics to disarmament to counter-terrorism.

When the 2011 uprising began, the Libyan leader's intentions were assessed through this historical analysis. The initial protests against Gaddafi were certainly met with brutal repression, including hundreds of killings and thousands of injuries by security forces.[13] However, it was claims by those in the uprising that Gaddafi was planning mass reprisals in rebel-held cities, along with news reports of Gaddafi's promise to 'go house to house' and '[c]apture the rats', that were cited by proponents of an intervention.[14] US President Obama, British Prime Minister Cameron, and

French President Sarkozy wrote a joint statement: 'We must never forget the reasons why the international community was obliged to act [...] By responding immediately, our countries halted the advance of Gaddafi's forces. The bloodbath that he had promised to inflict [...] has been prevented.'[15] British Foreign Secretary William Hague later argued that Benghazi was 'a city of hundreds of thousands of people [...] We are talking about vast numbers of people [...] There was therefore the possibility of immense bloodshed.'[16] US Secretary of State Hillary Clinton said the same thing at the time, that potentially 'tens of thousands of people' would be 'slaughtered.'[17]

The term bloodbath was not used by Gaddafi himself, who instead warned that intervention would mean 'a bloody war and thousands and thousands of Libyans will die.'[18] Politicians pointed to Gaddafi's rhetoric as evidence of his bloodbath intentions because they believed this interpretation fitted what kind of person he was. President Obama argued that *when someone like Gadhafi threatens a bloodbath* that could destabilise an entire region [...] then it's in our national interest to act.'[19] And as Hague stated in evidence to the Foreign Affairs Committee, '[i]t would be a brave assumption, *given the history of Gaddafi*, the situation and the disposition of forces, that his army would drive into Benghazi and they would all behave like pussycats.'[20] Gaddafi's history certainly showed that he responded to army revolts and armed rebellions with policies of summary executions and long prison sentences. And over the course of the 2011 war, human rights organisations uncovered multiple mass graves of detainees and protesters recently killed by government forces, ranging from 10 to 45 bodies at a time.[21] Larger massacres of city populations, however, were not uncovered and would have marked a change in his historical policy.

The reference to Gaddafi's background, then, appeared to be less about documented events than about an image of Gaddafi as vengeful or spiteful towards Libya's population. Hague understood Gaddafi's 'stated intention' was to exact 'revenge on the people of Benghazi'. Moreover, he told the Foreign Affairs Committee that even if the British Government lacked detailed intelligence on the politics of the uprising, 'the Gaddafi regime' itself 'did not understand the militias, the tribes, the movements and what was happening in their own country', again highlighting Gaddafi's distance or antipathy towards Libya's people.[22] On the US side, intelligence officials interviewed years later said that the CIA had 'little information' about 'Gadhafi's own intentions in repressing the rebellion' but that the Pentagon judged he was 'unlikely to risk world outrage by inflicting large civilian casualties'. In the view of one intelligence official, the NATO intervention 'was an intelligence-light decision' that was based on politicians' own speculation about a Libyan genocide.[23] But it was certainly a decision buoyed in public debate by intelligence assessments of Gaddafi's personality. Years after testifying on Saddam, Jerrold Post, founder of the CIA's personality analysis centre (Chapter 3), disseminated his view of Gaddafi. Again using personal biography, Post concluded that Gaddafi's actions reflected 'a borderline personality' that 'swings from intense anger to euphoria' and reacts to pressure by clinging to distorted beliefs. Post was nothing if not consistent: Bob Woodward reports that borderline personality disorder was the CIA's medical diagnosis of Gaddafi as far back as 1982. But more recently, Post thought, Gaddafi had 'lost touch with reality', as his self-image as 'the Muslim warrior courageously confronting insurmountable odds' rubbed against his loss of popular support. Post concluded that Gaddafi would 'go down in flames' to preserve that delusion.[24]

Compare this intelligence profile of Gaddafi as vengeful and a bad judge of geopolitics with the US and Britain's relations with Libya in the run-up to the 2011 intervention. The three countries' rapprochement happened just years after Gaddafi had brutally repressed a growing Islamist opposition movement, of both militant and moderate strands. Post-9/11 counter-terrorism therefore suited all countries concerned, with Britain and the US happy to designate this scattered and decimated Islamist opposition as a terrorist organisation despite its limited links to any international Islamist terrorism groups.[25] As co-operation increased from 2002, the CIA and MI6 began helping Libya's External Security Organisation to kidnap opposition activists living abroad; opponents of Gaddafi who had lived legally in Britain for years were detained as Britain tried to deport them to Tripoli; and Gaddafi's intelligence officers were allowed to work in Britain using British-gathered intelligence.[26] During the 2011 intervention, an MI5 memorandum dated February 2005 was uncovered among the rubble of Gaddafi's security services. Prepared in advance of an intelligence visit to Tripoli, the memorandum assessed that the kidnappings of Abdel Hakim Belhaj and Sami al-Saadi of the Islamist opposition (Chapter 4) had removed two figures who were opposed to their movement having any worldwide jihadist links, allowing the Islamist movement in Libya to increasingly fall under pro-jihadism influence.[27]

There has been no comment in the Anglosphere on whether Britain and the US's support for Gaddafi's repression of Islamism, or indeed their inadvertent boosting of international terrorism links in Libya, may have affected Gaddafi's perception of the uprising in 2011. Gaddafi made clear that he saw those protesting and revolting against him as under the influence of al-Qaeda and Osama bin Laden, 'the enemy who is manipulating people'.[28] As for vengeance, British Prime Minister David Cameron was well-known for his 'visceral dislike' of Gaddafi and approved of colleagues who followed their 'heart' on the issue of intervention rather than 'their briefings'.[29] Indeed, around the Cabinet, Michael Gove was overcome with 'messianic zeal', according to a fellow minister.[30] Cameron called out the previous Labour governments for having 'undermined our standing in the world' by 'sucking up' to Gaddafi, and by his own admission, the Libyan leader's response to the uprising 'stirred something' in him, since '[t]o us, raised in the 1980s', 'he was "Mad Dog" Gaddafi' who had helped the IRA and ordered the Lockerbie bombing. 'Remember what Qadhafi did', Cameron insisted.[31] All of which is to suggest that vengeance, counter-productiveness, and misunderstandings of geopolitics were neither unique to an 'Arab mind' dynamic nor disconnected from Libya's global relations, relations that *included* the influence of the Anglosphere on Libyan policies and Gaddafi's perceptions. Judging from the information that has so far been made public, intelligence analysis did little to confront this question of Libya's international sociology.

In fact, the historical record of assessments suggests that intelligence was likely to have reinforced policy-makers' image of Gaddafi. CIA analysis of Gaddafi in the mid-1980s judged the

Libyan leader's 'behaviour in the international arena' to be 'erratic and often ill-informed'. They attribute this to the man's 'personal philosophy' whereby he sees himself 'leader and agent of historic forces' in 'Third World politics'. The CIA's Office of Near East-South Asia Analysis concluded that Gaddafi was carrying out terrorism abroad because of the 'strong psychological effect' on him of exile opposition to his rule, and that US responses to this terrorism only 'feed [his] ego, which delights in confrontation and attention'.[32] President Reagan certainly received this message, as the CIA made a 15-minute film presentation 'which substituted for a written psychological profile', in order 'to show the nature of the beast'. An aide later commented: 'If you saw [the presentation], there's little doubt that [Gaddafi] had to go', which was what Reagan then attempted by authorising psychological and covert operations.[33] This long-established assessment of Gaddafi's vengefulness on the basis of his vulnerable psychology would certainly not have challenged calls for intervention in 2011, despite Gaddafi having no history of mass civilian reprisals.

Crucially, the CIA had long thought of the relationship between Gaddafi and the populations of the Middle East in terms of showmanship and mutual psychological need (Figure 5.1). Graham Fuller, vice chairman of the National Intelligence Council in 1986, wrote to the director of central intelligence on the psychology of the Libyan regime. While '[w]e talk a great deal' about Gaddafi's estimated 'public support', having 'accurately' assessed that he 'has managed to alienate most segments of his country', Fuller argued that actually 'in Arab politics popularity is not really the main issue. In the Arab political mind the critical perception is how *strong* the leader is, how invulnerable he appears to attack'. Fuller thought this went in both directions: Arab populations want evidence of Gaddafi's invulnerability, while Gaddafi is 'obsessed' with preserving this psychological sense' and will want to 'parade Western impotence' if he survives any Anglosphere 'military action'.[34] Analysts saw a feedback loop between the regular Arab mind's need for a strong leader and Gaddafi's need for popular approval. This judgement of an inner Arab logic to Gaddafi's longevity was made shortly before the US began a bombing campaign against Libya, first to try to provoke a Libyan response as a pretext for more extensive bombings, and then to try to kill Gaddafi.[35] Indeed, previous US assassination attempts on the Libyan leader are not mentioned by Fuller as something that might over time shape Gaddafi's perceptions of his own insecu-

Libya's Qadhafi: Vulnerabilities and Prospects

An Intelligence

This paper was
Office of Near
coordinated wi
the National I

Comments and
directed to the *Antiregime demonstration by Libyan exiles*

whether to strike. He is no longer restrained by the prospect of assuming the chairmanship of the OAU, but he is still seriously isolated in Arab circles, worried about US intentions, and preoccupied with Chad.

With the exception of Maqaryaf's National Salvation Front, and perhaps the LLO, none of the groups seem to be thinking of operations within Libya—the only kind of activity likely to have a perceptible impact on the regime. Few claim much support inside the country, and it is not clear that such followers as they may possess have any access to Qadhafi or to sensitive installations. The exile movements, in addition, are split by rivalries that reflect the social, geographical, and ideological strains within Libyan society as a whole.

The exiles are not Qadhafi's only external headache; he sees himself in a hostile world, ringed by enemies—chief among them Israel and the United States. From the disposition of Libyan defenses, we know he is worried about the possibility of a US thrust from the Mediterranean or an Israeli air attack—probably against the nuclear reactor at Tajura. His confrontation with the United States in the Gulf of Sidra in August 1981, Washington's reaction on learning of Libyan plans to assassinate President Reagan, the recent US response to a threat against Sudan, and Israel's raid on the Iraqi nuclear reactor in June 1981 have combined to feed those fears.

9   Secret

Figure 5.1   Intelligence made much of the psychological relationship between Gaddafi and Libyans. Whether discussing manipulated masses or angry opponents, the emphasis was always on Gaddafi's hurt ego and Arab emotions. (CIA, 'Libya's Qadhafi: Vulnerabilities and Prospects', 1983: cover, p. 9)

rity. Libyan political judgements of the US's influence, meanwhile, are translated into a 'psychological [effect]' of 'Western action' on Libyans' 'perception of [Gaddafi's] strength'.[36] It is the inner Arab logic that is key.

Fuller's memorandum concludes that while Gaddafi 'probably is more certain with each passing incident that he is safe' – those incidents are not detailed – the 'good news' is that 'such calculation may cause him to overplay his hand'.[37] And that is exactly how policy-makers judged the situation in 2011. William Hague recalls that despite Britain 'urging [...] the Gaddafi regime to change course immediately', members of Gaddafi's family had been 'under a misapprehension' for years that 'friendly' Britain would 'intervene on [their] behalf when [they] are in trouble'. Liam Fox adds that media stories of Gaddafi 'seek[ing] imperial power's help to crush Islamist uprisings in the east' were 'bizarre', proving for him that 'they [in Gaddafi's government] were capable of making phenomenal miscalculations about the intent of the international community'.[38] Notably, this intent was put to the world in the kind of self-aggrandising terms that would fit Gaddafi's own delusions of grandeur as intelligence analysts saw it. During British debate on Libya, Prime Minister Cameron publicly called ongoing events in the Middle East 'one of those once in a generation opportunities, a moment when history turns a page'. He believed the Libya intervention disproved widespread resignation that 'Britain actually couldn't do something like that any more', that 'we're on a path of certain decline'. 'I'm here to tell you that it isn't true'.[39]

We will have to wait for further inquiries or disclosures of documents to fully understand the role of intelligence assessments of Gaddafi in the Libya intervention. The evidence presented so far, though, suggests that a post-colonial model of the Middle East as self-contained and uniquely irrational had long been applied to Libyan politics and was influencing contemporary judgement. None of the intelligence which was absorbed by policy-makers appears to have challenged a racialised view of Gaddafi's motivations – that his was just another blinkered, emotional Arab dictatorship, which did not understand how geopolitics was supposed to work.

THE SOCIAL TURN – AN ENDLESS CIRCLE

The Libyan uprising which eventually toppled Gaddafi was part of the wave of revolutionary movements known as the Arab Spring. If anything was going to be called an intelligence surprise after the absence of Iraqi WMD, it was this seismic shift in Middle Eastern and African politics. Within weeks of demonstrators ousting President Ben Ali in Tunisia, President Obama was reported to have expressed 'disappoint[ment] with the intelligence community' over its failure to predict the revolt – this was denied by the White House – while the chair of the Senate Intelligence Committee claimed that events in Egypt and Tunisia 'should not have come upon us with the surprise that they did', given the protesters had been using public social media to organise.[40] MI6 was reported to have predicted that Hosni Mubarak would survive the mass street protests against his government – in fact, Mubarak was gone within three weeks.[41] A year after the Arab Spring began, the deputy director of the US Defence Intelligence Agency stated that analysts had overlooked signs of 'growing dissatisfaction', how opposition to autocracies in the Middle East and North Africa was 'bubbling over'. In Britain, the Intelligence and Security Committee concluded that agencies produced too little intelligence on Middle East countries, and that at the very least the community should have anticipated how 'the unrest would spread so rapidly across the Arab world'.[42] It is now accepted as 'common wisdom' that 'almost no one had anticipated the Arab revolutions, not even those whose business is monitoring such events', including '[i]ntelligence agencies, political establishments and think tanks'.[43]

So what is supposed to have gone wrong? And what is the link to the story of intelligence told in previous chapters? Of course, the first thing to note is that if the Arab Spring is an intelligence failure, it is something different from Iraq's WMD. The latter was about assessing the threat of a state, while the Arab Spring was about anticipating a shift in the social politics of multiple countries, a wave of action on an unprecedented scale against governments that resembled Saddam Hussein's in their autocracy and repressiveness. Intelligence scholars acknowledge that even the strategic surprise literature overwhelmingly addresses state military attacks, not popular uprisings.[44] But like with Iraq, it is good to start by listening to what the intelligence agencies say about their role in events. Some of their defences have logical truth. 'Specific triggers for how and when instability will lead to the collapse of various regimes cannot always be known and predicted', said Director of National Intelligence James Clapper, since '[w]e are not clairvoyant'. MI6 Chief John Sawers agreed: '[W]e are not crystal ball gazers', he said, pointing out that '[t]here was not a secret in somebody's safe in Cairo saying the Arab Spring was going to start in January 2011'.[45] Just uncovering the right hidden fact was not going to cut it.

It was not the file in the safe that analysts believed they should focus on in future. Instead, it was something more ephemeral: the culture of those Middle East societies who had authoritarian governments. While CIA agents stationed abroad 'spend their time chasing terrorists or arms shipments', it is 'the political Islam desk' back in the US that tries to follow 'social and demographic trends'. Perhaps, a former officer speculated, 'we are too fixated on terrorism [...] and not enough on the broad generational changes in the region'.[46] Others insisted that intelligence analysts had been following 'simmering unrest in the region that was the result of changing economic, demographic, and political conditions' for decades. 'We could all see the fault lines in Arab societies', said Sawers; the problem was 'predict[ing] when the earthquake would strike'.[47] Britain's Foreign Affairs Committee acknowledged that predicting the protests' timing was an unreasonable expectation. The committee nonetheless argued that the Foreign Office should have had closer contacts with intellectuals and civil society groups, in order to 'understand better [these] societies'. In testimony to the committee, former UN Deputy Secretary General and then Minister Mark Malloch Brown expressed the belief that Britain had lost 'its previous Arabist "touch and feel" for the region', with small embassy teams being unable to 'dig down deep enough'.[48]

This was the first link with Iraq: Once again, intelligence was asked to reinforce its knowledge of Arab societies and cultures. Chilcot's Inquiry concluded that Britain's post-invasion role in Iraq was hampered by a lack of intelligence on Iraq's 'political, cultural and ethnic background, and the state of society'. Former JIC Chair

John Scarlett had stated that analysts were aware of 'the fragility of the country and in particular the ethnic tensions' before the invasion, but that '[t]here wasn't a very detailed understanding or set of knowledge available.'[49] After the Arab Spring, intelligence scholars Uri Bar-Joseph and Rose McDermott pinned the 'failure to correctly estimate' these events on intelligence's 'lack of intimate understanding of foreign cultures.'[50] The mention of intimacy brings to mind CIA analyst William Tidwell's claim decades earlier that agents needed to get over their discomfort and integrate into non-Western parts of the world (Chapter 2). Fellow intelligence scholar Rotem Dvir has argued persuasively that the issue with popular uprisings is not the lack of information on when one event will spark a cascade of others, but that indicators of civilian unrest, from symbolic acts to demonstrations and riots, are generally not considered relevant for assessing the security situation in a country.[51] Again, recall analyst George Caldwell's argument in 1985 that analysts needed to look out for the erosion of political authority (Chapter 1). Three decades later, the conclusion was that analysts were still failing to keep up with countries' cultures.

This charge that intelligence needs more of a sociological, anthropological focus has found a receptive audience, similar to the way that mirror-imaging has been accepted as an important problem to overcome. In both cases, intelligence gaps are confronted through appeals to greater cultural sensitivity. But like the mirror-image concept, this idea of a 'social turn' in intelligence carries less progressive implications. For a start, echoes of past intelligence discussions should raise suspicions. As this book has argued, society and culture have *not* been overlooked in intelligence analysis of the Middle East and elsewhere. Analysts have constantly made arguments about how people in that part of the world behave and the roots of their behaviour in political education, emotion and religious sectarianism. In fact, there is evidence that intelligence organisations *did* warn policy-makers before the Arab Spring about the present conditions for mass rebellions. In the summer of 2010, President Obama commissioned a report on the potential for social unrest in the Middle East. In his memoirs, Obama states that this report was written by a National Security Council panel which held biweekly meetings with 'veteran diplomats and experts,' many of whom were 'predictably sceptical of the need for any change to US policy'. The panel's relationship with the intelligence services themselves remains unclear, although Obama argued at the time that '[w]e'd have to get buy-in from the Pentagon and the intel folks'. The report assessed four countries, most likely Jordan, Egypt, Bahrain, and Yemen, and concluded that Arab leaders' refusal to accept 'sweeping political changes' was making these countries 'ripe for popular revolt'.[52] Across the shore, Rubén Arcos and José-Miguel Palacios have written of a 2007 intelligence assessment by the European Union's Single Intelligence Analysis Capacity, which rejected the 'facade of apparent solidity [of] most regimes in the region' and argued that unrest in Egypt, Iran, Jordan, Saudi Arabia or Syria could 'easily spread from one country to another and rapidly take on a regional nature'. The assessment certainly predicted how the Arab Spring would cascade.[53]

It is the debate which took place around these warnings that points to the true significance of today's social turn. US officials told the *New York Times* that the 2010 report 'grapples with a problem that has bedevilled the White House's approach toward Egypt and other countries in recent days: how to balance American strategic interests and the desire to avert broader instability against the democratic demands of the protesters'. Intelligence analysis, in other words, had once again set itself the mission of analysing the world *through* the strategic aim of maintaining the region's alignment with US influence and policies. According to those involved in writing it, the report was a prompt for considering how to 'push for political change in countries with autocratic rulers *who are also valuable allies of the United States*'.[54] According to Obama, the report identified 'the United States' uncritical support of authoritarian regimes' as 'adversely affect[ing]' the 'US interests in stability across the Middle East and North Africa'. As with the January 2003 reflections by John Scarlett, this represents a moment of self-awareness. NSC analysts and policy-makers could glimpse the contradiction between keeping the Middle East oriented towards Anglosphere objectives, using a US-backed chain of autocrats, and growing popular dissatisfaction with those authoritarian governments and their policy priorities. But the policy conclusion was drawn quickly and narrowly: Obama planned that officials would

offer incentives to these governments in exchange for 'liberalis-
ing political and civic life', in order that those governments '*might
avoid* the destabilising uprisings, violence, chaos, and unpredictable outcomes that so often accompanied sudden change'. This aim
chimed with what experts told the NSC panel, that 'as unsavoury as
some of our Arab allies might be, the status quo served America's
core interests – something that wasn't guaranteed if *more populist
governments* took their place'.[55] The problem was not the support
of these autocrats; it was just that the US had not encouraged them
enough to placate popular opposition.

Even the historical awareness of the NSC panel speaks to this
disinterest in the international sociology of Middle East protest.
Obama reportedly pressed his advisers to 'study popular uprisings
in Latin America, Eastern Europe and Southeast Asia', in order to
figure out 'which ones worked and which did not'. Obama had in
mind 'Indonesia, where he spent several years as a child, which
ousted its longtime leader, Suharto, in 1998'.[56] It is a striking historical antecedent. President Suharto gave way to his vice-president
after more than three decades as president, having taken power
in 1965 through a military coup that involved 'one of the worst
mass murders of the twentieth century', according to the CIA.
This coup, along with Suharto's brutal, terrorising years in office,
were successful thanks to extensive US diplomatic and military
support, rationalised as a way to prevent a peasant-led revolution
opposed to US oil investors.[57] Indonesia's invasion and occupation
of East Timor in 1974, killing tens of thousands using US-supplied
military equipment, was long supported privately and then diplomatically by the US, despite the latter's leverage over Suharto.
While US consulate intelligence reported that the East Timorese
were strongly opposed to incorporation by Indonesia and wanted
self-determination, US and British analysts reasoned that the population were not ready for self-governance and that East Timor's
integration into Indonesia better suited 'regional stability'.[58]
Obama's chosen example, then, contained the same contradiction
that unfolded in 2010 over support for Middle Eastern authoritarian governments. Analysts struggled to reconcile interest in
knowledge of popular political opinion with a self-prescribed
purpose of helping to maintain the Anglosphere's influence and

power-position in the region. A focus on cultural life and social trends would only compound that contradiction if it risked revealing that those affected by US policy decisions in the so-called non-Western world were opposed to US priorities.

Yet this social turn remains a key proposition in discussion of improving intelligence: from proposals to combine massive social media datasets with social and cultural knowledge, in order to avoid future surprises like the Arab Spring; to methods for sensing behaviour and then constructing 'culturally-relevant mental models of another culture' over time.[59] Regardless of the individual merits of these proposals in terms of overcoming individual prejudice and challenging assumptions about social trends, the turn to cultural knowledge will confront the same three problems: one, that intelligence has two contradictory aims, of accurately understanding the world and of maintaining Anglosphere privilege; two, that the image of the Middle East as a self-contained equilibrium masks the negative role of Anglosphere power-projection; and three, that the idea of a mirror-imaging fallacy reduces the causes of others' political behaviour to an essentially different mind and culture. President Obama did not refer to Hosni Mubarak as 'an ally of ours' and 'very helpful' to the US, while warning Egyptian protesters not to violently resist their government's brutal security forces, because he received inaccurate assessments of Egyptian society. Nor was bad intel on culture the reason why Prime Minister Cameron allowed members of the former Egyptian Government to retain millions of pounds worth of property and business assets in Britain, an act of 'pure political profiteering' according to a lead Egyptian investigator into the siphoned funds.[60] Intelligence reinforced longstanding strategic principles on the Anglosphere's role in the world. As a result, it is more than likely that mass opposition to authoritarian state rulers and their US–British backers (Figure 5.2) – a form of popular geopolitical knowledge expressed in placards, chants, and protest songs at Cairo's Tahrir Square[61] – would never be able to overcome analysts' intellectual commitment to stabilising Anglosphere influence throughout and beyond the uprisings.

Indeed, a decade after the Arab Spring and two decades after intelligence analysts debated military action against Iraq, the

Figure 5.2   Protesters call for the US to end support for Hosni Mubarak during a solidarity march to the UN Plaza in San Francisco, 29 January 2011 (Steve Rhodes/Flickr, CC BY-NC-ND 2.0). Protesters in Egypt made the same demand.

equally momentous Russian invasion of Ukraine hints at the limits of intelligence's ability to 'turn' its gaze on the social world of other countries. On 21 July 2022, MI6 Chief Richard Moore commented publicly that Russian intelligence 'clearly *completely* misunderstood Ukrainian nationalism; they completely underestimated the degree of resistance that the Russian military would face'. Independent analysts agree that Russia 'undervalued Ukraine's social cohesion', a cohesion fostered institutionally since Ukraine's independence in 1991. This more recent 'civic culture' of 'societal unity' had stopped Russia from 'exploit[ing] fault lines' to gain local support.[62] It is not clear, however, that Ukraine's current international supporters had analysed the country any better. In May 2022, the US intelligence community was reported to be conducting an internal review after its agencies had underestimated the Ukrainian military's staying power and 'will to fight', with only one agency having accounted for the strength of feeling of opinion polls in eastern Ukraine.[63]

What is more significant than a common intelligence failure across Russia and the Anglosphere is how one of those sides is interpreting that shared failure. In the same July address, Richard

Moore prefaced his explanation of Russian intelligence's woes by saying that 'intelligence services reflect the societies they serve': 'I am answerable to democratically elected ministers, I'm answerable to parliamentarians, I'm answerable to judges'; 'It's a rather different system in Russia'. Specifically, '[o]ne thing that doesn't pay is to speak truth to power'.[64] Given that both Russia and the Anglosphere had failed to predict Ukrainian society's convergence around military resistance, this comparison between British parliamentary democracy and Russian autocracy does not necessarily prove that British society's institutions encourage better knowledge and awareness of the outside world. But what the comparison does do is trace Russia's bad war-making to an inferior state system, just as intelligence analysis in the twentieth century pinned Soviet policy on Russia's violent totalitarian history (Chapter 2). This argument is not so far from historical Orientalist accounts of a backward, despotic Eastern Europe whose worst qualities were fostered by the former Russian Empire.[65]

That historical echo may also help explain the Anglosphere's underestimation of Ukrainian resistance to Russia. Political scholarship on Eastern Europe has traditionally ignored the idea of Ukrainians' and Eastern Europeans' ability to sway geopolitical events, in favour of assuming that this region is simply acted upon and socially determined by Russian imperialism and US 'containment' policies. This denial of Eastern European abilities runs back to the long racialisation of the region's populations, as their language and customs became markers of inferior cultures.[66] Richard Moore hints at a wider angle to this story when he compares the number of Russian soldiers killed in Ukraine to Russia's 'ten years in Afghanistan in the 1980s'.[67] Former CIA agent Bruce Riedel, who helped to arm the guerrilla mujahideen groups in Afghanistan during the 1980s, has said that just as 'the Russians underestimated the Afghans', '[t]hey seem to have underestimated the Ukrainians today'.[68] Afghanistan seems to be the Anglosphere's preferred model for resistance in Ukraine: The extensive weapons being supplied to Ukraine has been compared to the arming of Afghanistan's mujahideen against the Soviets. Riedel argues that 'the role that Biden and company envision for the US' in Ukraine is to once again be 'quartermaster of the war', as it was in 1980s

Afghanistan.[69] But in both cases, mythic images of Easterners' emotive heroism mask a danger – fulfilled in Afghanistan, possible in Ukraine – that analysts overestimate their ability to corral and control the well-armed groups that come out of the war.[70] Indeed, historian Elisabeth Leake has demonstrated that the CIA underestimated the religious-political thought of the mujahideen and their unifying power once the Soviets would leave, having interpreted Afghanistan as a timeless tribal society and thereby ignored its changing social dynamics.[71] Those armed groups in Ukraine may similarly not agree to their region being acted upon once again.

Finally, the story of an intelligence success in predicting Putin's attack and thereby uniting the Western world against him may once more misread dramatic changes in the post-colonial world. Much has been made of how Russia's invasion has rallied many countries behind US and European geopolitical strategy. James Landale of the BBC has argued that whereas recently 'liberal democracies [were] uncertain of their focus and future', often 'question[ing] their alliances', war in Ukraine 'has reminded the West of what it represents – freedom, sovereignty and the rule of law', 'produc[ing] a united response to Russia's aggression'. Putin, says *The Atlantic*, has 'Accidentally Revitalised the West's Liberal Order'.[72] Intelligence has had a role to play here: Officials and analysts have told news outlets that declassifying intelligence is 'partly designed to shore up that Western unity'.[73] MI6 Chief Richard Moore echoes the sentiment: 'NATO has proved extraordinarily united in the face of [Russia's aggression]', with 'tectonic plates shifting in European security' towards greater and more widespread coherence, including Sweden and Finland joining the alliance.[74]

But that assessment of unity masks a larger trend: States across Asia, Africa, Latin America, and the oceans' islands are distancing themselves from *both* Russian imperialism *and* the Anglosphere's strategy in response. Beyond North America and Europe, few countries joined in the early sanctions policy against Russia. Indonesia's foreign ministry cautioned against 'blindly follow[ing] the steps taken by another country', while Argentina's foreign minister dismissed sanctions' ability to push actors towards 'a frank dialogue table that serves to save lives'.[75] A vote on 7 April 2022 to eject

Russia from the UN Human Rights Council saw 93 states in favour, 24 against, and 58 abstentions, with many smaller states wary of cutting off diplomatic and trade links with large parts of the world – especially with spiralling food and energy prices – by endorsing a US or Russian perspective.[76] Many of the governments which have abstained from votes such as these, 'governments representing a majority of the human population', have explained that they do not have the privilege of choosing to cut off desperately needed supply chains, not when they import huge amounts of the staple foods which their populations spend most of their income on. Nor do all states see punitive action against Russia as an upholding of sovereignty or the rule of law, not when Anglosphere states escape impunity for their own past crimes.[77]

Will US and British intelligence analysts face these post-colonial states' arguments head-on? Will they try to examine what a policy of 'bleeding Russia dry', that is, providing just enough arms to Ukraine to prolong the war – echoing US National Security Adviser Zbigniew Brzezinski's strategy towards the Soviets in Afghanistan – will do to the rest of the world's lives, livelihoods and then global political dynamics?[78] Or will these analysts dismiss a new non-alignment trend as ignorant cowardice, a reflection that the majority of the world's states are incapable of understanding geopolitics and of leading in international affairs, as agencies concluded in the 1950s and 1960s (Chapter 2)? The very public declassifications during this war have not yet given us an answer. Perhaps, in time, they will.

BEYOND ABOLITION

Is there a solution to this intelligence conundrum, this intellectual barrier against expressions from the post-colonial world that challenge the validity of Anglosphere supremacy? When those sceptical of state power confront the intelligence services, their usual solutions are to either better scrutinise these agencies or to abolish them altogether. Both ideas sit on a continuum of rearranging the pieces of the state security apparatus – at the milder end, add in an oversight committee here or there; at the headier end, remove the offending part of the bureaucracy – and both

therefore retain the standard view of the state intelligence relationship discussed in the Introduction. Critical debate over what to
do about intelligence nearly always rests on the assumption that
agencies' danger lies in their autonomous excess. They have grown
too large; they do things far beyond their intended function – they
are out of control.

Consider the most famous call for abolition in recent history,
US Senator Daniel Moynihan's long campaign against the CIA. It
is in the US that abolition has had the widest hearing – Robert
Jervis notes that while US intelligence has always been a conve-
nient scapegoat for politicians of all stripes, British elite scrutiny
of its secret services is much more cordial, much more Old Boys'
Club.[79] Moynihan, by contrast, is known for his legislative efforts
in 1991 and 1995 to have the CIA disbanded. The content of his
proposed legislation, however, was to move intelligence work under
the remit of the State Department. As critics retorted, Moynihan
did not explicitly explain how this shuffle would improve intelligence performance, especially on politicisation.[80] Moynihan's
one criticism that got most public attention was that the agency
had gained too much political strength over decades and was
now hampering post-Cold War US foreign policy. In Congressional committees and in his book *Secrecy*, he judged that the CIA
was 'an information-gathering organisation that had *lost its way*
and succumbed to the lure of audacious, but invariably disastrous,
covert operations'.[81] Moynihan, who was certainly no anti-security
progressive, wanted above all to preserve the US state's sovereignty
over planning geopolitics: In his address to Congress proposing his
1995 bill, he emphasised that the State Department 'must function
as the primary agency in formulating and conducting foreign
policy'.[82] The problem for him, then, was that the CIA had too
much bureaucratic power, in league with presidents or not, and its
secrecy let it get away with it.

But Moynihan's story of intelligence gets more complicated
around his other major criticism: that in his view, '[f]or a quarter
century, the CIA has been repeatedly wrong about the major
political and economic questions entrusted to its analysis'. His
primary example was of the CIA overestimating the Soviet Union's
economic sustainability. The closest Moynihan comes to an organ-

isational solution to bad analysis is his idea that intelligence agencies' lack of transparency breeds their own insularity and ignorance: In his words, secrecy 'causes hardening of the arteries of the mind. It hinders true scholarship and hides mistakes'.[83] This argument has an ironic predecessor: It was those analysts tasked with scrutinising the behaviour of so-called Arab regimes who also blamed secrecy for their targets' supposed lack of international skill. By turning the accusation against the US, however, Moynihan reached the limits of a bureaucratic critique of intelligence. Like the Arabists and Sovietologists before him, Moynihan traced the failure to inwardness and thereby cut intelligence off from the world that made it, that shaped its outlook and fed in turn on its ideas. The social life of intelligence was reduced to the closed doors of Langley headquarters. Transparency might stop insularity but it does not necessarily produce clarity: Moynihan belittled intelligence expertise by pointing out that the CIA's Soviet misperception 'was the conventional wisdom among economists, generally', leaving it unclear, at least by his own logic, how greater openness would have avoided the error.[84] But inadvertently, then, Moynihan's criticisms raises the question of how intelligence analysis relates to the wider world.

This book has argued that intelligence's importance for the Anglosphere is not bureaucratic but a matter of shared imagination. Intelligence analysis has provided policy-makers with a way of understanding the revolutionary changes of the post-war, post-colonial world in a way that preserved the legitimacy of the few states that still dominated the rest. Analysts looked out at the preponderance of US–British possessions and influence in the world. They concluded that their purpose now was to figure out how all of it could be preserved. This analytical focus was both shaped by and in turn re-made assumptions about racial inequality, the global colour line between a minority of colonial states and the majority of the world's non-white population. With this combination of political focus and racial assumptions, geopolitics started to look like it *needed* the Anglosphere to remain supreme, in order to secure something called stability. Analysis made certain ways of holding on to supremacy seem possible, and acceptable. These possibilities evolved through the tumultuous post-war period of decolonisation, across the diplomatic and military conflicts of the so-called Cold War, and up to the post-9/11 priority of disciplining unruly Arab autocracies. Intelligence has worked to keep the *political identity* of Anglosphere states, in symbiosis with international hierarchies, from falling apart in the face of resistance to these states' dominance.

From this perspective, the concept of intelligence failure – the idea that agencies are best judged in terms of whether they really are any good at discovering the truth of current events – has been beneficial rather than damaging to the geopolitical status quo.[85] If intelligence analysis is about re-telling and adapting stories of the state's place in the world, then from a policy-maker's perspective, intelligence fails not simply when it is inaccurate but when it does not play a useful enough role in securing the state's presumed position in international relations. The details of that failure – misreading another government's plans, underestimating missile numbers, even being too pessimistic about the future – are less important than the untouched implication that the world out there, with those hard-to-read plans and missiles and good fortunes, is self-defined and unchanging, something we simply find as it is – and where it just so happens that the analyst's state is already on top. Categorising an event as a failure is a way of reasserting the taken-for-granted legitimacy of the world and of that position. What the category of failure leaves unspoken, then, is that successful intelligence would preserve current international hierarchies.

Dissenting from Anglosphere foreign policy aims means asking what role intelligence analysis plays in allowing statespersons to think that those aims are possible and justifiable. Any attempt by dissenters to use the failure category as a mode of critique will struggle to avoid debating whether there were better ways for intelligence to secure British or US geopolitical status in this or that situation. Failing at something, after all, implies a worthy objective. Consider how public debate in the decades after the invasion of Iraq has sought to find 'lessons' from this intelligence failure. When the Iraq Inquiry was launched in 2009, John Chilcot explained that it would produce 'lessons [which] will help ensure that, *if we face similar situations in future*, the government of the day is best equipped to respond to those situations in the most effective manner *in the best interests of the country*.[86] For such a momentous event as the Iraq War, this mission is quite a vague commitment. What situation is being singled out here – a non-existent threat from a Middle Eastern regime? A prime minister willing to prosecute war before diplomatic options have been exhausted? The reader is left to decide. But the refrain of 'lessons for next time' expresses adamantly that Britain and the US have a right to consider military interventions in the Middle East. On the day Chilcot's report was released, a BBC *Newsnight* panel drew the lesson that 'given the state' of 'a very complicated country like Iraq' at the time, 'you would have needed a total occupation of Iraq' to bring about the desired new government. The future objective for politicians should therefore be to 'regain [public] trust', 'if we are to do [a military intervention] again'.[87]

British interests, though, were carefully prescribed in post-Chilcot discussion. The inquiry's report concludes that while the idea of Iraq passing on WMD to terrorists was not supported in intelligence assessments, the intelligence services had warned Tony Blair of the increased potential for international terrorism should Britain and the US invade. Subsequent statements from security and intelligence officials concur that this is exactly what happened.[88] But there has been no suggestion that the Anglosphere should therefore reduce its political–military–economic footprint in the Middle East and cede decision-making about security to others. When asked on *Newsnight* what the British public should think about the intelligence failure as documented by Chilcot, David Omand, who was Government Communication Headquarters director and a JIC member at the time of the invasion, responded that the public should acknowledge intelligence's role in thwarting several unnamed terrorist plots in Britain over the last 18 months.[89] An increased threat, yes, but at least the services were keeping a lid on them. US debate is even narrower: A recent 'net assessment' of the 'War on Terror', by two experts on grand strategy, concludes that the US 'has mostly achieved its fundamental strategic objective', namely to protect itself from terrorist attacks, albeit with a 'major humanitarian travesty' in Iraq. They acknowledge that 'the problems of Salafist violence and regional instability are significantly worse', partly because the invasion of Iraq 'inflam[ed] anti-Americanism' and turned that country 'into a training ground for the next generation of zealots'. This constitutes 'a strategic danger given American interests in the Middle East'. As a solution, they propose 'maintaining numerous regional footholds with military and intelligence capabilities' while 'empower[ing] committed local forces'.[90] Again, intelligence on a self-inflicted increase in terrorism does not challenge the wisdom or legitimacy of deciding how the Middle East should be organised.

Finally, what about the parts of those pre-invasion reports that are not accused of having come out of pressure or manipulation? No one has questioned why the intelligence community insisted that Saddam Hussein was motivated by a childish anti-Western hatred. No one has criticised analysts for assessing that Saddam was irrational. If the Iraq intelligence had been successful rather than a failure, these ideas would still have remained. This is the other success of intelligence failure, that the concept fits so easily within the racial thinking of intelligence analysts about geopolitics and other states' obscure cultures that it turns attention away from the validity of those assumptions. That is about more than over-emphasising capabilities or overlooking intentions. It is about the stories officials tell themselves and others of what their own country and other societies represent in the world.

Instead of basing dissent around the concept of failure, it is more fruitful to consider Patrick Moynihan's much earlier thoughts on intelligence analysis, decades before his famous legislative bouts. As detailed by Paul McGarr, during Moynihan's tenure as ambassador to India in the 1970s, he came to view CIA operations in Asia as only intensifying popular opposition to US influence. Not only did covert action tend to leak out and embolden popular anti-imperialism, but the CIA seemed uninterested in challenging its own assumptions or its arrogance – 'in a year of trying to get [the CIA] to *think* about Indian Communism for me, they have not been able to do so'.[91] Moynihan saw a blowback effect, where CIA beliefs and actions ended up fuelling further Indian paranoia about US motives. Those who want to dissent from British and US geopolitics should approach intelligence analysis with this kind of arrogance and blowback in mind. Even when intelligence highlights possible blowback, as in the Iraq invasion's contribution to terrorism, their self-ascribed purpose and belief in the danger of mirror-imaging will stop that blowback from forcing a fundamental rethink of the arrogance. This is a view of the world shaped by and contributing to ideologies of racial inequality. Regional cultures just do not understand the Anglosphere's actions. The colour line, which is propped up by intelligence analysis, is immovable because of others' faulty geopolitical sense. Dissenting from intelligence has to mean breaking this racist conviction.

Looking out from Moynihan's position in India, if we want to break that conviction, one appropriate abolitionist source is actually once again W. E. B. Du Bois. Du Bois' idea of the colour line running down the middle of the twentieth century was inspired by his historical appreciation for the role of slavery's abolition in revolutionary anti-colonialism. Abolitionism was not just about respectable liberal calls for citizenship. It was also led by slave runaways, international revolts and declarations of independence, which segued into anti-colonial uprisings. With slavery having financed early European imperialism, these revolts and independence movements opposed the appropriation of land from indigenous communities. Moreover, slavery's abolition in Britain and the US was followed by reinvigorated colonialism that produced the global colour line, including the material inequality of the world. For Du Bois, therefore, anti-colonialism in the twentieth century needed to finish the work that abolitionism had started.[92] This is how we should define intelligence abolition: not as removing an organisational arm of the state, but as following the lead of contemporary anti-colonial revolt by challenging the intellectual defences of the global colour line.

And what does that revolt sound like? People judged by analysts to be ignorant, emotional, and illogical are just as capable of assessing geopolitics as well as what Britain and the US should do in response – as indeed they do, as they expressed during the Arab Spring, and as indeed polling repeatedly demonstrates. A 2018 poll by the Arab Opinion Index across eleven countries in the Middle East and North Africa found that 75% of citizens saw Israel and the United States as the biggest threats to their own national security. Lest this be seen as xenophobic Arab conservatism, 76% also said that democracy was the most appropriate system of governance for their country.[93] In 2020, a YouGov poll across 18 MENA countries dared to ask respondents what *they* thought was the most critical issue facing the United States. The most popular answer, at 32%, was white nationalism. Radical Islamic terrorism was down at 5%.[94] It does not take an analytical genius to cross-reference these views and make a reasonable recommendation about future Anglosphere policy. If the assessments of intelligence agencies get in the way of thinking this through, the answer is not simply those agencies' abolition. The answer is challenging the wider shared political assumptions that undergird agencies' analysis, which ultimately means challenging the right of some states to retain their inherited advantage and to use it to dictate the destinies of others.

Notes

INTRODUCTION

1. Mark Trevelyan, 'Russia Declares Expanded War Goals Beyond Ukraine's Donbas'. *Reuters*, 20 July 2022. www.reuters.com/world/europe/lavrov-says-russias-objectives-ukraine-now-go-beyond-donbas-2022-07-20.
2. Rebecca Kheel, 'Despite Having Misjudged Russia's "Hollow Force", Intelligence Officials Say Putin Is Still an "Evolving" Threat', *Military.com*, 10 May 2022. www.military.com/daily-news/2022/05/10/despite-having-misjudged-russias-hollow-force-intelligence-officials-say-putin-still-evolving-threat.html.
3. Henry Foy and John Paul Rathbone, 'Intelligence Failures Hamper Russia's Ukraine Mission', *Financial Times*, 1 March 2022. www.ft.com/content/ba440d90-b0ba-4a73-a138-9cb1229b6cac; Mia Jankowicz, 'Putin Purged Large Numbers of FSB Agents in Retribution for Poor Ukraine Intelligence, Russia Expert Says', *Business Insider* 12 April 2022. www.businessinsider.com/putin-purges-fsb-over-ukraine-failures-bellingcat-expert-2022-4.
4. Stephen Collinson, 'Western Spy Agencies Weaponize Intelligence in Attempt to Undermine Putin', *CNN*, 1 April 2022. https://edition.cnn.com/2022/04/01/politics/western-spy-agencies-intelligence-putin-ukraine-war/index.html; Dan Sabbagh, 'Why is GCHQ Saying Putin Has Been Misinformed About Ukraine War?', *The Guardian*, 31 March 2022. www.theguardian.com/world/2022/mar/31/why-is-gchq-saying-putin-has-been-misinformed-about-ukraine-war.
5. Raffaello Pantucci, 'Western Intelligence Was Mocked After Iraq. With Ukraine, it Has Redeemed itself', *The Telegraph*, 24 February 2022. www.telegraph.co.uk/world-news/2022/02/24/western-intelligence-mocked-iraq-ukraine-has-redeemed.
6. Neveen Shaaban Abdalla, Philip H. J. Davies, Kristian Gustafson, Dan Lomas, and Steven Wagner, 'Intelligence and the War in Ukraine: Part 1', *War on the Rocks*, 11 May 2022. warontherocks.com/2022/05/intelligence-and-the-war-in-ukraine-part-1.
7. Zach Dorfman, 'CIA applies Lessons From Iraq 'Debacle' in Information Battle Over Russian Invasion of Ukraine', *Yahoo! News*, 23 March 2022. https://news.yahoo.com/cia-applies-lessons-from-iraq-debacle-in-information-battle-over-russian-invasion-of-ukraine-090001168.html.
8. Abdalla et al., 'Intelligence and the War in Ukraine'.

9. Mark M. Lowenthal and Ronald A. Marks, 'Intelligence Analysis: Is It As Good As It Gets?'. *International Journal of Intelligence and CounterIntelligence*, 28:4 (2015): p. 663.
10. Mark A. Jensen, 'Intelligence Failures: What Are They Really and What Do We Do about Them?' *Intelligence and National Security*, 27:2 (2012): pp. 263, 274–278.
11. Abdalla et al., 'Intelligence and the War in Ukraine'. Original emphasis.
12. Amy Mackinnon, 'Has Putin Lost the Plot?', *Foreign Policy*, 4 March 2022. https://foreignpolicy.com/2022/03/04/putin-mental-state-russia-ukraine-future-actions-predictions; Quint Forgey and Alexander Ward, 'Avril Haines Gets Inside Putin's Head', *Politico*, 8 March 2022. www.politico.com/newsletters/national-security-daily/2022/03/08/avril-haines-gets-inside-putins-head-00015278.
13. Abdalla et al., 'Intelligence and the War in Ukraine'.
14. Mackinnon, 'Has Putin Lost the Plot?'
15. Katie Bo Lillis, 'Top US Spy Chief Says War In Ukraine Will Likely Become "More Unpredictable and Escalatory"', *CNN*, 10 May 2022. https://edition.cnn.com/2022/05/10/politics/haines-ukraine-russia-hearing/index.html.
16. Gordon Corera, 'Ukraine War: Western Agents Seek to Get Inside Putin's Head', *BBC News*, 20 March 2022. www.bbc.com/news/world-europe-60807134.
17. Jack Holmes, 'Is Putin Crazy? Or Did He Just Get Some Bad Intel?', *Esquire*, 9 March 2022. www.esquire.com/news-politics/a39376114/is-putin-crazy-or-bad-intel.
18. Dan Sabbagh, 'Why is GCHQ Saying'; Collinson, 'Western Spy Agencies'.
19. 'Secret Intelligence Has Unusually Public Role in Ukraine War', *Associated Press*, 3 April 2022. https://economictimes.indiatimes.com/news/defence/secret-intelligence-has-unusually-public-role-in-ukraine-war; Corera, 'Ukraine War'.
20. 'Iraq Body Count', n.d. www.iraqbodycount.org.
21. Lily Hamourtziadou and Bülent Gökay, 'The Deadly Legacy of 20 Years of US "War on Terror" in Iraq', *Open Democracy*, 10 September 2021. www.opendemocracy.net/en/north-africa-west-asia/the-impact-of-the-war-on-terror-on-iraq-state-economy-and-civilian-deaths.
22. Marina Calculli, 'Middle East Security: The Politics of Violence after the 2003 Iraq War'. In Louise Fawcett (ed.), *International Relations of the Middle East*, fifth edition (Oxford: Oxford University Press, 2019): pp. 226–245.
23. Judith Betts and Mark Pythian, *The Iraq War and Democratic Governance: Britain and Australia go to War* (London: Palgrave Macmillan, 2020): pp. 120–140.
24. Public Administration and Constitutional Affairs Committee, *Lessons still to be learned from the Chilcot Inquiry* (London: House of Commons, 2017): p. 7.

25. Quoted in PACAC, *Lessons Still to be Learned from the Chilcot Inquiry*: p. 6.
26. Bill Rolston and Phil Scraton, 'In the Full Glare of English Politics: Ireland, Inquiries and the British State'. *British Journal of Criminology*, 45 (2005): pp. 551–553.
27. Quoted in Betts and Pythian, *The Iraq War and Democratic Governance*: pp. 140–141.
28. Joshua Rovner, *Fixing the Facts: National Security and the Politics of Intelligence* (London: Cornell University Press, 2011): pp. 137–139.
29. The most sophisticated of this latter category is Mark Pythian, 'Intelligence Failure as a Mutually Reinforcing Politico-Intelligence Dynamic: The Chilcot Report and the Nature of the Iraq WMD Intelligence Failure'. *British Yearbook of International Law*, 87:1 (2017): pp. 196–215.
30. Richard Aldrich, 'Whitehall and the Iraq War: the UK's Four Intelligence Enquiries'. *Irish Studies in International Affairs*, 16 (2005): pp. 73–88; Rovner, *Fixing the Facts*: p. 139.
31. Alan Doig, '45 Minutes of Infamy? Hutton, Blair and the invasion of Iraq'. *Parliamentary Affairs*, 58:1 (2005): pp. 109–123; Eunan O'Haplin, 'British Intelligence and the Case for Confronting Iraq: Evidence from the Butler and Hutton Reports'. *Irish Studies in International Affairs*, 16 (2005): pp. 89–102.
32. Steven Kettell, 'Who's Afraid of Saddam Hussein? Re-examining the "September Dossier" Affair'. *Contemporary British History*, 22:3 (2008): pp. 407–426.
33. Piers Robinson, 'Learning from the Chilcot report: Propaganda, Deception and the "War on Terror"'. *International Journal of Contemporary Iraqi Studies*, 11:1–2 (2017): pp. 47–73.
34. Alistair Campbell, 'Now Chilcot Says it Too: We Did Not 'Sex Up' Intelligence in the WMD Dossier', *The Guardian*, 6 July 2016. www.theguardian.com/commentisfree/2016/jul/06/chilcot-we-did-not-sex-up-wmd-dossier.
35. Quoted in PACAC, *Lessons Still to be Learned from the Chilcot Inquiry*: p. 6.
36. Owen Thomas, 'Good Faith and (Dis)Honest Mistakes? Learning from Britain's Iraq War Inquiry'. *Politics*, 37:4 (2017): pp. 375–378.
37. Anna Stavrianakis, 'Searching for the Smoking Gun? Methodology and Modes of Critique in the Arms Trade'. In Mariene de Goede, Esmé Bosma and Polly Pallister-Wilkins (eds.), *Secrecy and Methods in Security Research: A Guide to Qualitative Fieldwork* (London: Routledge, 2020): p. 240.
38. Simon Jenkins, 'A Very British Inquiry: A Chat in a Whitehall Club'. *The Guardian*, 8 December 2009. www.theguardian.com/uk/2009/dec/08/chilcot-inquiry-john-scarlett.

39. David Meadows, 'Latin Intelligence?' *rogueclassicism*, 20 January 2011. https://rogueclassicism.com/2011/01/20/latin-intelligence.

40. Thomas, 'Good Faith and (Dis)Honest Mistakes?': pp. 373–375.

41. Thomas, 'Good Faith and (dis)Honest Mistakes?': p. 378.

42. A recent argument of the CIA's unaccountable power is Elizabeth Goitein, 'How the CIA Is Acting Outside the Law to Spy on Americans', *Brennan Center for Justice*, 15 February 2022. www.brennancenter.org/our-work/analysis-opinion/how-cia-acting-outside-law-spy-americans. An influential example of the private army critique is Chalmers Johnson, *The Sorrows of Empire: Militarism, Secrecy, and the End of the Republic* (London: Macmillan, 2007): p. 11.

43. Peter Gill, 'Thinking about Intelligence Within, Without, and Beyond the State'. *All Azimuth*, 3:2 (2014): p. 13; Len Scott and R. Gerald Hughes, 'Intelligence, Crises and Security: Lessons from History?'. *Intelligence and National Security*, 21:5 (2006): p. 663.

44. Glenn Greenwald, *No Place to Hide: Edward Snowden, the NSA, and the US surveillance state* (London: Hamish Hamilton, 2014); Geoff Martin and Erin Steuter, *Drone Nation: The Political Economy of America's New Way of War* (London: Lexington Books, 2017): pp. 30–31.

45. For discussion of this sociological debate on the state, see Rafael Khachaturian, 'Bringing What State Back In? Neo-Marxism and the Origin of the Committee on States and Social Structures'. *Political Research Quarterly*, 72:3 (2019): pp. 714–726.

46. Christopher Richard Moran and Andrew Hammond, 'Bringing the 'Social' in from the Cold: Towards a Social History of American Intelligence'. *Cambridge Review of International Affairs*, 34:5 (2021): pp. 616–636.

47. 'Transcript of hearing – Tony Blair'. The Iraq Inquiry, 21 January 2011: p. 13. Emphasis added.

48. Tony Blair, 'Full Text: Tony Blair's Speech', *The Guardian*, 18 March 2003. www.theguardian.com/politics/2003/mar/18/foreignpolicy.iraq1.

49. James J. Wirtz, 'Robert Jervis: Remembering the Dean of Intelligence Studies'. *Intelligence and National Security*, doi:10.1080/02684527.2022. 2055707: pp. 1–9.

50. Robert Jervis, 'Reports, Politics, and Intelligence Failures: The Case of Iraq'. *Journal of Strategic Studies*, 29:1 (2006): pp. 41–44.

51. Jervis, 'Reports, Politics, and Intelligence Failures': pp. 39, 41, 44.

52. Peter Schouten, 'Theory Talk #12: Robert Jervis on Nuclear Weapons, Explaining the non-Realist Politics of the Bush Administration and US Military Presence in Europe', *Theory Talks*, 24 July 2008. www.theory-talks.org/2008/07/theory-talk-12.html. Original emphasis.

53. 'Decolonization', United Nations, n.d. www.un.org/en/global-issues/decolonization.

54. 'Decolonization of Asia and Africa, 1945–1960', US Department of State Office of the Historian, n.d. https://history.state.gov/milestones/1945-1952/asia-and-africa.
55. Kerem Nisancioglu, 'Racial Sovereignty'. *European Journal of International Relations*, 26:S1 (2020): pp. 42–45; Alina Sajed, 'Race and International Relations – What's in a Word? A Debate Around John Hobson's *The Eurocentric Conception of World Politics*'. *Postcolonial Studies*, 19:2 (2016): pp. 168–172.
56. T. D. Harper-Shipman, K. Melchor Quick Hall, Gavriel Cutipa-Zorn, and Mamyrah A. Dougé-Prosper, 'Forum: Stripping Away the Body: Prospects for Reimagining Race in IR'. *International Studies Review*, 23 (2021): pp. 2019–2047.
57. Biana Gonzalez-Sobrino, and Devon R. Goss, 'Exploring the Mechanisms of Racialization Beyond the Black-White Binary'. *Ethnic and Racial Studies*, 42:4 (2019): pp. 505–510.
58. Ann Laura Stoler, 'Affective States'. In David Nugent and Joan Vincent (eds.), *A Companion to the Anthropology of Politics* (Oxford: Blackwell, 2007): pp. 4–20; Nisancioglu, 'Racial Sovereignty': pp. 45–48.
59. Patrick Wolfe, 'Race and Racialisation: Some Thoughts'. *Postcolonial Studies*, 5:1 (2002): pp. 51–62.
60. Tamar Blickstein, 'Affects of Racialization'. In Jan Slaby and Christian von Scheve (eds.), *Affective Societies: Key Concepts* (London: Routledge, 2019): pp. 153–156.
61. Ann Laura Stoler has used the Netherlands Indies colonies to detail both the 'discrepant and *changing* criteria by which racial superiority and attendant European privilege were assigned' and how colonial subjects' 'cultural sensibilities, physical being, and political sentiments called into question' those criteria. Stoler, *Carnal Knowledge and Imperial Power: Race and the Intimate in Colonial Rule* (London: University of California Press, 2010): pp. 39, 79. Original emphasis.
62. As famously argued in Aimé Césaire, *Discourse on Colonialism*, trans. Joan Pinkham (New York: Monthly Review Press, 2000).
63. Srdjan Vucetic, *The Anglosphere: A Genealogy of a Racialized Identity in International Relations* (Stanford, CA: Stanford University Press, 2011): pp. 1–4.
64. Gargi Bhattacharyya, *Dangerous Brown Men: Exploiting Sex, Violence and Feminism in the War on Terror* (London: Zed Books, 2008): pp. 96–104.
65. Tarak Barkawi and Keith Stanski, 'Introduction: Orientalism and War'. In Barkawi and Stanski (eds.), *Orientalism and War* (London: C. Hurst & Co., 2012): pp. 1–6.
66. Derek Bryce, 'The Absence of Ottoman, Islamic Europe in Edward W. Said's *Orientalism*'. *Theory, Culture & Society*, 30:1, 2013: 99–121.

67. Tariq Amin-Khan, 'New Orientalism, Securitisation and the Western Media's Incendiary Racism'. *Third World Quarterly*, 33:9, 2012: pp. 1597–1600.
68. Sophia Dingli, 'Is the Failed State Thesis Analytically Useful? The Case of Yemen'. *Politics*, 33:2, 2013: pp. 91–100.
69. Dina Rezk, *The Arab World and Western Intelligence: Analysing the Middle East, 1956–1981* (Edinburgh: Edinburgh University Press, 2018).
70. Debra Thompson, 'Through, Against and Beyond the Racial State: The Transnational Stratum Of Race'. *Cambridge Review of International Affairs*, 26:1 (2013): pp. 136–141.
71. W. E. B. Du Bois, *The Souls of Black Folk* (Chicago: McClurg, 1903): p. 13.
72. W. E. B. Du Bois, 'The Color Line Belts the World'. In Bill V. Mullen and Cathryn Watson (eds.), *W. E. B. Du Bois on Asia: Crossing the World Color Line* (Jackson: University Press of Mississippi, 2005): pp. 33–4.
73. Du Bois, 'The Color Line Belts the World'.
74. Bill V. Mullen, *W.E.B. Du Bois: Revolutionary across the Color Line* (London: Pluto Press, 2016): pp. 89–104.
75. Chester Bowles, 'The Ominously Changing Balance of Power in Asia', Memorandum to Allen Dulles, 28 March 1955. CIA: FOIA ERR.
76. Jan Eckel, 'Human Rights and Decolonization: New Perspectives and Open Questions'. *Humanity*, 1:1 (2010) pp. 111–135.
77. Bradley R. Simpson, 'Self-Determination, Human Rights, and the End of Empire in the 1970s'. *Humanity*, 4:2 (2014): pp. 239–260.
78. Herbert Feis, 'Anthony Eden and the Cacophony of Nations'. *Foreign Affairs*, 44:1 (1965): pp. 78, 82, 88.
79. As a form of cultural racism, Orientalism in particular treats populations on the other side of the colour line as if they would accept their inability to govern themselves. If those people reject that idea, that can be used to reinforce the claim that they are ill-tempered, unreasonable, too irrational to make political decisions. Arjun Chowdhury, 'Shocked by War: The Non-Politics of Orientalism'. In Tarak Barkawi and Keith Stanski, *Orientalism and War* (London: C. Hurst & Co., 2012): pp. 33–37.
80. Alina Sajed, 'Re-remembering Third Worldism: An Affirmative Critique of National Liberation in Algeria'. *Middle East Critique*, 28:3 (2019): pp. 243–260.
81. Gurminder K. Bhambra, *Connected Sociologies* (London: Bloomsbury, 2014): pp. 3–6.
82. Catherine Hall and Sonya Rose, 'Introduction: Being at Home with the Empire'. In Hall and Rose (eds.), *At Home with the Empire: Metropolitan Culture and the Imperial World* (Cambridge: Cambridge University Press, 2006): pp. 23–26.
83. Antoinette Burton, 'Who Needs the Nation? Interrogating 'British' History'. In Catherine Hall (ed.), *Cultures of Empire: A Reader* (New York: Routledge, 2000): pp. 137–153; Hall and Rose, 'Introduction': pp. 22–23.

84. Gurminder K. Bhambra, 'Undoing the Epistemic Disavowal of the Haitian Revolution: A Contribution to Global Social Thought'. *Journal of Intercultural Studies*, 37:1 (2016): pp. 1–16.

85. Chowdhury, 'Shocked by War': pp. 36–37.

86. William Hague, 'What's Really Going On in Vladimir Putin's Head', *New York Post*, 17 February 2022. https://nypost.com/2022/02/17/a-break-down-of-whats-going-on-in-vladimir-putins-head.

87. 'William Hague Rejects Iraq 'Abuse' Complaint to ICC', *BBC News*, 12 January 2014. www.bbc.com/news/uk-25703723.

88. Corera, 'Ukraine war'.

89. Yaroslav Trofimov, 'Russia's Turn to Its Asian Past', *The Wall Street Journal*, 6 July 2018.

CHAPTER 1

1. J. K. Gardiner, 'The Use of the Term "Middle East"'. Memo to Joint Intelligence Sub-Committee, JIC/365/46, 21 March 1946. TNA: CAB 176/10.

2. Joint Intelligence Sub-Committee, 'Minutes of the 14th meeting of the Sub-Committee (Deputy Directors)', JIC (46) 14th meeting (o), 22 March 1946. TNA: CAB 81/94.

3. T. Haddon, 'Use of the Term "Middle East"'. Memo to Joint Intelligence Sub-Committee, JIC/429/46, 5 April 1946. TNA: CAB 176/10.

4. Michael S. Goodman, 'Creating the Machinery for Joint Intelligence: The Formative Years of the Joint Intelligence Committee, 1936–1956'. *International Journal of Intelligence and CounterIntelligence*, 30 (2017): pp. 67–69.

5. W. B. Fisher, 'Unity and Diversity in the Middle East'. *Geographical Review*, 37:3 (1947): p. 415.

6. M. A. Fitzsimons, 'Conflicts in the Middle East'. *The Review of Politics*, 19:2 (1957): p. 260–261.

7. Roderic H. Davison, 'Where Is the Middle East?'. *Foreign Affairs*, 38:4 (1960): p. 666.

8. G. C. L. Bertram, 'Long Term Development in the "Middle East"'. *The Geography Journal*, 109:1/3 (1947): pp. 109–112.

9. Goodman, 'Creating the Machinery for Joint Intelligence': pp. 72–73.

10. Philip H. J. Davies, 'Twilight of Britain's Joint Intelligence Committee?'. *International Journal of Intelligence and CounterIntelligence*, 24 (2011): pp. 427–431.

11. Rhodri Jeffreys-Jones, 'Why Was the CIA Established In 1947?'. *Intelligence and National Security*, 12:1 (1997): pp. 21–24.

12. Robert Mandel outlines intelligence scholars' story of a Cold War enemy focus followed by a 'War on Terror' one in 'On Estimating Post-Cold War Enemy Intentions'. *Intelligence and National Security*, 24:2 (2009): pp.

194–215. Eminent intelligence scholar Mark Phythian takes this story as a given when he details just how challenging is the intelligence target of al-Qaeda compared to the Soviet Union. Phythian, 'Intelligence Analysis Today and Tomorrow'. *Security Challenges*, 5:1 (2009): pp. 67–83.

13. Daniel Wirls narrates the late 1970s rise of neo-conservative US officials and their extremely antagonistic analysis of Soviet intentions. Wirls notes the parallel between their rise and the intelligence debate of the late 1940s and early 1950s. Daniel Wirls, *Buildup: The Politics of Defense in the Reagan Era* (Cornell: Cornell University Press, 1992): pp. 21–28. If the dominant story of Western intelligence does lean on the idea of a deceptively belligerent USSR, then in an important sense neo-conservatism won the battle for Cold War history.

14. Quoted in W. Taylor Fain, *American Ascendance and British Retreat in the Persian Gulf Region* (London: Palgrave Macmillan, 2008): p. 31.

15. Memorandum by the Chief of the Division of South Asian Affairs (Hare), 5 November 1947. *Foreign Relations of the United States (FRUS), 1947, The Near East and Africa*, volume 5, document 402.

16. 'The British and American Positions', Memorandum Prepared in the Department of State, n.d. *FRUS, 1947, The Near East and Africa*, Volume 5, Document 394; Memorandum by the Under Secretary of State (Acheson) to the Secretary of State, 9 October 1945. *FRUS: Diplomatic Papers, 1945, The Near East and Africa*, volume 8, document 20.

17. On Britain's (and France's) imperialist decolonisation: Robert Gildea, *Empires of the Mind: The Colonial Past and the Politics of the Present* (Oxford: Oxford University Press, 2019): pp. 68–96. On the US's 'informal empire' during this period: Hideki Kan, 'Informal Empire and the Cold War'. *The Journal of Imperial and Commonwealth History*, 49:3 (2021): pp. 576–606.

18. On field agent 'Arabists' see Hugh Wilford, *America's Great Game: The CIA's Secret Arabists and the Shaping of the Modern Middle East* (New York: Basic Books, 2013). On local intelligence and counter-subversion, see Rory Cormac, *Confronting the Colonies: British Intelligence and Counterinsurgency* (Oxford: Oxford University Press, 2014); and Chikara Hashimoto, *The Twilight of the British Empire: British Intelligence and Counter-Subversion in the Middle East, 1948–1963* (Edinburgh: Edinburgh University Press, 2017).

19. See the discussion between Anders Stephanson and Odd Arne Westad on the politics of 'Cold War' as an historical concept: Stephanson, 'Cold War Degree Zero' and Westad, 'Exploring the Histories of the Cold War: A Pluralist Approach', in Joel Isaac and Duncan Bell (eds.), *Uncertain Empire: American History and the Idea of the Cold War* (Oxford: Oxford University Press, 2012): pp. 19–49 and 51–59.

20. John Kent details policy-makers' back-and-forth on these issues in 'British Foreign Policy and Military Strategy: The Contradictions of

Declining Imperial Power and the Baghdad Pact, 1947–55'. *Middle Eastern Studies*, 56:5 (2020): pp. 730–743.

21. Wesley K. Wark, *The Ultimate Enemy: British Intelligence and Nazi Germany, 1933–1939* (Cornell: Cornell University Press, 2010): pp. 18–19.

22. Donald Cameron Watt, 'British Intelligence and the Coming of the Second World War in Europe'. In Ernest R. May (ed.), *Knowing One's Enemies: Intelligence Assessment Before the Two World Wars* (Princeton, NJ: Princeton University Press, 1985): pp. 263–265.

23. Michael Goodman, 'Learning to Walk: The Origins of the UK's Joint Intelligence Committee'. *International Journal of Intelligence and CounterIntelligence*, 21:1 (2008): p. 45.

24. Goodman, 'Creating the Machinery for Joint Intelligence': p. 70.

25. 'Centralised Intelligence', n.d. TNA: CAB 163/6.

26. V. Cavendish-Bentinek, 'Charter for the JIC', 13 July 1944: pp. 5–6. TNA: CAB 163/6.

27. Letter from S. N. Shoosmulh to V. F. W. Cavendish-Bentinek, 29 March 1941. TNA: CAB 163/8.

28. V. Cavendish-Bentinek, Letter to Joint Intelligence Sub-Committee, JIC/1584/43. TNA: CAB 163/6.

29. Philip H. J. Davies, 'Organizational politics and the Development of Britain's Intelligence Producer/Consumer Interface'. *Intelligence and National Security*, 10:4 (1995): p. 127.

30. V. Cavendish-Bentinek and Denis Capel-Dunn, 'The Intelligence Machine', Report to the Joint Intelligence Sub-Committee, 10 January 1945. TNA: CAB 163/6.

31. Goodman, 'Creating the Machinery for Joint Intelligence': p. 79.

32. Joint Intelligence Sub-Committee, 'Russia's Strategic Interests and Intentions, from the Point of View of Her Security', JIC (44)467, 18 December 1944. Reprinted in Richard J. Aldrich, Rory Cormac and Michael S. Goodman, *Spying on the World: The Declassified Documents of the Joint Intelligence Committee, 1936–2013* (Edinburgh: Edinburgh University Press, 2014): pp. 123–147.

33. Joint Intelligence Sub-Committee, 'Russia's Strategic Interests and Intentions', JIC (46)1(O), 1 March 1946. TNA: CAB 81/132.

34. JIC, 'Russia's Strategic Interests and Intentions': pp. 2, 6–7.

35. Larry A. Valero, 'The American Joint Intelligence Committee and Estimates of the Soviet Union, 1945–1947'. *Studies in Intelligence*, 44:3 (2000).

36. Michael Warner, 'The Creation of the Central Intelligence Group'. *Studies in Intelligence*, 39:5 (1996): p. 114.

37. Woodrow Kuhns, 'The Office of Reports and Estimates: CIA's First Center for Analysis'. *Studies in Intelligence*, 51:2 (2007): p. 28.

38. Ludwell Montague, 'Comment on the Dulles-Jackson Report', 11 February 1949. CIA: FOIA ERR.
39. Central Intelligence Agency, 'Comments by The Central Intelligence Agency on "Conclusions and Recommendations" of A Report to the National Security Council by Mr. Allen W. Dulles, Chairman, Mr. William H. Jackson, Mr. Mathias F. Correa Entitled "The Central Intelligence Agency and National Organisation for Intelligence"', 28 February 1949: pp. 18–19. Emphasis added. CIA: FOIA ERR.
40. Fain, *American Ascendance and British Retreat*: pp. 25–27.
41. Malvyn P. Leffler, 'The American Conception of National Security and the Beginnings of the Cold War, 1945–48'. *The American Historical Review*, 89:2 (1984): pp. 346–381.
42. The historian Michael J. Hogan calls this the 'ideology of national security' because it emerged as a formalised belief system, a set of assumptions about the US position in the world, which bounded its advocates together in a collective self-image. Hogan, *A Cross of Iron: Harry S. Truman and the Origins of the National Security State, 1945–1954* (Cambridge: Cambridge University Press, 1998): pp. ix–x.
43. Emily S. Rosenberg, 'Commentary: The Cold War and the Discourse of National Security'. *Diplomatic History*, 17:2 (1993): pp. 278–280.
44. CIA, 'Comments by the Central Intelligence Agency': pp. 21, 23, 26.
45. Minutes of the first meeting of the National Security Council, 26 September 1947. *FRUS, 1945–50, Emergence of the Intelligence Establishment*, document 225.
46. Jackson, 'Origin and Nature of the "CIA Review of the World Situation"', 1950: pp. 7, 10–11. CIA: FOIA ERR.
47. Jackson, 'Origin and Nature': pp. 13–14.
48. Jackson, 'Origin and Nature': p. 21.
49. Ludwell Montague, 'Review of the World Situation as it Relates to the Security of the United States', CIA 1, 26 September 1947: pp. 3, 5, 6. Since the CIA Director Roscoe Hillenkoetter presented the report at the first NSC meeting, the minutes of that meeting attribute the report to him. The CIA's internal history, however, attributes it to Montague.
50. Sidney W. Souers, 'Policy Formulation for National Security'. *The American Political Science Review*, 43:3 (1949): p. 542.
51. Montague, 'Review of the World Situation', CIA 1: pp. 2, 3. CIA: FOIA ERR.
52. George Caldwell, 'The Mob Is In The Streets'. *Studies in Intelligence*, Winter 1985: pp. 33–35. The author is redacted in the declassified file but is cited openly by other articles in *Studies in Intelligence*.
53. Gregor Davey, 'Conflicting Worldviews, Mutual Incomprehension: The Production of Intelligence Across Whitehall and the Management of Subversion During Decolonisation, 1944–1966'. *Small Wars &*

Insurgencies, 25:3 (2014): p. 546; G. H. Green, 'Potential Trouble Spots', JIC/199/53, 24 January 1953. TNA: CAB 176/40.

54. Robert F. Byrnes, 'Harvard, Columbia, and the CIA: My Training in Russian Studies'. *Russian History/Histoire Russe*, 15:1 (1988): p. 109.

55. Official Committee on the Middle East, 'Anglo-American Discussions on Middle East Policy', OME (57) 27 (Revise), 12 April 1957: pp. 3–4. TNA: CAB 134/2339.

56. Goodman, 'Creating the Machinery for Joint Intelligence': p. 73.

57. P. Gleadell, Note on 'Forecast of the World Situation in 1956/60', JIC (47) 42 (O) (T. of R), 25 July 1947. TNA: CAB 158/1.

58. P. Gleadell, Note on 'Forecast of the World Situation in 1960', JIC (47) 42 (O) Supplementary T. of R, 10 October 1947. TNA: CAB 158/1; P. Gleadell, Note on 'Strategic Intentions of a Certain Power – 1956/60', JIC (47) 43 (O) (Terms of Reference), 25 July 1947. TNA: CAB 158/1.

59. Joint Intelligence Committee, 'Forecast of the World Situation in 1957', JIC (47) 42 (O) (Final), 12 June 1948: pp. 6–7, 24–25, 33. TNA: CAB 158/1.

60. JIC, 'Forecast of the World Situation in 1957': p. 47. Emphasis added.

61. JIC, 'Forecast of the World Situation in 1957': p. 25, 33, 46.

62. Joint Intelligence Committee, Minutes of 38th meeting of the Committee, JIC (48) 38th Meeting (O), 28 April 1948: pp. 2–3. TNA: CAB 159/3. The paragraph appears on p. 25 of the 'Forecast'.

63. Andrew J. Williams, *France, Britain and the United States in the Twentieth Century: Volume 2, 1940–1961. A Reappraisal* (London: Palgrave Macmillan, 2020): pp. 185–195.

64. Office of Research and Estimates, 'The Break-Up of the Colonial Empires and its Implications for US Security', ORE 25–48, 3 September 1948: pp. 1, 12. Emphasis added. CIA: FOIA ERR.

65. ORE, 'The Break-Up of the Colonial Empires': pp. 1–2, 3. Emphasis added.

66. ORE, 'The Break-Up of the Colonial Empires': pp. 2, 5.

67. ORE, 'The Break-Up of the Colonial Empires': pp. 2, 5, 11.

68. Thomas Borstelmann, *The Cold War and the Colour Line: American Race Relations in the Global Arena* (London: Harvard University Press, 2001): pp. 70–75.

69. ORE, 'The Break-Up of the Colonial Empires': pp. 8, 13.

70. Joint Intelligence Committee, 'Review of the Middle East and North Africa', JIC (51) 88 (Final), 27 June 1952: pp. 3–5. TNA: CAB 158/13.

71. JIC, 'Review of the Middle East and North Africa': p. 4, 5. Emphases added.

72. Bernard Burrows, 'Implications for the Persian Gulf of Possible Changes in the Constitutional and Political Position of Aden Colony and Protectorate', Memorandum to Official Committee on the Middle East, OME (58) 30, 27 May 1958: pp. 2–3. TNA: CAB 134/2342.

73. Joint Intelligence Committee, 'Commitments in Iraq', Note by the Secretary, JIC (53) 121 (Terms of Reference), 23 December 1953. TNA: CAB 158/16.
74. Joint Intelligence Committee, 'Commitments in Iraq', JIC (53) 121 (Final), 6 February 1954: pp. 1, 3, 6. TNA: CAB 158/16.
75. Allen Dulles, 'The Asian-African Conference', NSC Briefing, 5 April 1955: pp. 1-2. CIA: FOIA ERR.
76. Central Intelligence Agency, 'Estimate of the World Situation', National Intelligence Estimate 100-3-57, 29 January 1957: pp. 1, 6-9. CIA: FOIA ERR. On Africa, the proposal is even more contradictory: the CIA recommends that European governments 'implement liberal colonial policies' to try to 'exert a moderating influence on nationalist movements', pushing them away from 'an anti-Western direction' (9).
77. Joint Intelligence Committee, Minutes of the ninety-fifth meeting of the Committee, JIC (51) 95th Meeting, 13 September 1951: pp. 4-5. Emphasis added. TNA: CAB 159/1.
78. Davey, 'Conflicting Worldviews, Mutual Incomprehension': pp. 548-552.
79. For discussion, see Douglas Little, 'Mission Impossible: The CIA and the Cult of Covert Action in the Middle East'. *Diplomatic History* 28:5 (2004): pp. 663-701.
80. Official Committee on the Middle East, 'Future Middle East Policy', Note by the Foreign Office, OME (57) 23 (Reviso), 16 April 1957: Annex. TNA: CAB 134/2339.
81. For example, see Maurice Jr. M. Labelle, 'A New Age of Empire? Arab 'Anti-Americanism', US Intervention, and the Lebanese Civil War of 1958'. *The International History Review*, 35:1 (2013): pp. 42-69.
82. Nathan J. Citino, 'Historiographical Review: The Middle East and the Cold War'. *Cold War History*, 19:3 (2019): pp. 441-456.
83. R. D. J. Scott Fox, 'Saudi Arabia: Annual Review for 1950', ES 1011/1, 19 March 1951: pp. 29, 32. TNA: FO 464/5.
84. Anthony Eden, 'Egypt: The Alternatives', Memorandum by the Secretary of State for Foreign Affairs, C (53) 65, 16 February 1953. TNA: CAB 129/59.
85. G. C. Peden, 'Suez and Britain's Decline as a World Power'. *The Historical Journal*, 55:4 (2012): pp. 1082-1093.
86. Gregory Winger, 'Twilight on the British Gulf: The 1961 Kuwait Crisis and the Evolution of American Strategic Thinking in the Persian Gulf'. *Diplomacy & Statecraft*, 23 (2012): pp. 660-664.
87. Roland Popp, 'Accommodating to a Working Relationship: Arab Nationalism and US Cold War Policies in the Middle East, 1958-60'. *Cold War History*, 10:3 (2010): pp. 397-427; Janick Marina Schaufelbuehl, Sandra Bott, Jussi Hanhimäki, and Marco Wyss, 'Non-Alignment, the Third Force, or Fence-Sitting: Independent Pathways in the Cold War'. *The International History Review*, 37:5 (2015): pp. 906-908.

88. Quoted in Simon C. Smith, 'Britain's Decision to Withdraw from the Persian Gulf: A Pattern Not a Puzzle'. *Journal of Imperial and Commonwealth History*, 44:2 (2016): pp. 330–332.

89. 'The future of the United Kingdom in World Affairs', Memorandum for Cabinet Policy Review Committee, PR (56) 3, 1 June 1956. Reprinted in David Goldsworthy (ed.), *British Documents on the End of Empire, Series A Volume 3: The Conservative Government and the End of Empire, 1951–1957* (London: HMSO, 1994): pp. 61, 67–68, 70–71.

90. Joint Intelligence Committee, 'The Outlook for the Persian Gulf Area Over the Next Six Months', JIC (58) 85 (Final), 21 August 1958: pp. 1–2, Annex p. 2. TNA: CAB 158/34.

91. JIC, 'The Outlook for the Persian Gulf Area': Annex pp. 1, 3, 4.

92. Joint Intelligence Committee, 'Likely Developments in the Persian Gulf and their Probable Effects for British Interests', JIC (68) 35 (Final), 7 June 1968: pp. 1–2, 4. TNA: CAB 158/70.

93. In 1959, the CIA produced 14 National Intelligence Estimates and Special National Intelligence Estimates on the Middle East, Compared to 13 for the Soviet Bloc. United States Intelligence Board, 'Estimates Produced During 1959 with Notations Regarding USIB Release to Foreign Governments', UIB-D-17.5/2, 25 January 1960. CIA: FOIA ERR.

94. CIA, 'Estimate of the World Situation', NIE 100-3-57: pp. 1, 3–4, 6–8. CIA: FOIA ERR.

95. Joint Intelligence Committee, 'The Soviet Threat', JIC (A) (72) 34, 13 October 1972: p. 11. TNA: CAB 186/12.

96. National Security Council, 'Statement by the National Security Council of Long-Range US Policy Toward the Near East', NSC 5801/1, 24 January 1958. *FRUS, 1958–1960, Near East Region*, volume 12, document 5.

97. Central Intelligence Agency, 'Estimate of the World Situation', NSC Briefing, 20 March 1958: p. 3. CIA: FOIA ERR.

98. See Thomas Borstelmann, *The Cold War and the Colour Line: American Race Relations in the Global Arena* (London: Harvard University Press, 2001): pp. 70–75.

99. Willard C. Matthias, *America's Strategic Blunders: Intelligence Analysis and National Security Policy, 1936–1991* (University Park, PA: The Pennsylvania State University Press, 2001): pp. 136–137.

100. CIA, 'Estimate of the World Situation', NSC Briefing, 20 March 1958: pp. 3–4, 9. CIA: FOIA ERR.

101. Joint Intelligence Committee, 'The Probable Sequence of Events Over the Next Six Months in the Area of Concern to Commander British Forces Arabian Peninsula', JIC (58) 89 (Final), 28 August 1958: pp. 1–2. TNA: CAB 158/34.

102. JIC, 'The Probable Sequence of Events': p. 3.

103. JIC, 'The Probable Sequence of Events': p. 7.

NOTES

104. Official Committee on the Middle East, 'Future Middle East Policy':
p. 1.
105. Joint Intelligence Committee, 'The Possible Consequences of the Early
Collapse or Overthrow of the Government in Iraq', JIC (58) 114, 5
December 1958: p. 3. TNA: CAB 158/34.
106. Central Intelligence Agency, 'Main Currents in the Arab World',
National Intelligence Estimate, NIE 30-59 ADVON, 25 August 1959:
cover, pp. 1–3. CIA: FOIA ERR.
107. CIA, 'Main Currents in the Arab World': pp. 3–4. Emphasis added.
108. JIC, 'The Possible Consequences': pp. 4–6.
109. Stephen Blackwell, 'A Desert Squall: Anglo-American Planning for
Military Intervention in Iraq, July 1958–August 1959'. *Middle Eastern
Studies*, 35:3 (1999): pp. 1–18.
110. JIC, 'The Possible Consequences': pp. 4–6.
111. Conclusions of Cabinet meeting, C.C. 55 (58), 14 July 1958: p. 3. TNA:
CAB 128/32.
112. Joint Intelligence Committee, 'Consequences in the Middle East of
Anglo/American Withdrawal from Jordan and the Lebanon', JIC (58)
103 (Final), 16 October 1958: pp. 5–6. TNA: CAB 158/34.
113. JIC, 'Consequences in the Middle East': pp. 2, 6.
114. Nigel John Ashton, 'A Microcosm of Decline: British Loss of Nerve
and Military Intervention in Jordan and Kuwait, 1958 and 1961. *The
Historical Journal*, 40:4 (1997): pp. 1069–1083.
115. JIC, 'Consequences in the Middle East': pp. 3, 6.
116. Conclusions of Cabinet meeting, C.C. 59 (58), 16 July 1958: p. 4–5.
TNA: CAB 128/32.
117. Central Intelligence Agency, 'The Middle East Crisis', Special National
Intelligence Estimate, SNIE 30-2-58, 22 July 1958. *FRUS, 1958–1960,
Near East Region*, Volume 12, document 27.

CHAPTER 2

1. 'Gen. William Tidwell, 81, Dies'. *The Washington Post*, 17 June 1999,
www.washingtonpost.com/archive/local/1999/06/17/gen-william-
tidwell-81-dies/dcca6096-e742-407c-bd4f-0524b2d1938c; James G.
Blight and David A. Welch, 'What can Intelligence Tell Us About the
Cuban Missile Crisis, and What Can the Cuban Missile Crisis Tell Us
About Intelligence?'. *Intelligence and National Security*, 13:3 (1998): p. 7.
2. W. A. Tidwell, 'Horrible Thought'. *Studies in Intelligence*, 2:1 (1958):
pp. 65–70.
3. Joshua Rovner and Austin Long strongly critique the 9/11 Commission
Report's lack of rigour, asking how imagination could be institutionalised
and then evaluated as to its proper scope and extent: 'how can
the Intelligence Community ensure that it is being appropriately

217

imaginative?'. Rovner and Long, 'The Perils of Shallow Theory: Intelligence Reform and the 9/11 Commission'. *International Journal of Intelligence and CounterIntelligence*, 18:4 (2005): p. 617.

4. W. A. Tidwell, 'Kim or Major North?'. *Studies in Intelligence*, 2:2 (1958): pp. 37–42. Emphasis added.

5. Ralph Riposte, 'New Anachronism'. *Studies in Intelligence*, 2:2 (1958): pp. 43–44.

6. R. E. Buttall, 'Communications To The Editors'. *Studies in Intelligence*, 3:1 (1959): n.p. Emphasis added.

7. Tidwell, 'Horrible Thought': p. 70.

8. See Osamah F. Khalil, *America's Dream Palace: Middle East expertise and the rise of the national security state* (London: Harvard University Press, 2016): pp. 151–157, 160–164.

9. Lauren Witlin, 'Of Note: Mirror-Imaging and Its Dangers'. *SAIS Review*, XXVIII:1 (2008): p. 89.

10. Frank Watanabe, 'Fifteen Axioms for Intelligence Analysts'. *Studies in Intelligence*, 40:5 (1997): p. 46, original emphasis.

11. For discussion, see Christopher J. Lee, 'Between a Moment and an Era: The Origins and Afterlives of Bandung', in Christopher J. Lee (ed.), *Making a World after Empire: The Bandung moment and its political afterlives* (Athens: Ohio University Press, 2010): pp. 1–42. On escaping the Cold War lens, see NAM participant S. K. Singh, 'Non-Alignment: Past, Present and Future'. *South African Journal of International Affairs*, 1:1 (1993): pp. 23–34.

12. Asher Orkaby, 'The North Yemen Civil War and the Failure of the Federation of South Arabia'. *Middle Eastern Studies*, 53:1 (2017): pp. 69–83.

13. Abdel Razzaq Takriti, *Monsoon Revolution: Republicans, sultans, and Empires in Oman, 1965–1976* (Oxford: Oxford University Press, 2013).

14. Matthew Connelly, *A Diplomatic Revolution: Algeria's fight for Independence and the Origins of the Post-Cold War Era* (Oxford: Oxford University Press, 2002); James Mark, Péter Apor, Radina Vučetić, and Piotr Osęka, "We Are with You, Vietnam': Transnational Solidarities in Socialist Hungary, Poland and Yugoslavia'. *Journal of Contemporary History*, 50:3 (2015): pp. 439–464.

15. For an assessment of these interventions' humanitarian credentials, see Douglas Eisner, 'Humanitarian Intervention in the Post-Cold War Era'. *Boston University International Law Journal*, 11:1 (1993): pp. 200–206.

16. Siba Grovogui, 'A Revolution Nonetheless: The Global South in International Relations'. *The Global South*, 5:1 (2011): p. 176.

17. Eric Gettig, '"Trouble Ahead in Afro-Asia": The United States, the Second Bandung Conference, and the Struggle for the Third World, 1964–1965'. *Diplomatic History*, 39:1 (2015): pp. 129–135; Pak K. Lee and Cecilia Ducci, 'No Humanitarian Intervention in Asian Genocides:

How Possible and Legitimate?'. *Third World Quarterly*, 41:9 (2020): pp. 1582–1583.

18. Stephen Mettler, 'Return of the Bear: Learning from Intelligence Analysis of the USSR to Better Assess Modern Russia'. *American Intelligence Journal*, 35:2 (2018): p. 33.

19. Gerald K. Haines and Robert E. Leggett (eds.), *Watching the Bear: Essays on CIA's Analysis of the Soviet Union* (Washington DC: Center for the Study of Intelligence, 2003); Michael S. Goodman, *Spying on the Nuclear Bear: Anglo-American Intelligence and the Soviet Bomb* (Stanford CA: Stanford University Press, 2008).

20. Joint Intelligence Committee, 'Russia's Strategic Interests and Intentions', JIC (46) 1 (O) Final, 1 March 1946: p. 2. TNA: CAB 81/132.

21. JIC, 'Russia's Strategic Interests and Intentions': p. 2.

22. JIC, 'Russia's Strategic Interests and Intentions': p. 6.

23. Joint Intelligence Committee, 'Soviet Interests, Intentions and Capabilities – General', JIC (47) 7/2 Final, 6 August 1947: pp. 5–6. Emphasis added. TNA: CAB 158/1.

24. JIC, 'Soviet Interests, Intentions and Capabilities': pp. 1, 3.

25. Intelligence Advisory Committee, 'Minutes of Meeting', IAC-M-89, 1 December 1952: p. 2. CIA: FOIA ERR.

26. Central Intelligence Agency, 'Probable Consequences of the Death Of Stalin and of the Elevation Of Malenkov to Leadership in the USSR', SE-39, 9 March 1953: p. 3. CIA: FOIA ERR.

27. See Khalil, *America's Dream Palace*: pp. 146–151.

28. Central Intelligence Agency, '[redacted] Consultants' Discussion', Staff Memorandum 336, 26 March 1953: pp. 1, 4, 6, 7. CIA: FOIA ERR. The name of the consultants' group is redacted but the structure and form of the meeting, as well as reference to the 'Inn' where they meet, point clearly to the Princeton Consultants as they are detailed in the public record.

29. CIA, '[redacted] Consultants' Discussion': pp. 2–4.

30. Alan J. P. Crick, 'Away With Capabilities!'. *Studies in Intelligence*, 1:2 (1956): pp. 35–39. Original emphasis.

31. As Arjun Chowdhury outlines, once your knowledge is designed to maintain racist superiority, you cannot imagine that others are equal. They therefore cannot technically be battlefield 'rivals'. Chowdhury, 'Shocked by War: The Non-Politics of Orientalism', in Tarak Barkawi and Keith Stanski (eds.), *Orientalism and War* (London: Hurst & Co, 2012): pp. 21–28.

32. Michael S. Goodman, 'Creating the Machinery for Joint Intelligence: The Formative Years of the Joint Intelligence Committee, 1936–1956'. *International Journal of Intelligence and CounterIntelligence*, 30:1 (2017): p. 82 n. 39.

33. See Sunny Xiang, *Tonal Intelligence: The Aesthetics of Asian Inscrutability During the Long Cold War* (Columbia: Columbia University Press, 2020): pp. 25–52.

34. Joint Intelligence Committee, 'Anti-Soviet Communism', JIC (53) 119, 29 December 1953: p. 5. TNA: CAB 158/16.

35. Joint Intelligence Committee, 'Review of Assessments of Communist Intentions Made Since January 1947 by the Joint Intelligence Committee', JIC (51) 87 (Final), 12 December 1951: Annex pp. 4–5. TNA: CAB 158/13.

36. A. D. Wilson, 'Chinese Reactions to the Sending of American Forces to the Lebanon and of British Forces to Jordan', Letter to Selwyn Lloyd, 28 July 1958. TNA: FO 371/133356.

37. Kyle Haddad-Fonda assesses these protests' mix of government corralling and popular solidarity: 'The Domestic Significance of China's Policy Toward Egypt, 1955–1957'. *The Chinese Historical Review*, 21:1 (2014): pp. 56–62.

38. Cyrus H. Peake, 'History's Role in Intelligence Estimating'. *Studies in Intelligence*, 3:1 (1959): p. 90.

39. Dina Rezk, *The Arab World and Western Intelligence: Analysing the Middle East, 1956–1981* (Edinburgh: Edinburgh University Press, 2017): pp. 2–5.

40. Michael S. Goodman, *The Official History of the Joint Intelligence Committee – Volume I: From the approach of the Second World War to the Suez crisis* (London: Routledge, 2014): pp. 371–377. On Nasser, the CIA and the State Department: Scott Lucas and Alistair Morey, 'The Hidden 'Alliance': The CIA and MI6 before and after Suez'. *Intelligence and National Security*, 15:2 (2000): pp. 97–100.

41. Joint Intelligence Committee, Minutes of Meeting, JIC (52) 101st Meeting, 17 September 1952: p. 2. TNA: CAB 159/12.

42. 'Situation in Egypt: Future Developments', JIC/2171/52, 24 September 1952: pp. 1–2. TNA: CAB 176/38.

43. Joint Intelligence Committee, 'Perimeter Review', JIC (52) 84th Meeting, 31 July 1952: Annex p. 6; 'Perimeter Review', JIC (52) 105th Meeting, 25 September 1952: Annex p. 4; 'Perimeter Reviews', JIC (52) 142nd Meeting, 18 December 1952: Annex pp. 5–6; Joint Intelligence Committee Middle East, 'The Egyptian Situation', JIC (M.E.) (53)–38 (Final), 18 May 1953. TNA: CAB 159/12 and DEFE 28/42.

44. Associated Press, 'Egypt's Tiger and Fox'. *The New York Times*, 2 April 1956: p. 3.

45. Joint Intelligence Committee, Minutes of Meeting, JIC (54) 17th Meeting, 25 February 1954: p. 4. TNA: CAB 159/15.

46. Goodman, *The Official History*: p. 376.

47. Joint Intelligence Committee, Minutes of Meeting, JIC (55) 96th Meeting, 8 December 1955: p. 3. TNA: CAB 159/21.

48. Minutes of meeting, JIC (56) 5th Meeting, 12 January 1956: pp. 8–9. TNA: CAB 159/22.

49. Joint Intelligence Committee, Minutes of meeting, JIC (56) 8th Meeting, 19 January 1956: pp. 4–5. TNA: CAB 159/22.

50. Goodman, The Official History: pp. 377–386; Lucas and Morey, 'The Hidden "Alliance".

51. Joint Intelligence Committee, 'Factors Affecting Egypt's Policy in the Middle East and North Africa', JIC (56) 20 (Final), 4 April 1956: p. 1, Annex pp. 3–4. TNA: CAB 158/23.

52. Joint Intelligence Committee, 'Nasser's Achievements, Aims and Future Policies', JIC (59) 23 (Final), 11 June 1959: pp. 13–14. TNA: CAB 134/2343.

53. Humphrey Trevelyan, 'Conversation between Her Majesty's Ambassador and the Egyptian Prime Minister on May 26, 1956', JE 1053/40–43, 27 May 1956. Emphases added. TNA: FO 407/235.

54. Joint Intelligence Committee, 'The Implications of Egyptian Nationalisation of the Suez Canal', JIC (56) 80 (Draft), 31 July 1956: pp. 1–2; 'Egyptian Nationalisation of the Suez Canal Company', JIC (56) 80 (Final), 2 August 1956: p. 1. TNA: CAB 158/25.

55. Humphrey Trevelyan, 'Egyptian Motives', JE 14211/1333, 1 September 1956. TNA: FO 407/235.

56. United States Intelligence Board, 'Post-Mortem on NIE 30-59', USIB-D-15.2/30, 26 August 1959; Central Intelligence Agency, 'Terms of Reference: NIE 36/61', 13 April 1961: p. 2. CIA: FOIA ERR.

57. Central Intelligence Agency, 'Nasser and the Future of Arab Nationalism', NIE 36-61, 27 June 1961. FRUS, 1961–1963, Near East, volume 27, document 68. CIA: FOIA ERR.

58. Peake, 'History's Role in Intelligence Estimating': pp. 86, 88.

59. Sherman Kent, 'A Crucial Estimate Relived'. Studies in Intelligence, 8:2 (1964): pp. 9–10, 15.

60. Willard C. Matthias, 'How Three Estimates Went Wrong'. Studies in Intelligence, 12:1 (1968): pp. 29–31.

61. M. K. Evans, 'Afghanistan: "The Hug of the Bear"', Letter to A. A. Duff, 11 November 1968: p. 2; P. W. M. Vereker, 'Afghanistan: "The Hug of the Bear"', 20 November 1968. TNA: FCO 37/332.

62. Joint Intelligence Committee, 'Likely Developments in the Persian Gulf and their Probable Effects for British Interests', JIC (68) 35 (Final), 7 June 1968: pp. 1–4. TNA: CAB 158/70.

63. Uri Bronfenbrenner, 'The Mirror Image in Soviet-American Relations: A Social Psychologist's Report'. Journal of Social Issues, 17 (1961): pp. 45–56.

64. For example: Ole R. Holsti, 'The Belief System and National Images: A Case Study'. Journal of Conflict Resolution, 6:3 (1964): pp. 244–252; William Eckhardt and Ralph K. White, 'A Test of the Mirror-Image

Hypothesis: Kennedy and Khrushchev'. *Journal of Conflict Resolution*, 11:3 (1967): pp. 325–332; Ralph K. White, 'Three Not-So Obvious Contributions of Psychology to Peace'. *Journal of Social Issues*, 25:4 (1969).

65. Nehemiah Jordan, 'International Relations and the Psychologist'. *Bulletin of the Atomic Scientists*, 19:9 (1963): pp. 29–33; Jerome D. Frank, *Sanity and Survival: Psychological Aspects of War and Peace* (New York: Random House, 1964).

66. Foreign and Commonwealth Office Middle East Research Department, 'Military Regimes in the Middle East (including the Sudan): Their Origin, Policy and Prospects', LR 6/12, 22 July 1960: pp. 3–5, 9. TNA: FO 464/60.

67. Anthony Marc Lewis, 'Re-Examining Our Perceptions On Vietnam'. *Studies in Intelligence*, 17:1 (1973): pp. 1–5. Original emphases.

68. Lewis, 'Re-Examining Our Perceptions': p. 3. Emphases added.

69. Dennis J. Duncanson, 'Vietnam – Inscrutable East?'. *International Affairs*, 44:4 (1968): p. 735.

70. See David C. Engerman, *Know Your Enemy: The Rise and Fall of America's Soviet Experts* (Oxford: Oxford University Press, 2009): pp. 249–253.

71. Engerman, *Know Your Enemy*: p. 264–266, 272–274.

72. On Sovietology debates, see Engerman, *Know Your Enemy*: pp. 206–232.

73. Richard B. Foster and Richard Pipes, 'Soviet National Strategy as it Applies to Foreign Policy: a Working Hypothesis'. In *Summary Volume: Soviet Strategy and Foreign Policy*, Stanford Research Institute, SSC-TN-2625-11, August 1975: 1–2.

74. This research programme's first Director has since detailed its results: H. E. Puthoff, 'CIA-Initiated Remote Viewing Program at Stanford Research Institute'. *Journal of Scientific Exploration*, 10:1 (1996): pp. 63–76.

75. 'Experiments – Uri Geller at SRI, 4–11 August, 1973': pp. 2–3. CIA: FOIA ERR.

76. James Dornan, 'Detente and Soviet Policy in Europe: A Comment on Recent Research'. In *Summary Volume*: pp. 7–10.

77. Richard Pipes, 'Detente: Moscow's View'. In *Summary Volume*: pp. 29–31.

78. Richard Pipes, 'Detente: Moscow's View'. In *Summary Volume*: pp. 33–39. Emphasis added; Dornan, 'Detente and Soviet Policy in Europe'. In *Summary Volume*: p. 7.

79. Quoted in Engerman, *Know Your Enemy*: p. 279.

80. Benjamin B. Fischer, '"We May Not Always Be Right, but We're Never Wrong": US Intelligence Assessments of the Soviet Union, 1972–91'. In Paul Maddrell (ed.), *The Image of the Enemy: Intelligence analysis of adversaries since 1945* (Washington, DC: Georgetown University Press, 2015): pp. 103–104, 119.

81. 'Issues Paper: Bias in CIA Intelligence Analysis', Center for the Study of Intelligence, 27 January 1977: p. 2. CIA: FOIA ERR.

82. 'Interagency Estimates of the Soviet Threat – Task 1', Memorandum from Chief, Production Assessment and Improvement Division, 10 January 1977. CIA: FOIA ERR.
83. 'Trend Analysis of "Soft Data" 1974–1975', Report by Production Assessment and Improvement Division, n.d.: pp. 1–2. CIA: FOIA ERR.
84. Chief, Production Assessment and Improvement Division, Draft paper on national estimates process, 24 January 1977: pp. 4–5. Emphases added. CIA: FOIA ERR.
85. H. G. Balfour Paul, Letter to Near East and North African Department, 27 August 1973. TNA: FCO 93/82.
86. A. J. M. Craig, Letter to H. G. Balfour Paul, 14 September 1973. TNA: FCO 93/82.
87. 'The Nicoll Report: The JIC and the Warning of Aggression': pp. 1–2. The report is reprinted in Michael S. Goodman, 'The Dog That Didn't Bark: The Joint Intelligence Committee and Warning of Aggression'. *Cold War History*, 7:4 (2007): pp. 536–551.
88. 'The Nicoll Report': pp. 2–5.
89. 'The Nicoll Report': pp. 2–5.
90. 'The Nicoll Report': p. 12.
91. Chief, Production Assessment and Improvement Division, 'JJM Views on B Team Report', note to D/OPEI, 27 January 1977. CIA: FOIA ERR.
92. Christopher J. Fettweis, 'Misreading the Enemy'. *Survival*, 57:5 (2015): p. 49.
93. Anne Hessing Cahn, 'Team B: The Trillion Dollar Experiment'. *Bulletin of the Atomic Scientists*, 49:3 (1993): pp. 22–27.
94. Uri Bar-Joseph, 'The Politicization of Intelligence: A Comparative Study'. *International Journal of Intelligence and CounterIntelligence*, 26:2 (2013): p. 351.
95. Cahn, 'Team B': p. 26.
96. John Prados, 'Team B: The Trillion Dollar Experiment'. *Bulletin of the Atomic Scientists*, 49:3 (1993): p. 28.
97. Lawrence Freedman, 'The CIA and the Soviet threat: The politicization of estimates, 1966–1977'. *Intelligence and National Security*, 12:1 (1997): p. 138.
98. Chalmers Johnson, 'The CIA and Me'. *Bulletin of Concerned Asian Scholars*, 29:1 (1997): p. 36.
99. Fischer, 'We May Not Always Be Right': p. 105.
100. Richards J. Heuer Jr., *Psychology of Intelligence Analysis* (Washington DC: Center for the Study of Intelligence, 1999): pp. 70–71.
101. Heuer Jr., *Psychology of Intelligence Analysis*: p. 71. Original emphasis.

CHAPTER 3

1. 'Ex-Israeli Intel Chief Admits Role in Assassination of Iran's Qassem Soleimani'. *Haaretz*, 20 December 2021. www.haaretz.com/

israel-news/2021-12-20/ty-article/israeli-intel-chief-takes-responsibility-for-assassination-of-irans-soleimani/0000017f-dc7a-df9c-a17f-fe7a86f80000; Dan Sabbagh, 'RAF Intelligence Base Linked to US Drone Strike on Iranian General Qassem Soleimani'. *The Guardian*, 2 October 2021. www.theguardian.com/uk-news/2021/oct/02/raf-intelligence-base-linked-to-us-drone-strike-on-iranian-general-qassem-soleimani.

2. John Cassidy, 'The Real Backstory of Why Trump Ordered the Killing of Sulemani is Becoming More Clear'. *The New Yorker*, 10 January 2020. www.newyorker.com/news/our-columnists/the-real-backstory-of-why-trump-ordered-the-killing-of-suleimani-is-becoming-more-clear; Elliot Setzer, 'White House Releases Report Justifying Soleimani Strike'. *Lawfare*, 14 February 2020. www.lawfareblog.com/white-house-releases-report-justifying-soleimani-strike.

3. Falih Hassan and Alissa J. Rubin, 'Pro-Iran Clash At US Embassy Ends in Baghdad'. *The New York Times*, 2 January 2020, A1; Julian Borger, 'US troops deployed to Middle East after Baghdad embassy siege'. *The Guardian*, 1 January 2020. www.theguardian.com/world/2020/jan/01/us-troops-fire-teargas-to-disperse-protesters-at-baghdad-embassy.

4. Justin Baragona, 'Tucker Slams Soleimani Intel: Now We Trust the Deep State?' *Daily Beast*, 6 January 2020. www.thedailybeast.com/tucker-carlson-slams-soleimani-intel-and-asks-now-we-trust-the-deep-state; Veronica Stracqualursi, 'Menendez on Iran intelligence: 'The last thing we need is another weapons of mass destruction moment'. *CNN*, 7 January 2020. https://edition.cnn.com/2020/01/07/politics/bob-menendez-trump-iran-intelligence-cnntv/index.html; David A. Graham, 'It's 2003 All Over Again'. *The Atlantic*, 6 January 2020. www.theatlantic.com/ideas/archive/2020/01/its-beginning-to-look-a-lot-like-2003/604477.

5. Karen DeYoung, 'Senior administration officials struggle to explain intelligence behind killing of Soleimani'. *The Washington Post*, 13 January 2020. www.washingtonpost.com/national-security/senior-administration-officials-struggle-to-explain-intelligence-behind-killing-of-soleimani/2020/01/12/daf7e896-3582-11ea-bf30-ad313e4ec754_story.html; Sheren Khalel and Umar A Farooq, 'Was it Legal?: What US and International Law say about Trump's strike on Soleimani'. *Middle East Eye*, 3 January 2020. www.middleeasteye.net/news/was-it-legal-what-us-and-international-law-says-about-trumps-strike-soleimani.

6. Brian T. Connor, '9/11 – A New Pearl Harbor? Analogies, Narratives, and Meanings of 9/11 in Civil Society'. *Cultural Sociology*, 6:1 (2012): pp. 3–25; T. Christopher Jespersen, 'Analogies at War: Iraq and Vietnam'. *OAH Magazine of History*, 27:1 (2013): pp. 19–22.

7. Tom O'Connor, Naveed Jamali and James Laporta, 'Iran Government Played Direct Role in Instigating US Embassy Demonstration in

Iraq, Intelligence Officials Say'. *Newsweek*, 31 December 2019. www.newsweek.com/iran-role-iraq-protests-embassy-officials-1479926.

8. James Risen, Tim Arango, Farnaz Fassihi, Murtaza Hussain and Ronen Bergman, 'A Spy Complex Revealed'. *The Intercept*, 18 November 2019. https://theintercept.com/2019/11/18/iran-iraq-spy-cables.

9. Tim Arango, Ronen Bergman and Ben Hubbard, 'Qassim Soleimani, Master of Iran's Intrigue, Built a Shiite Axis of Power in Mideast'. *The New York Times*, 3 January 2020. www.nytimes.com/2020/01/03/obituaries/qassem-soleimani-dead.html.

10. Arango et al., 'Qassim Soleimani'; Rasha Al Aqeedi, 'Qassim Soleimani: The Vincible General'. *New Lines Magazine*, 3 January 2021. https://newlinesmag.com/essays/the-vincible-general.

11. Ali Younes, '"Iran is not afraid": Why Tehran dismisses US threats over Iraq'. *Al-Jazeera*, 1 January 2020. www.aljazeera.com/news/2020/1/1/iran-is-not-afraid-why-tehran-dismisses-us-threats-over-iraq.

12. Risen et al., 'A Spy Complex Revealed'.

13. John Bolton, *The Room Where It Happened: A White House Memoir* (New York: Simon & Schuster, 2020).

14. Christian Høj Hansen and Troels Burchall Henningsen, 'Whose Proxy War? The Competition Among Iranian Foreign Policy Elites in Iraq'. *Small Wars & Insurgencies*, doi:10.1080/09592318.2022.2064152 (2022): pp. 14–17. Veteran Middle East journalist Patrick Cockburn described the so-called Iran Cables as 'disappointing', saying that the Iranian policies they revealed were 'mostly known and not very sinister', being 'the policy of the Iraqi government anyway'. Slava Zilber, 'Patrick Cockburn on Iran, Iraq, and ISIS'. *LA Progressive*, 4 January 2020. www.laprogressive.com/the-middle-east/patrick-cockburn.

15. Aaron Blake, 'When the United States and Qasem Soleimani Worked Together'. *The Washington Post*, 3 January 2020. www.washingtonpost.com/politics/2020/01/03/when-united-states-qasem-soleimani-worked-together.

16. Patrick Cockburn, 'Blundering into War'. *London Review of Books*, 42:2, 23 January 2020. www.lrb.co.uk/the-paper/v42/n02/patrick-cockburn/blundering-into-war.

17. Quoted in Taif Alkhudary, '"No to America … No to Iran": Iraq's Protest Movement in the Shadow of Geopolitics'. *LSE Middle East Centre Blog*, 20 January 2020. https://blogs.lse.ac.uk/mec/2020/01/20/no-to-americano-to-iran-iraqs-protest-movement-in-the-shadow-of-geopolitics.

18. National Intelligence Council, 'Five-Year Regional Outlook: Middle East and North Africa'. *Global Trends 2040*, NIC-2021-02482, February 2021. www.dni.gov/index.php/gt2040-home/gt2040-5-year-regional-outlooks/mena; Arwa Ibrahim, 'Muhasasa, the political system reviled by Iraqi protesters'. *Al Jazeera*, 4 December 2019.

www.aljazeera.com/news/2019/12/4/muhasasa-the-political-system-reviled-by-iraqi-protesters.

19. Hassan and Rubin, 'Pro-Iran Clash at US Embassy Ends in Baghdad'.

20. Michael S. Goodman, 'The Dog That Didn't Bark: The Joint Intelligence Committee and Warning of Aggression'. *Cold War History*, 7:4 (2007): pp. 537–538.

21. On the coup as an intelligence failure: Jeffrey G. Karam, 'Missing Revolution: The American Intelligence Failure in Iraq, 1958'. *Intelligence and National Security*, 33:6 (2017): pp. 693–709.

22. Brandon Wolfe-Hunnicutt, *The Paranoid Style in American Diplomacy: Oil and Arab nationalism in Iraq* (Stanford, CA: Stanford University Press, 2021): pp. 46–55; Simon C. Smith, *Britain's Revival and Fall in the Gulf: Kuwait, Bahrain, Qatar, and the Trucial States, 1950–71* (London: Routledge/Curzon, 2004): pp. 37–39.

23. 'Memorandum of Discussion at the 402nd Meeting of the National Security Council'. 17 April 1959. *FRUS, 1958–1960*, volume 12, document 176.

24. Roland Popp, 'Accommodating to a Working Relationship: Arab Nationalism and US Cold War Policies in the Middle East, 1958–60'. *Cold War History*, 10:3 (2010): pp. 403–407; Brandon Wolfe-Hunnicutt, 'Embracing Regime Change in Iraq: American Foreign Policy and the 1963 Coup d'état in Baghdad'. *Diplomatic History*, 39:1 (2015): pp. 100–106.

25. Richard John Worrall, "Coping with a Coup d'Etat': British Policy towards Post-Revolutioary Iraq, 1958–63'. *Contemporary British History*, 21:2 (2007): pp. 173–199.

26. Quoted in Richard A. Mobley, 'Gauging the Iraqi Threat to Kuwait in the 1960s'. *Studies in Intelligence*, 45:5 (2001): pp. 21–23; and Dina Rezk, *The Arab World and Western Intelligence: Analysing the Middle East, 1956–1981* (Edinburgh: Edinburgh University Press, 2017): pp. 91–95.

27. Joint Intelligence Committee, 'Supply of British Military Equipment and Training Assistance to Iraq', JIC (63) 33 (Final), 5 April 1963. TNA: CAB 158/49. On US support for Iraq's first Ba'athist government, including its extensive human rights violations: Weldon C. Matthews, 'The Kennedy Administration and Arms Transfers to Ba'thist Iraq'. *Diplomatic History*, 43:3 (2019): pp. 469–492.

28. Richard Sale, 'Saddam Key in Early CIA Plot'. *United Press International*, 10 April 2003. www.globalpolicy.org/component/content/article/169/36408.html.

29. 'Iraq: Internal Stresses and the Search for the Bogeyman'. Research Memorandum RNA–6 from the Director of the Bureau of Intelligence and Research (Hughes) to Secretary of State Rogers, 14 February 1969. *FRUS, 1969–1976*, volume E–4, document 251. Emphasis added.

30. 'Iraq: Internal Stresses and the Search for the Bogeyman'.

31. Central Intelligence Agency, 'Iraq Under Baath Rule, 1968–1976', Office of Political Research, November 1976: p. 3. CIA: FOIA ERR.

32. Joint Intelligence Committee, 'The Outlook for the Persian Gulf up to 1978', JIC (A) (73) 10, 11 May 1973: pp. 4, 6, 15. TNA: CAB 186/15.

33. Joint Intelligence Committee, 'The Arab-Israel Military Balance and its Political Implications up to the End of 1973', JIC (A) (69) 16 (Final), 25 April 1969: p. 25. TNA: CAB 186/2.

34. A. J. Wilton, 'Kuwait – Iraq', Letter to P. R. H. Wright, 25 July 1973: p. 1. TNA: FCO 8/1992.

35. CIA, 'Iraq Under Baath Rule': p. 7.

36. Bryan R. Gibson, *Sold Out? US Foreign Policy, Iraq, the Kurds, and the Cold War* (London: Palgrave Macmillan, 2015): 104–105, 128.

37. JIC Working Party on Intelligence Implications of Recently Announced Policy Decisions, Minutes of meeting, JIC (SWP) (68) 1st Meeting, 22 January 1968. TNA: CAB 182/72.

38. Joint Intelligence Committee, 'The Threat to Kuwait', JIC (63) 81 (Final), 17 October 1963: pp. 4–5. TNA: CAB 158/50.

39. Cited in Ash Rossiter, '"Screening the Food from the Flies": Britain, Kuwait, and the Dilemma of Protection, 1961–1971'. *Diplomacy & Statecraft*, 28:1 (2017): p. 93.

40. D. F. Hawley, 'Iraq: Annual Review for 1970', Diplomatic Report No. 57/71, NEQ 1/4, 4 January 1971: pp. 2–3. TNA: FCO 17/1532. Emphasis added.

41. 'Some Notes on Iraqi Politics'. Memorandum Prepared in the Central Intelligence Agency, 5 September 1973. *FRUS, 1969–1976*, volume 27, document 232.

42. 'Some Notes on Iraqi Politics'.

43. Joint Intelligence Committee Middle East, 'Weekly Intelligence Review No. 12 of 1963', 22 March 1963: p. 3. TNA: CAB 191/5; Roger Allen, Letter to R. S. Crawford, 1039/9/63, 26 February 1963: p. 2. TNA: FO 371/168738.

44. A. J. Wilton, 'Kuwait-Iraq Relations', 3/5, 29 August 1973: p. 1. TNA: FCO 8/1992.

45. Hawley, 'Iraq: Annual Review for 1970': p. 3.

46. 'Some Notes on Iraqi Politics'.

47. A. J. D. Stirling, 'Iraq/Soviet Union', 020/303/1, 12 September 1978: p. 3. TNA: FCO 8/3234.

48. Joint Intelligence Committee, 'The Outlook for Kuwait', JIC (A) (70) 41, 13 January 1971: pp. 2, 5, 8, 12. TNA: CAB 186/6.

49. 'Some Notes on Iraqi Politics'.

50. R. G. Giddens, 'Ba'athism', Letter to I. T. M. Lucas, O11/1, 26 July 1976: p. 1. TNA: FCO 8/2778.

51. J. A. N. Graham, 'Iraq: Annual Review for 1976', Diplomatic Report No. 112/77, NBR 014/2, 6 January 1977: pp. 2–3. TNA: FCO 8/3008; 'Iraq:

Annual Review for 1974', Diplomatic Report No. 53/75, NBR 1/4, 6 January 1975: p. 3. TNA: FCO 8/2539.

52. G. G. Arthur, Letter to A. A. Acland, 3/4, 16 January 1971. TNA: FCO 8/1579. Emphases added.

53. Hawley, 'Iraq: Annual Review for 1970': p. 5. Original emphases.

54. Hawley, 'Iraq: Annual Review for 1970': pp. 1, 4.

55. H. G. Balfour Paul, 'Iraq: Annual Review for 1971', Diplomatic Report No. 151/72, NEQ 1/3, 2 February 1972: pp. 1, 2, 4. TNA: FCO 17/1728.

56. Graham, 'Iraq: Annual Review for 1976': p. 4.

57. Graham, 'Iraq: Annual Review for 1974': pp. 2–3, 6. Emphasis added.

58. Joint Intelligence Committee, 'The Likely Effect of a Postponement of British Military Withdrawal on the Security Situation in the Gulf', JIC (A) (70) 49, 8 December 1970: pp. 2, 4, 8, 10. TNA: CAB 186/6.

59. 'The Persian Gulf: The End of Pax Britannica'. Intelligence Memorandum Prepared in the Central Intelligence Agency, 21 September 1972. *FRUS, 1969–1976*, volume 24, document 122; 'Iraq-Persian Gulf: Iraq Looks at the Gulf'. Intelligence Note RNAN Prepared in the Bureau of Intelligence and Research, 16 July 1970. *FRUS, 1969–1976*, volume E-4, document 271.

60. Joint Intelligence Committee, 'The Soviet Threat to CENTO', JIC (A) (72) 35, 8 December 1972: pp. 12, 14. TNA: CAB 186/12.

61. JIC, 'The Arab-Israel Military Balance': pp. 24–25, 28.

62. Joint Intelligence Committee, 'Subversive Activity in the Persian Gulf', 8/JIC/4082, 28 March 1968: pp. 1–3. TNA: CAB 163/73.

63. 'Subversive Activity in the Persian Gulf', Letter to Joint Intelligence Committee, J/326/1, 1 May 1968: Attachment p. 2. TNA: CAB 163/73.

64. Joint Intelligence Committee, 'Likely Developments in the Persian Gulf and their Probable Effects for British Interests', JIC (68) 35 (Final), 7 June 1968: p. 2. TNA: CAB 158/70.

65. CIA, 'Iraq Under Baath Rule': pp. 5–6, 29.

66. Dina Rizk Khoury, 'The Security State and the Practice and Rhetoric of Sectarianism in Iraq'. *International Journal of Contemporary Iraqi Studies*, 4:3 (2010): pp. 325–338.

67. 'Iraq-Persian Gulf: Iraq Looks at the Gulf'.

68. JIC, 'Likely Developments in the Persian Gulf', p. 3; 'The Outlook for the Persian Gulf': p. 16.

69. 'Military Supply Policy for the Lower Persian Gulf States'. Memorandum from the President's Assistant for National Security Affairs (Kissinger) to President Nixon, 14 August 1972. *FRUS, 1969–1976*, volume 24, document 119. Historian Mark Curtis compiles National Archives documents on Britain–Iran relations through the 1960s and 1970s: 'Iran, 1964–1979'.http://markcurtis.info/wp-content/uploads/2018/01/pro.Iran-1964-79.-for-Declassified.pdf.

70. 'Iraq: Iraqi Politics in Perspective'. National Security Council Briefing Paper Prepared for President Nixon, 18 May 1972. *FRUS, 1969–1972*, volume e-4, document 308.

71. 'Leading Personalities in Iraq, 1979', NBR 010/1: p. 49. FCO 8/3401.

72. R. G. Giddens, 'Ba'athism': pp. 1–2.

73. H. G. Balfour Paul, 'Assassination of Hardan Tikriti', Letter to R. M. Evans, 17 April 1971: pp. 1–2. TNA: FCO 8/1659. The 'Very Iraqi' comment is written in the margins by R. M. Evans of the FCO's Near Eastern Department.

74. Brandon Wolfe-Hunnicutt, 'Oil Sovereignty, American Foreign Policy, and the 1968 Coups in Iraq'. *Diplomacy & Statecraft*, 28:2 (2017): pp. 245–248.

75. CIA, 'Iraq Under Baath Rule': pp. iii, 1.

76. CIA, 'Iraq Under Baath Rule': pp. 2, 30.

77. CIA, 'Iraq Under Baath Rule': p. 11.

78. CIA, 'Iraq Under Baath Rule': pp. 8–10, 19, 20.

79. CIA, 'Iraq Under Baath Rule': pp. 15, 19.

80. CIA, 'Iraq Under Baath Rule': pp. 30–31, 36.

81. Hal Brands discusses Saddam's reaction to this covert support: 'Making the Conspiracy Theorist a Prophet: Covert Action and the Contours of United States-Iraq Relations'. *The International History Review*, 33:3 (2011): pp. 386–393.

82. CIA, 'Iraq Under Baath Rule': p. 19.

83. J. A. N. Graham, 'Ba'athist Iraq: Non-Aligned or Fellow-Traveller?', Diplomatic Report No. 139/77, NBR 030/1, 1 February 1977: pp. 2–4. TNA: FCO 8/3018.

84. Graham, 'Ba'athist Iraq': pp. 3–4.

85. I. T. M. Lucas, 'Ba'athist Iraq: Non-Aligned or Fellow Traveller?', Letter to J. A. N. Graham, NBR/030/1, 1 March 1977: p. 2. Original emphasis. TNA: FCO 8/3018. Lucas is himself citing a *Times* editorial on the subject.

86. 'Leading Personalities in Iraq': p. 49.

87. JIC, 'The Outlook for the Persian Gulf': pp. 15–16.

88. I. T. M. Lucas, 'Ba'athism', 4 June 1976. TNA: FCO 8/2778. Emphasis added.

89. CIA, 'Iraq Under Baath Rule': p. 8.

90. Lucas, 'Ba'athist Iraq': pp. 1–2.

91. Chad E. Nelson, 'Revolution and War: Saddam's Decision to Invade Iran'. *Middle East Journal*, 72:2 (2018): pp. 248–252; Ofra Bengio, 'Shi'is and Politics in Ba'thi Iraq'. *Middle Eastern Studies*, 21:1 (1985): pp. 6–7.

92. Nelson, 'Revolution and War': pp. 252–255.

93. Hal Brands, 'Saddam Hussein, the United States, and the Invasion of Iran: Was There a Green Light?' *Cold War History*, 12:2 (2012): pp. 325–327; Christian Emery, *US Foreign Policy and the Iranian Revolution: The Cold*

War dynamics of engagement and strategic alliance (London: Palgrave Macmillan, 2013): pp. 181–182.

94. Michael S. Goodman, 'The Dog That Didn't Bark': pp. 537–538.
95. On the Iranian revolution: William J. Daugherty, 'Behind the Intelligence Failure in Iran'. *International Journal of Intelligence and CounterIntelligence*, 14 (2001): pp. 449–484.
96. 'Iran-Iraq Conflict'. Alert Memorandum issued by the Director of Central Intelligence, 17 September 1980: p. 1. CIA: FOIA ERR.
97. 'Prospects for Escalation of Iran-Iraq Conflict'. Memorandum Prepared by Office of Political Analysis and Office of Strategic Research, 22 September 1980: pp. 1, 3. CIA: FOIA ERR.
98. 'Iraq: Saddam Hussein's Rule and Protracted War'. Memorandum by Office of Political Analysis, 10 October 1980: p. 1. CIA: FOIA ERR.
99. 'Implications of Various Outcomes of the Iran-Iraq War'. Special National Intelligence Estimate, SNIE 34/36.2-80, 20 October 1980: p. 5. CIA: FOIA ERR.
100. 'Implications of Various Outcomes': p. 5.
101. Goodman, 'The Dog That Didn't Bark': pp. 537, 538.
102. 'Iraq: A Handbook'. Reference Aid, Directorate of Intelligence, NESA 82-10620, December 1982: p. 31. Emphasis added. CIA: FOIA ERR.
103. 'Iraq: A Handbook': p. 31.
104. Brands, 'Making the Conspiracy Theorist a Prophet': pp. 393–400.
105. Daniel Salisbury, 'Arming Iran from the Heart of Westminster? The Iranian Military Procurement Offices, Rumours and Intelligence, 1981–1987'. *Intelligence and National Security*, 35:7 (2020): pp. 1042–1058.
106. 'When moral argument is imperative'. *The Guardian*, 12 March 1990; Robert Fisk, 'Letter from Baghdad: Personality Cult in Stylish Shades'. *The Times*, 29 July 1985; Walker, 'Liberal screen'; Peter Sluglett, 'Iraqi Leader Gives Impersonation of a Good Democrat'. *The Independent*, 1 April 1989.
107. 'Rape of the Gulf'. *The Sunday Times*, 5 August 1990; Andrew Marshall, 'The Invasion of Kuwait: Oil markets Nervous as they Await Iraq's Next Move'. *The Independent*, 4 August 1990.
108. Jack Anderson and Dale Van Atta, 'Saddam Hussein's House of Horrors'. *The Washington Post*, 13 August 1990; Elaine Sciolino, 'US Remains at a Loss Trying to Predict Saddam Hussein's Next Move'. *The New York Times*, 15 August 1990: A18.
109. John Scali, 'CIA's Profile of Saddam Hussein'. *Good Morning America*, 28 August 1990; Richard Norton-Taylor, 'Giving Saddam the Benefit of the Doubt'. *The Guardian*, 22 August 1990; 'CIA Evaluation of Saddam Was Based on Community Assessment'. *Associated Press*, 17 May 1991.
110. Jerrold M. Post, 'Saddam Hussein of Iraq: A Political Psychology Profile'. *Political Psychology*, 12:2 (1991): p. 279.
111. Post, 'Saddam Hussein of Iraq': p. 280.

112. Post, 'Saddam Hussein of Iraq': pp. 281, 285, 288.
113. Post, 'Saddam Hussein of Iraq': p. 282.
114. Post, 'Saddam Hussein of Iraq': p. 286.
115. Najib Ghadbian, 'Some Remarks on the Distorting Literature about Saddam Hussein'. *Political Psychology*, 13:4 (1992): pp. 783–789. Ghadbian also notes factual inaccuracies and selective sourcing in Post's testimony, which damage its scholarly integrity but allowed it to bolster pro-war public policy.
116. Post, 'Saddam Hussein of Iraq': p. 286.
117. Post, 'Saddam Hussein of Iraq': pp. 280, 284.
118. Post, 'Saddam Hussein of Iraq': p. 285.
119. 'Iraq's Saddam Husayn: The Next Six Weeks'. Special National Intelligence Estimate, SNIE 36.2-90, Director of Central Intelligence, December 1990: p. iii.
120. 'Iraq's Saddam Husayn': pp. 1, 3. Emphasis added.
121. 'Iraq's Saddam Husayn': pp. 1–2.
122. 'Iraq's Saddam Husayn': pp. 3–4, 6.
123. Just a few years after the Gulf War, military advisers were explaining that Saddam's 'elimination' was 'never a war aim' but was certainly 'a war hope'. In private discussions before the war, Prime Minister Thatcher and President Bush agreed that 'this guy is going to have to go' if Persian Gulf insecurity 'was ever to be resolved'. Michael Sterner, 'Closing the Gate: The Persian Gulf War Revisited'. *Current History*, 96 (1997): p. 14; C. D. Powell, 'The Gulf Crisis: The Military Option'. Record of Conversation between Prime Minister Thatcher and President Bush, 30 September 1990: p. 5. TNA: PREM 19/3084.
124. Roger Morgan, 'Adequate Influence on the Outside World'. *Government and Opposition*, 33:4 (1998): p. 528.
125. Morgan, 'Adequate Influence': p. 528; 'Chairmanship of JIC', Minute to Margaret Thatcher, 27 January 1983. TNA: PREM 19/1127.
126. Percy Cradock, 'Implications of Iraqi Withdrawal from Kuwait'. Briefing for Prime Minister, Jp 01233, 12 December 1990: pp. 2–3. TNA: PREM 19/3440.
127. Richard H. Jacobs, 'A Chronology of the Gulf War', *Arab Studies Quarterly*, 13:1/2 (1991): pp. 147, 149; Arthur Clark, *The ABCs of Human Survival: A Paradigm for Global Citizenship* (Edmonton: AU Press, 2010: pp. 143–148.
128. Percy Cradock, 'Iraq'. Minute to Prime Minister, 27 July 1990, 27 July 1990: p. 1. Emphasis added. TNA: PREM 19/3073. Fellow JIC member Gordon Barrass confirms that this 'customary' minute detailed 'the JIC's deliberations' on Iraq the previous day. 'Britain and the 1991 Gulf War Witness Seminar – Session 1: 11.30–12.45: origins of the Conflict up to Desert Shield'. *Air Power Review*, First Gulf War 25th Anniversary – Special Edition (2016): p. 41.

129. Percy Cradock, 'Gulf Crisis: Visit to Washington'. Note to Prime Minister, Jp 01239, 18 December 1990: p. 2. TNA: PREM 19/3440.
130. 'Conveying Messages to Saddam Hussein'. Message from Foreign Ministry Washington to Foreign and Commonwealth Office, 15 October 1990: pp. 1–2. Emphases added. TNA: PREM 19/3084. Of course, this misreading of states' military movements is precisely what Anglosphere analysts flagellated themselves for in subsequent years – due, as they saw it, not to their own cultural myopia but to Saddam's deception.
131. Cradock, 'Implications of Iraqi Withdrawal': p. 2; C. D. Powell, 'The Gulf', Letter to Simon Webb, 23 October 1990: p. 2. TNA: PREM 19/3085.
132. 'No End of Lessons on Iraq'. The New York Times, 23 September 1990: p. E20.
133. Percy Cradock, 'Meeting with HRH Prince Bandar – 21 August'. Minute for Prime Minister Thatcher, Jp 01095, 22 August 1990: p. 2. TNA: PREM 19/3077; 'Britain and the 1991 Gulf War Witness Seminar – Session 1': p. 48.
134. James J. Wirtz, 'Miscalculation, Surprise and American Intelligence after the Cold War. International Journal of Intelligence and CounterIntelligence, 5:1 (1991): pp. 3–6. The article was published simultaneously in Studies in Intelligence.
135. Wirtz, 'Miscalculation, Surprise and American Intelligence': pp. 4–5.
136. Wirtz, 'Miscalculation, Surprise and American Intelligence': pp. 8, 9, 12.
137. Wirtz, 'Miscalculation, Surprise and American Intelligence': p. 13.
138. Toby Dodge, 'Saddam Hussein and US Foreign Policy: Diabolical Enemy Images, Policy Failure and the Administrations of Bush Senior and Junior'. In Lawrence Freedman and Jeffrey H. Michaels (eds.), Scripting Middle East Leaders: The impact of Leadership Perceptions on US and UK foreign policy (New York: Bloomsbury, 2013): pp. 124–126.
139. Louise Kettle, 'Between Franks and Butler: British Intelligence Lessons from the Gulf War'. Intelligence and National Security, 31:2 (2016): p. 208.
140. Wirtz, 'Miscalculation, Surprise and American Intelligence': pp. 2–3.
141. Norman Cigar, 'Iraq's Strategic Mindset and the Gulf War: Blueprint for Defeat'. Journal of Strategic Studies, 15:1 (1992): p. 1.
142. Lawrence Freedman and Efraim Karsh, 'How Kuwait Was Won: Strategy in the Gulf War'. International Security, 16:2 (1991): pp. 15–19.
143. Powell, 'The Gulf Crisis: The Military Option': pp. 1, 2–3; Cradock, 'Gulf Crisis: Visit to Washington': p. 3.
144. Christopher Brady, 'Intelligence Failures: Plus Ça Change'. Intelligence and National Security, 8:4 (1993): pp. 91, 94.
145. Freedman and Karsh, 'How Kuwait Was Won': pp. 10–11.
146. Efraim Karsh and Inari Rautsi, Saddam Hussein: A Political Biography (New York: Grove Press, 1991): pp. 228–229.

147. Weston Kosova and Melinda Liu, 'Reading Saddam's Mind'. *Newsweek*, 128:13 (1996): p. 34.
148. Rodric Braithwaite, 'Foreign Policy and the Art of Intelligence'. *Contemporary British History*, 12:2 (1998): p. 150.
149. Anthony James Joes, Review of John Hughes-Wilson, *Military Intelligence Blunders. Intelligence and National Security*, 16:1 (2001): p. 356; John Hughes-Wilson, *Military Intelligence Blunders* (New York, NY: Carroll & Graf, 1999): pp. 322, 341. Emphasis added.
150. Iraq Inquiry, *The Report of the Iraq Inquiry* (London: Her Majesty's Stationary Office, 2016): Executive Summary p. 69, Section 4.1 p. 9.
151. Committee of Privy Counsellors, *Review of Intelligence on Weapons of Mass Destruction* (London: Her Majesty's Stationary Office, 2004): pp. 41, 46.
152. Iraq Inquiry, *The Report of the Iraq Inquiry*: Executive Summary p. 10.

CHAPTER 4

1. 'Transcript of Hearing – SIS4, part 2'. The Iraq Inquiry, n.d.: p. 1. As explained in the Acknowledgements, intelligence reports and witness transcripts referenced in this Chapter originally come from the Iraq Inquiry's website, which is now archived by the National Archives. This material is now available at both the National Archive's UK Government Web Archive (https://webarchive.nationalarchives.gov.uk/search) and the University of Exeter's Warnings from the Archive website (https:// warningsfromthearchive.exeter.ac.uk).
2. Oliver Wright, 'MI6 Made Secret Plan for Anti-Saddam Coup in December 2001', 13 May 2011, www.independent.co.uk/news/uk/politics/mi6-made-secret-plan-for-antisaddam-coup-in-december-2001-2283432.html.
3. 'Transcript of hearing – SIS4, part 2': pp. 46, 48.
4. 'Transcript of hearing – SIS4, part 2': pp. 1–3. Emphasis added.
5. 'Transcript of hearing – SIS4, part 2': pp. 7–9. Original emphasis.
6. 'Transcript of hearing – SIS4, part 2': pp. 2–3, 7.
7. Hugh Clout and Cyril Gosme, 'The Naval Intelligence Handbooks: A Monument in Geographical Writing'. *Progress in Human Geography*, 27:2 (2003): pp. 153–173.
8. Naval Intelligence Division, *Iraq and the Persian Gulf* (London: Routledge, 2014 [1944]): pp. 7, 10, 12. The researcher formerly of the Anglo-Iranian Oil Company is listed as a contributor on page 643.
9. Naval Intelligence Division, *Iraq and the Persian Gulf*: pp. 335–336, 349.
10. Ian Black, 'MI6 Man Who Saved Gaddafi Risks Being Mired in an Intelligence Minefield', *The Guardian*, 6 September 2011, www.theguardian.com/world/2011/sep/06/libya-mastermind-wmd-triumph-minefield.
11. 'Transcript of hearing – SIS4, part 2': pp. 46–47.

12. Richard Norton-Taylor details the renditions, their fallout, and Allen's role: *The State of Secrecy: Spies and the Media in Modern Britain* (London: I.B. Tauris, 2020): pp. 240–249.

13. Iraq Inquiry, *The Report of the Iraq Inquiry* (London: Her Majesty's Stationary Office, 2016): Executive Summary pp. 69–76.

14. Judith Betts and Mark Pythian, *The Iraq War and Democratic Governance: Britain and Australia go to war* (London: Palgrave Macmillan, 2020): pp. 171–180.

15. Richard J. Aldrich, Rory Cormac and Michael S. Goodman, *Spying on the World: The declassified documents of the Joint Intelligence Committee, 1936–2013* (Edinburgh: Edinburgh University Press, 2014): p. 389.

16. Joint Intelligence Committee, 'Iraq: Chemical and Biological Weapons Programmes', 19 April 2000: p. 1.

17. JIC, 'Iraq: Chemical and Biological Weapons Programmes': p. 2.

18. Joint Intelligence Committee, 'Iraqi WMD Programmes: Status and Vulnerability', 10 May 2001: pp. 1–5. Original emphasis.

19. Joint Intelligence Committee, 'Iraq: Prospects for Co-operation with UNSCR 1284', 1 November 2000: pp. 1–4. Original emphases.

20. JIC, 'Iraq: Prospects for Co-operation': p. 4. Original emphases.

21. Joint Intelligence Committee, 'Iraq: Saddam 63 Not Out', 10 May 2000: pp. 1–3.

22. Joint Intelligence Committee, 'Impact of the NFZs on Iraqi Persecution', 13 December 2000: pp. 2–3.

23. JIC, 'Iraq: Regional Rapprochement': pp. 1–3. Original emphases.

24. Joint Intelligence Committee, 'Iraq: Regional Attitudes', 19 April 2002: pp. 1–2.

25. Kamil Mahdi, 'Iraq's Economic Reforms in Perspective: Public Sector, Private Sector and the Sanctions'. *International Journal of Contemporary Iraqi Studies* 1:2 (2007): pp. 213–231; Jean Drèze and Haris Gazdar, 'Hunger and Poverty in Iraq, 1991'. *World Development*, 20:7 (1992): pp. 921–945; International Committee for the Red Cross, *Iraq: 1989–1999, a Decade of Sanctions*, 14 December 1999. www.icrc.org/en/doc/resources/documents/report/57jqap.htm; Muhammed Akunjee and Asif Ali, 'Healthcare under Sanctions in Iraq: An Elective Experience'. *Medicine, Conflict and Survival* 18:3 (2002): pp. 249–257.

26. Joint Intelligence Committee, 'Iraq: Economic Sanctions Eroding', 14 February 2001: pp. 2, 4.

27. Joint Intelligence Committee, 'Iraq: Impact of Smarter Sanctions', 8 March 2001: pp. 1, 3, 4. Original emphases.

28. Joint Intelligence Committee, 'Iraq's Military Capabilities', 1 December 2000: p. 4.

29. Joint Intelligence Committee, 'Iraq After September 11 – The Terrorist Threat', 28 November 2001: pp. 2–4. Original emphases.

30. Joint Intelligence Committee, Minutes of meeting, 28 November 2001. Quoted in Iraq Inquiry, *The Report of the Iraq Inquiry*: Section 3.1 p. 353.
31. JIC, 'Iraq After September 11': p. 4.
32. Joint Intelligence Committee, 'Iraq: Saddam Under the Spotlight', 27 February 2002: pp. 1–5.
33. Joint Intelligence Committee, Minutes of Meeting, 27 February 2002. Quoted in Iraq Inquiry, *The Report of the Iraq Inquiry*: Section 3.2 p. 412.
34. Joint Intelligence Committee, 'Iraq: The Return of UN Weapons Inspectors', 11 October 2002: pp. 2, 6.
35. Iraq Inquiry, *The Report of the Iraq Inquiry*: Section 3.5 p. 334, Section 3.6 pp. 10–11; Letter from private secretary for 'C' to John Scarlett, 14 November 2002.
36. Defence Intelligence Service, 'Saddam Hussein – DIS Psychological Profile, Updated', 14 November 2002: pp. 1–2, 4–5, 8. Original emphasis.
37. DIS, 'Saddam Hussein': pp. 3–5.
38. DIS, 'Saddam Hussein': pp. 1, 5.
39. JIC, 'Iraq: Saddam's Diplomatic and Military Options': p. 2.
40. JIC, 'Iraq After September 11': pp. 3–4.
41. Joint Intelligence Committee: 'Iraqi Use of Chemical and Biological Weapons – Possible Scenarios', 9 September 2002: pp. 2, 5.
42. Joint Intelligence Committee, Minutes of Meeting, 4 September 2002: p. 2. Emphasis added.
43. Iraq Inquiry, *The Report of the Iraq Inquiry*: Section 4.2, p. 157.
44. JIC, Minutes of meeting, 4 September 2002: p. 3.
45. JIC, 'Iraqi Use of Chemical and Biological Weapons': p. 2.
46. JIC, 'Iraqi Use of Chemical and Biological Weapons': p. 3.
47. JIC, 'Iraqi Use of Chemical and Biological Weapons': pp. 3, 5.
48. Iraq Inquiry, *The Report of the Iraq Inquiry*: Section 4.2, p. 161.
49. Iraq Inquiry, *The Report of the Iraq Inquiry*: Section 4.2, p. 163.
50. Iraq Inquiry, *The Report of the Iraq Inquiry*: Section 3.1, pp. 361–367.
51. Letter from Richard Dearlove's Private Secretary to Sir David Manning, 3 December 2001: pp. 2, 3, 6.
52. Joint Intelligence Committee, 'Iraq: Regime Cohesion', 4 July 2002: p. 2.
53. JIC, 'Iraq: Regime Cohesion': pp. 1–4. Emphases added.
54. Joint Intelligence Committee, 'Iraq: Regime Cohesion Under Pressure', 14 November 2002: pp. 1–3. Emphasis added.
55. JIC, 'Iraq: Regime Cohesion': pp. 2–4.
56. Joint Intelligence Committee, Minutes of Meeting, 3 July 2002. Quoted in Iraq Inquiry, *The Report of the Iraq Inquiry*: Section 3.3 p. 32.
57. Iraq Inquiry, *The Report of the Iraq Inquiry*: Section 3.4, pp. 102–103, Section 6.1 p. 185.
58. Defence Intelligence Service, 'Removing Saddam', 5 March 2002: pp. 9–10.
59. DIS, 'Removing Saddam': pp. 1, 7, 9.

60. DIS, 'Saddam Hussein': pp. 1, 5.

61. Iraq Inquiry, *The Report of the Iraq Inquiry*: Section 4.1, p. 54.

62. Joint Intelligence Committee, 'Iraq: Continuing Erosion of Sanctions', 25 July 2001: pp. 4–5. Original emphases.

63. JIC, 'Iraq: Regime Cohesion Under Pressure': p. 3.

64. 'Transcript of hearing – SIS4, part 1'. The Iraq Inquiry, n.d.: pp. 7, 23–24, 36. Emphasis added.

65. 'Transcript of hearing – John Scarlett'. The Iraq Inquiry, 8 December 2009: pp. 29–30, 32–33. Emphases added.

66. 'Transcript of hearing – John Scarlett': pp. 32–33, 52–53.

67. JIC, 'Iraq: Saddam's Diplomatic and Military Options': pp. 2, 3, 5.

68. Joint Intelligence Committee, 'Iraq: Military Options', 6 December 2002: p. 2.

69. JIC, 'Iraq: Military Options': pp. 1, 2, 4.

70. Iraq Inquiry, *The Report of the Iraq Inquiry*: Executive Summary: pp. 19–21.

71. Iraq Inquiry, *The Report of the Iraq Inquiry*: Section 3.6: pp. 51–54.

72. Iraq Inquiry, *The Report of the Iraq Inquiry*: Section 4.3: pp. 304–306.

73. Joint Intelligence Committee, Minutes of meeting, 18 December 2002. Quoted in Iraq Inquiry, *The Report of the Iraq Inquiry*: Section 3.6 p. 57.

74. Iraq Inquiry, *The Report of the Iraq Inquiry*: Section 3.6 p. 57.

75. Joint Intelligence Committee, 'An Initial Assessment of Iraq's WMD Declaration', 18 December 2002: p. 5.

76. Letter from John Scarlett to Julian Miller, 3 January 2003.

77. Iraq Inquiry, *The Report of the Iraq Inquiry*: Section 3.6 p. 92.

78. Letter from Julian Miller to JIC members, 13 January 2003: pp. 1–4.

79. Joint Intelligence Committee, 'Iraq: The Emerging View from Baghdad', 29 January 2003: pp. 1–2.

80. 'Transcript – SIS1'. The Iraq Inquiry, 2010: pp. 16, 56.

81. JIC, 'Iraq: The Emerging View': pp. 2, 4.

82. JIC, 'Iraq: The Emerging View': p. 4.

83. John Scarlett, 'Iraq: JIC Assessment and Personal Observations', Jp28, 30 January 2003: p. 1; Iraq Inquiry, *The Report of the Iraq Inquiry*: Section 4.3 p. 335.

84. Scarlett, 'Iraq: JIC Assessment and Personal Observations'; 'Transcript of Hearing – John Scarlett and Julian Miller'. The Iraq Inquiry, 5 May 2010: p. 57.

85. Scarlett, 'Iraq: JIC Assessment': p. 1. Emphasis added.

86. Letter from Julian Miller to JIC members: p. 3.

87. Scarlett, 'Iraq: JIC Assessment': p. 1. Emphasis added.

88. Scarlett, 'Iraq: JIC Assessment': p. 2.

89. Scarlett, 'Iraq: JIC Assessment': pp. 2, 4, 5.

90. 'Transcript of hearing – John Scarlett': pp. 49–50. Emphases added.

91. 'Transcript of hearing – William Ehrman and Tim Dowse'. The Iraq Inquiry, 25 November 2009: pp. 11, 15–16, 27–29.
92. Stephen Farrell, 'Iraqi planes found buried in desert'. *The Times*, 2 August 2003.
93. Andrew Brown, 'Use Abandoned British Army Equipment to Save Iraqi Refugees, Say Campaigners'. *The Guardian*, 16 October 2014.
94. 'Transcript of hearing – William Ehrman and Tim Dowse': pp. 54–55. Emphases added.
95. 'Transcript of hearing – William Ehrman and Tim Dowse': pp. 36–37.
96. Quoted in John Hughes-Wilson, *Military Intelligence Blunders* (New York: Carroll & Graf Publishers, 1999): pp. 341–342. Emphases added.

CONCLUSION

1. John Prados, 'How Qaddafi Came Clean'. *Bulletin of the Atomic Scientists*, 61:1 (2005): pp. 28, 30–31.
2. Yehudit Ronen, 'Libya's Conflict with Britain: Analysis of a Diplomatic Rupture'. *Middle Eastern Studies*, 42:2 (2006): pp. 271–283.
3. Yehudit Ronen, 'Britain's Return to Libya: From the Battle of a-Alamein in the Western Libyan Desert to the Military Intervention in the 'Arab Spring' Upheaval'. *Middle Eastern Studies*, 49:5 (2013): p. 686.
4. Debora Valentina Malito, 'Interventions and Sovereignty Limitations in Libya'. In Ruth Hanau Santini, Abel Polese and Rob Kevlihan (eds.), *Limited Statehood and Informal Governance in the Middle East and Africa* (London: Routledge): pp. 106–107.
5. Christopher Andrew, 'British Official Perceptions of Muammar Gaddafi, 1969–2011'. In Lawrence Freedman and Jeffrey H. Michaels (eds.), *Scripting Middle East Leaders: The Impact of Leadership Perceptions on US and UK Foreign Policy* (New York: Bloomsbury, 2013): pp. 207–208.
6. John Godfrey, 'Al-Qadhafi and the Reform 'Vision Thing', Cable from Tripoli Embassy to US Department of State, 18 November 2008. www. wikileaks.org/plusd/cables/08TRIPOLI896_a.html.
7. On these two dynamics, see Alison Pargeter, 'Libya: Reforming the Impossible?'. *Review of African Political Economy* 33:108 (2006): pp. 219–235.
8. Elizabeth Fritschle, 'Qadhafi's calls for African and Muslim unity resonate in Libya', Cable from Tripoli Embassy to US Department of State, 2 May 2007. www.wikileaks.org/plusd/cables/07TRIPOLI421_a.html.
9. Mona Damluji, '"Securing Democracy in Iraq": Sectarian Politics and Segregation in Baghdad, 2003–2007'. *Traditional Dwellings and Settlements Review* 21:2 (2010): pp. 71–87; Nils B. Weidmann and Idean Salehyan, 'Violence and Ethnic Segregation: A Computational Model Applied to Baghdad'. *International Studies Quarterly* 57 (2013): pp. 52–64.

10. Gene A. Cretz, 'Insight into Qadhafi's life from an American Businessman', Cable from Tripoli Embassy to US Department of State, 18 November 2009. www.wikileaks.org/plusd/cables/09TRIPOLI920_a.html.

11. Gene A. Cretz, 'A Glimpse Into Libyan Leader Qadhafi's Eccentricities', Cable from Tripoli Embassy to US Department of State, 29 September 2009. www.wikileaks.org/plusd/cables/09TRIPOLI771_a.html. This cable gained by far the most press attention when leaked by Wikileaks.

12. Chris Stevens, 'Qadhafi Development Foundation Director Sounds Warning on Terrorist Threat, Bilateral Ties', Cable from Tripoli embassy to US Department of State, 31 December 2007. www.wikileaks.org/plusd/cables/07TRIPOLI1066_a.html. Emphasis added.

13. John Zarocostas, 'Libyan Hospitals are Overstretched Treating Thousands of Victims of Violent Crackdown'. BMJ, 342 (2011): d1245.

14. Quoted in Derek Chollet and Ben Fishman, 'Who Lost Libya? – A Close Call'. Foreign Affairs, 94:3 (2015): p. 154.

15. 'Libya Letter by Obama, Cameron and Sarkozy: Full Text'. BBC News, 15 April 2011. www.bbc.com/news/world-africa-13090646.

16. 'Oral evidence: Libya – William Hague and Liam Fox'. Foreign Affairs Committee, 1 December 2015. http://data.parliament.uk/writtenevidence/committeeevidence.svc/evidencedocument/foreign-affairs-committee/libya-examination-of-intervention-and-collapse-and-the-uks-future-policy-options/oral/25384.html.

17. Quoted in Kelly Riddell and Jeffrey Scott Shapiro, 'Hillary Clinton Libya War Genocide Narrative Rejected by US Intelligence'. The Washington Times, 29 January 2015. www.washingtontimes.com/news/2015/jan/29/hillary-clinton-libya-war-genocide-narrative-rejec.

18. Quoted in 'Gaddafi Threatens Bloodbath in Libya', ABC (Sydney), 2 March 2011. www.abc.net.au/news/2011-03-02/gaddafi-threatens-bloodbath-in-libya/1964900.

19. Quoted in Jillian Harding, 'In weekly address, Obama Makes Case for Libya'. CNN, 26 March 2011. https://politicalticker.blogs.cnn.com/2011/03/26/in-weekly-address-obama-makes-case-for-libya. Emphasis added.

20. Foreign Affairs Committee, Libya: Examination of Intervention and Collapse and the UK's Future Policy Options (London: House of Commons, 2016): pp. 13–15.

21. Ronald Bruce St John, 'From the February 17 Revolution to Benghazi: Rewriting History for Political Gain'. The Journal of North African Studies, 21:3 (2016): pp. 362–365; 'Libya: Mass Grave Yields 23 Bodies', Human Rights Watch, 14 September 2011. www.hrw.org/news/2011/09/14/libya-mass-grave-yields-34-bodies.

22. 'Oral Evidence: Libya – William Hague and Liam Fox'.

23. Riddell and Shapiro, 'Hillary Clinton Libya War'.

24. Jerrold Post, 'Qaddafi Under Siege', *Foreign Policy*, 15 March 2011. https://
foreignpolicy.com/2011/03/15/qaddafi-under-siege-2/; Bob Woodward,
'Don't Make the Libya Problem Worse', *The Washington Post*, 2 February
1986.
25. Pargeter, 'Libya': pp. 221, 230–231.
26. The extent of this cooperation was laid bare by intelligence documents
found in Libya after the 2011 intervention: Ian Cobain, 'How Britain did
Gaddafi's Dirty Work', *The Guardian*, 9 November 2017. www.theguardian.
com/news/2017/nov/09/how-britain-did-gaddafis-dirty-work-libya.
27. Cobain, 'How Britain did Gaddafi's Dirty Work'.
28. 'Gaddafi says Protesters are on Hallucinogenic Drugs', *Reuters*, 24
February 2011.
29. Cecil G. Parker, 'The UK National Security Council and Misuse of
Intelligence By Policy Makers: Reducing the Risk?' *Intelligence and
National Security*, 35:7 (2020): p. 996.
30. Patrick Wintour and Nicholas Watt, 'David Cameron's Libyan
War: Why The PM Felt Gaddafi had to be Stopped', *The Guardian*,
2 October 2011. www.theguardian.com/politics/2011/oct/02/david-
cameron-libyan-war-analysis.
31. David Cameron, *For The Record* (London: William Collins, 2019):
pp. 274–275; Grant Dawson, '"No Future for Libya with Gaddafi":
Classical Realism, Status and Revenge in the UK Intervention in Libya'.
Cambridge Review of International Affairs, doi:10.1080/09557571.2021.1
888879 (2019): p. 14.
32. Central Intelligence Agency, 'The Roots of Libyan Foreign Policy:
Qadhafi and His Advisors', Memorandum for Director of Intelligence,
5 March 1985; 'Libya's Qadhafi: Vulnerabilities and Prospects', NESA
83-10117, June 1983: pp. iii–iv. CIA: FOIA ERR.
33. Seymour Hersh, 'Target Qaddafi', *The New York Times Magazine*, 22
February 1987.
34. Graham E. Fuller, 'Qadhafi – The Psychological State of the Regime', NIC
00099-86, 7 January 1986: pp. 1–2. Original emphasis. CIA: FOIA ERR.
35. Noam Chomsky, *Pirates and Emperors, Old and New: International
Terrorism in the Real World* (London: Pluto Press, 2002): pp. 89–92;
Saskia Van Genugten, *Libya in Western Foreign Policies, 1911–2011*
(London: Palgrave Macmillan, 2016): pp. 112–113.
36. Fuller, 'Qadhafi': p. 1.
37. Fuller, 'Qadhafi': p. 1.
38. 'Oral evidence: Libya – William Hague and Liam Fox'.
39. Quoted in Dawson, 'No Future for Libya with Gaddafi': p. 9.
40. Kimberly Dozier, 'Obama Criticizes Spy Agencies for Not Seeing Revolts',
Associated Press, 5 February 2011.
41. Marc Ambinder, 'An Intelligence Failure in Egypt?', *The Atlantic*,
5 February 2011.

42. Ken Dilanian, 'US Intelligence Official Acknowledges Missed Arab Spring Signs', *Los Angeles Times*, 19 July 2012; Intelligence and Security Committee, *Annual Report 2011-2012* (London: House of Commons, 2012): pp. 13–14.

43. Asef Bayat, 'The Arab Spring and its Surprises'. *Development and Change*, 44:3 (2013): pp. 587–601.

44. Rotem Dvir, 'Post Factum Clarity: Failure to Identify Spontaneous Threats'. *Intelligence and National Security*, 34:4 (2019): p. 576.

45. Dilanian, 'US Intelligence Official'; 'Transcript of Evidence – Iain Lobban, Andrew Parker and John Sawers', Intelligence and Security Committee, 7 November 2013: p. 3.

46. Ambinder, 'An Intelligence Failure'; Dozier, 'Obama criticizes spy agencies'.

47. Ambinder, 'An Intelligence Failure'; 'Transcript of evidence – Iain Lobban, Andrew Parker and John Sawers': p. 3.

48. Foreign Affairs Committee, *British foreign policy and the 'Arab Spring'* (London: House of Commons, 2012): pp. 19–20.

49. Iraq Inquiry, *The Report of the Iraq Inquiry* (London: Her Majesty's Stationary Office, 2016): Executive Summary p. 134; 'Transcript of Hearing – John Scarlett'. The Iraq Inquiry, 8 December 2009: pp. 33–34.

50. Uri Bar-Joseph and Rose McDermott, *Intelligence Success and Failure: The human factor* (Oxford: Oxford University Press, 2017): p. 243.

51. Dvir, 'Post Factum Clarity': pp. 576–594.

52. Mark Landler, 'Secret Report Ordered by Obama Identified Potential Arab Uprisings', *The New York Times*, 17 February 2011: p. A14; Barack Obama, *A Promised Land* (New York: Crown, 2020): p. 637.

53. Rubén Arcos and José-Miguel Palacios, 'The Impact of Intelligence on Decision-Making: The EU and the Arab Spring'. *Intelligence and National Security*, 33:5 (2018): pp. 740, 743–744.

54. Landler, 'Secret Report'.

55. Obama, *A Promised Land*: p. 637. Emphasis added.

56. Landler, 'Secret Report'.

57. Noam Chomsky, 'Indonesia, Master Card in Washington's Hand'. *Indonesia*, 66 (1998): pp. 1–5.

58. Brad Simpson, ' 'Illegally and Beautifully': The United States, the Indonesian Invasion of East Timor and the International Community, 1974–76'. *Cold War History*, 5:3 (2005): pp. 281–315. Simpson describes the U.S, Britain, Australia and New Zealand view as a belief that 'East Timor was too small and too primitive to merit self-governance' (p. 281).

59. Kevjn Lim, 'Big Data and Strategic Intelligence'. *Intelligence and National Security*, 31:4 (2016): pp. 619–635; Louise J. Rasmussen, Winston R. Sieck and Robert R. Hoffman, 'Cultural Knowledge for Intelligence Analysts: Expertise in Cultural Sensemaking'. *American Intelligence Journal*, 31:2 (2013): p. 28.

60. Mounira Soliman, 'The Reception of US Discourse on the Egyptian Revolution: Between the Popular and the Official'. In Alex Lubin and Marwan M. Kraidy (eds.), *American Studies Encounters the Middle East* (Chapel Hill: University of North Carolina Press, 2016): p. 146; Jack Shenker, 'Scandal of Mubarak regime millions in UK', *The Guardian*, 2 September 2012. www.theguardian.com/world/2012/sep/02/scandal-mubarak-regime-millions-assets-uk.

61. Soliman, 'The Reception of US Discourse': pp. 146–152.

62. 'Fireside Chat with Richard Moore'. The Aspen Security Forum, Colorado, USA, 21 July 2021. Original emphasis. www.aspensecurityforum.org; Ethan S. Burger, 'Ukrainian National Identity and Russian Intelligence Failure', *The Institute of World Politics*, 25 April 2022. www.iwp.edu/events/ukrainian-national-identity-and-russian-intelligence-failure.

63. Katie Bo Lillis and Natasha Bertrand, 'US Intelligence Community Launches Review Following Ukraine and Afghanistan Intel Failings'. *CNN*, 13 May 2022. https://edition.cnn.com/2022/05/13/politics/us-intelligence-review-ukraine/index.html.

64. 'Fireside Chat with Richard Moore'.

65. Gražina Bielousova, 'Western Disorientations: The Vanishing East of South America and Eastern Europe'. *Acta Academiae Artium Vilnensis*, 105 (2022): pp. 12–23.

66. Maria Mälksoo, 'The Postcolonial Moment in Russia's War Against Ukraine'. *Journal of Genocide Research*, doi:10.1080/14623528.2022.2074 947 (2022): pp. 1–11.

67. 'Fireside Chat with Richard Moore'.

68. Quoted in Griff Witte, 'In Putin's Ukraine quagmire, echoes of Soviet failure in Afghanistan'. *The Washington Post*, 2 April 2022. www.washingtonpost.com/world/2022/04/02/ukraine-afghanistan-russia-parallels-quagmire.

69. Witte, 'In Putin's Ukraine Quagmire'.

70. Taz Ali, 'Ukraine Could Follow Afghanistan into Years of Turmoil as West Adopts "Mujahideen Model" with Weapons'. *i*, 19 March 2022. https://inews.co.uk/news/world/ukraine-follow-afghanistan-turmoil-west-adopts-mujahideen-model-weapons-1522113.

71. Elisabeth Leake, 'Spooks, Tribes, and Holy Men: The Central Intelligence Agency and the Soviet Invasion of Afghanistan'. *Journal of Contemporary History*, 53:1 (2018): pp. 240–262.

72. James Landale, 'Ukraine War: The West is United for Now – But What If It Splits?'. *BBC News*, 27 April 2022. www.bbc.co.uk/news/world-61237762; Kori Schake, 'Putin Accidentally Revitalized the West's Liberal Order'. *The Atlantic*, 28 February 2022. www.theatlantic.com/international/archive/2022/02/vladimir-putin-ukraine-invasion-liberal-order/622950.

73. Jill Lawless and Aamer Madhani, 'Secret Intelligence has Unusually Public Role in Ukraine War'. *Associated Press*, 3 April 2022.

74. 'Fireside Chat with Richard Moore'.
75. Quoted in David Adler, 'The West v Russia: Why the Global South Isn't Taking Sides'. *The Guardian*, 28 March 2022. www.theguardian.com/commentisfree/2022/mar/10/russia-ukraine-west-global-south-sanctions-war.
76. Humberto Márquez, 'War in Ukraine Triggers New International Non-Alignment Trend'. *IPS News*, 20 June 2022. www.ipsnews.net/2022/06/war-ukraine-triggers-new-international-non-alignment-trend.
77. Howard W. French, 'Why the World Isn't Really United Against Russia'. *Foreign Policy*, 19 April 2022. https://foreignpolicy.com/2022/04/19/russia-ukraine-war-un-international-condemnation; Siddarth Tripathi, 'Seeing Beyond 'Either/Or': Global South's Dilemmas on the Ukraine Crisis'. *Global Cooperation Research – A Quarterly Magazine*, 4:1 (2022). www.gcr21.org/publications/gcr/gcr-quarterly-magazine/qm-1/2022-articles/qm-1-2022-tripathi-seeing-beyond-either/or-global-souths-dilemmas-on-the-ukraine-crisis.
78. Helena Malikyar, 'Russia-Ukraine war: Is Washington reprising the Soviet-Afghan playbook?'. *Middle East Eye*, 11 March 2022. www.middleeasteye.net/opinion/russia-ukraine-war-washington-reprising-soviet-afghan-playbook.
79. Robert Jervis, 'Commentary: The Butler Report'. In R. Gerald Hughes, Peter Jackson, and Len Scott (eds.), *Exploring Intelligence Archives: Enquiries into the secret state* (London: Routledge, 2008): pp. 310–311.
80. Daniel P. Moynihan, 'Do We Still Need the CIA?' and Bud Shuster, 'Independence Means Integrity', *The New York Times*, 19 May 1991: p. E17.
81. Paul McGarr, '"Do We Still Need the CIA?" Daniel Patrick Moynihan, the Central Intelligence Agency and US Foreign Policy'. *History*, 100:340 (2015): p. 292. Emphasis added.
82. Quoted in McGarr, '"Do We Still Need the CIA?"': p. 291.
83. McGarr, '"Do We Still Need the CIA?"': p. 291; Moynihan, 'Do We Still Need the CIA?'
84. Moynihan, '"Do We Still Need the CIA?"'
85. Elsewhere, I have discussed how the intelligence failure concept ties together Intelligence Studies as an academic discipline, how it encourages scholars to take the suspicious Hobbesian anarchy of the world as given and to focus on how well intelligence reads this anarchy or not: Hager Ben Jaffel, Alvina Hoffman, Oliver Kearns and Sebastian Larsson, 'Collective Discussion: Toward Critical Approaches to Intelligence as a Social Phenomenon'. *International Political Sociology*, 14 (2020): pp. 328–331.
86. Quoted in Public Administration and Constitutional Affairs Committee, *Lessons still to be learned from the Chilcot Inquiry* (London: House of Commons, 2017): p. 7. Emphases added.
87. Roula Khalaf and Rory Stewart, *BBC Newsnight*, BBC 2, 6 July 2016.

88. Jeremy H. Keenan, 'UK Foreign Policy and Intelligence in the Post-Truth Era: Radical Violent Extremism and "Blow-Back"'. *State Crime Journal*, 6:2 (2017): pp. 193–197.

89. David Omand, *BBC Newsnight*, BBC 2, 6 July 2016.

90. Hal Brands and Michael O'Hanlon, 'The War on Terror Has Not Yet Failed: A Net Assessment After 20 Years'. *Survival*, 63:4 (2021): pp. 33–54.

91. Quoted in McGarr, "Do We Still Need the CIA?": p. 284. Original emphasis.

92. Jesse Olsavsky, 'The Abolitionist Tradition in the Making of W. E. B. Du Bois's Marxism and Anti-Imperialism'. *Socialism and Democracy*, 32:3 (2018): pp. 27–33.

93. 'Poll: 75% of Arabs see Israel, US as Biggest Threats to Security', *Middle East Monitor*, 13 July 2018. www.middleeastmonitor.com/20180713-poll-75-of-arabs-see-israel-us-as-biggest-threat-to-security.

94. Ephrem Kossaify, 'Arabs see Iran Among Top Three Threats to US Interests: Poll', *Arab News*, 26 October 2020. www.arabnews.com/node/1754596/middle-east.

Index

11 September 2001 attacks, 68, 176, 177
  as changing the 'calculus of risk', 139,
    144–5; and Pearl Harbour, 101
9/11 Commission, 68

Aden Protectorate uprising (1960s), 71
Afghanistan War (2001), 159, 173
Africa
  nationalist movements, 113, 215
    n. 76
Afro-Asian Peoples' Solidarity
  Movement, 71
Algerian War of Independence, 71
Algiers Accord (1975), 119
Allen, Mark (SIS4), MI6 officer
  intelligence assessments on Iraq
    regime change, 158, 161; Libya
    renditions, 143–4; and MI6's
    Cold War record, 140; racialised
    reading of Ba'athist Iraq, 140–1,
    158, 161–2
Anglo-Persian Oil Company
  and British intelligence, 141, 233 n.
    8
anti-colonialism
  defined as an infection in
    intelligence, 49, 65; dismissed
    as irrational, 42–9, 51–2, 59, 65;
    and international politics, 49;
    political consciousness, 49–53;
    self-determination demands, 24,
    44; *see also* decolonisation
Arab nationalism
  judged as emotional and irrational,
    44, 83, 85, 86–7, 142, 148–9
Arab Spring, 178
  initial intelligence assessments, 187;
    intelligence warnings, 189–91

Arab Street concept, 148, 158
Asher, Jeff, former CIA analyst, 3
Asia
  judged as easily-manipulated, 78–9;
    see also China, Vietnam
Atlee, Clement, 30

Ba'ath Party, Iraq, 107
  and Arabism, 121; political
    ideology, 111–14, 119, 136
Ba'athist Government, Iraq
  as secretive and insular, 110–11,
    136, 141, 149; internal power
    struggles, 108–9; sect politics,
    115, 140; US support for Kurdish
    genocide, 107, 226 n. 26; *see also*
    Regime concept
Bandung Conference (1955), 51, 71
Belhaj, Abdel Hakim, Libya rendition
  target, 143–4, 183
Blair, Tony, 158, 160, 169, 200
  meetings with Muammar Gaddafi,
    177; and rogue states, 166; and
    Hussein, Saddam, 14, 152, 165
Bolton, John, US national security
  adviser
  on Iran Revolutionary Guard
    Corps, 103
Bowles, Chester, US Ambassador to
  India, 23
Britain
  Cabinet discussion of Jordan and
    Arab nationalism (1958), 63;
    'counter-subversion' in colonies,
    53, 56; empire, elite attitude
    towards, 36–37; intelligence on
    British Empire, 45–6; role in
    Middle East, *see* Middle East

Ehrman, William, Foreign Office
director general of defence and
intelligence, 172
intelligence gaps on Iraq, 174–5
European Union
Single Intelligence Analysis
Capacity on Middle East
instability, 190

Ford, Gerald, 91
Foreign Affairs Committee, Britain,
181
Arab Spring and intelligence, 188
Foreign Intelligence Advisory Board,
US, 91
Foreign Office (FO), Britain, 121, 172,
188
Counter-Proliferation Department,
172; Middle East Department,
121, 122; Middle East Research
Department on military coups,
86–7
Fox, Liam, British Defence Secretary
Gaddafi's world perceptions, 186
Freedman, Lawrence, scholar and
Chilcot Inquiry member
Hussein, Saddam, behaviour during
Gulf War, 137; Iraqi WMDs and
perception of regional threat,
173; Team B CIA exercise, 97
Fuller, Graham, vice chairman of US
National Intelligence Council
psychology of Gaddafi's Libya,
184–5

Gaddafi, Muammar
ego, 184; erratic, 178, 180, 182,
184; influenced by Anglosphere
actions, 183; insular misreadings
of world politics, 179–80;
intelligence gaps on, 182; and
the IRA, 177, 183; and Islam,
182, 183; lacking politics, 178–9;
and the Lockerbie bombing,

177, 183; mentally unstable,
182; and sectarianism, 179; and
uprising in Libya (2011), 180–2;
US assassination attempts,
184–5; vengeful, 181; WMD
programmes, 177; see also Libya
Geller, Uri, 89, 90
General Dynamics
military equipment contract with
Libya, 177–8
geopolitics, see intelligence analysis;
Middle East and North Africa
(MENA)
Gove, Michael, British Minister under
David Cameron, 183
Government Communication
Headquarters (GCHQ)
propaganda in Ukraine war, 5
Grovogui, Siba 71–2
Gulf War (1990), 126–34, 174
in Intelligence and Strategic Studies
literature, 134–8, 175; and Iraq
regime change, 231 n. 123

Hague, William, British Foreign
Affairs Secretary
Muammar Gaddafi, 181–2, 186;
potential for massacres in
Benghazi (2011), 181
Haines, Avril, Director of US National
Intelligence, 4
Heuer, Richards J.
Psychology of Intelligence Analysis,
98
Hillenkoetter, Roscoe, Director of US
Central Intelligence, 213 n. 49
Hughes-Wilson, John, British Colonel,
138
Hussein, Saddam
aggressive and vengeful, 165, 168;
assassination attempt against
Qasim, 107; Ba'ath Party/
Government role, 108–9,
117–19, 146–7, 151, 159, 161,

of, 32, 46; conservative Islam vs. revolutionary Arabism, 114–15, 125; definition in post-war intelligence, 30–2, 45–6; geopolitical importance for US and Britain, 33–4, 41–2, 56, 191; Iraq War impact, 8, 200–201; instability, *see* intelligence analysis; and liberal democracy, 59, 86–7, 161–2, 202–3; popular views of US and security, 202–3; proxy conflicts, 103–4; racialised as emotional, 44–5, 51, 148–50, 157, 172, 184–5; self-contained equilibrium, 21–2, 25, 35–6, 55–9, 60–6, 69, 85, 111–12, 122, 150, 157, 163–4, 170, 176, 192; US support for authoritarian states, 190; *see also* Arab nationalism; intelligence analysis; Pan-Arabism

Miller, Julian, Head of JIC Assessments Staff, 155

Hussein, Saddam, 'errors of judgement', 166–7, 170; Hussein, Saddam, JIC view, 157–8

Ministry of Defence (MoD), Britain, 155, 164

mirror-imaging concept, 26, 163, 192
antecedents, 85; and Gaddafi, Muammar, 180; and Hussein, Saddam, 124, 166, 168–9, 172–3; importance in intelligence analysis and Intelligence Studies, 70, 98, 189; racialisation, 70–1, 92, 136, 166; Regimes, internalised to, 135–6; and Russia/Soviet Union, 88–91; self-delusion of superiority, 92, 94, 135–6, 168–9; social psychology, 86; *see also* intelligence analysis; Pipes, Richard, historian; Team B, CIA exercise (1976)

Montague, Ludwell, CIA officer, 41–2, 213 n. 49

Moore, Richard, MI6 Chief
intelligence and society, 193–4; Russian intelligence in Ukraine, 193; world response to Russian invasion of Ukraine (2022), 195

Moynihan, Daniel, US Ambassador to India and Senator
blowback against US covert action in Asia (1970s), 201; criticism of CIA (1990s), 197–8

Nasser, Gamal, President of Egypt, 54, 61, 81
intelligence focus on, 80; irrational, 83–4; lacking geopolitical sense, 82–3; links with CIA and State Department, 80; and Qasim, Abd al-Karim, 107

National Intelligence Council, US, 103, 184

National Intelligence Estimates, 39, 57
'Arab world, the', 61–2, 65–6; Hussein, Saddam, 124, 129–31; neoconservative criticism, 91; *see also* Central Intelligence Agency

national security concept, 40–1, 203 n. 42

National Security Council (NSC), 40, 41–2, 58, 107
panel on Middle East social unrest (2010), 189–90

Naval Intelligence, Britain
Handbook on Iraq and the Persian Gulf (1944), 141–2

Nehru, Jamal, President of India
Middle East concept, 32

neoconservatives, US political movement
criticism of CIA, 91; and intelligence history, 211 n. 13; and Iran, 103; and mirror-imaging

Thanks to our Patreon subscriber:

Ciaran Kane

Who has shown generosity and
comradeship in support of our publishing.

Check out the other perks you get by subscribing
to our Patreon – visit patreon.com/plutopress.
Subscriptions start from £3 a month.